Theories of the Symbol

TZVETAN TODOROV

Theories of the Symbol

TRANSLATED BY CATHERINE PORTER

CORNELL UNIVERSITY PRESS
ITHACA, NEW YORK

Originally published in French under the title
Théories du symbole, © 1977 by Editions du Seuil.
The publisher gratefully acknowledges the financial assistance of the
French Ministry of Culture in defraying part of the cost of translation.

First published 1982 by Cornell University Press.
First printing, Cornell Paperbacks, 1984.

*The paper in this book is acid-free, and meets the guidelines
for permanence and durability of the Committee on Production
Guidelines for Book Longevity of the Council on Library Resources.*

Printed in the United States of America

Library of Congress Cataloging in Publication Data
TODOROV, TZVETAN, 1939–
    Theories of the symbol.

    Translation of: Théories du symbole.
    Includes index.
    1. Semiotics—Addresses, essays, lectures.
2. Rhetoric—Addresses, essays, lectures.
P99.T613 1982   001.51   81-17420
ISBN 0-8014-1192-0   AACR2

Contents

CONTENTS

Translator's Note

Under the author's direction, certain material that appeared in the original French version of this work, *Théories du symbole* (Paris: Seuil, 1977), has been deleted from the translation: a detailed presentation of the rhetorical theories of Du Marsais, Beauzée, Condillac, and Fontanier (chapter 3), a detailed analysis of Freud's descriptive work in *Jokes and Their Relation to the Unconscious* (chapter 8), and an appendix providing a study of Freud's work on enunciation. The remaining text of *Théories du symbole*, revised slightly by the author, has been translated in full.

In this translation I have quoted from published English texts or standard English translations wherever possible, supplementing (or, occasionally, replacing) the bibliographic reference given in the French text with the corresponding English reference. For quoted material where no English-language reference is indicated, I have translated from the French, consulting the original-language text where appropriate and feasible.

For their help in tracking down sources and standard translations, I thank Neil Hertz, Giuseppe Mazzotta, Pietro Pucci, and Linda Waugh of Cornell University; for his advice on thorny bits of Latin, Arnold Lewin of the State University of New York,

College at Cortland; for his careful reading of the whole and many helpful suggestions, Philip Lewis of Cornell University.

CATHERINE PORTER

Ithaca, New York

Introduction

The *symbol*—the thing itself, not the word—is the object of this book. The reader will find here not a history of the term "symbol" but studies devoted to thinkers who have reflected on phenomena that, in our day, are usually called "symbolic." Moreover, as we shall be concerned, most of the time, with theories bearing upon the *verbal* symbol, we shall frequently oppose the latter to the sign. Because this book consists of studies of the various ways of grasping and defining "symbolic" phenomena, a liminary definition is not called for here. It should suffice to indicate that symbolic evocation is grafted onto direct signification, and that certain uses of language, such as poetry, cultivate it more than others. The notion of the symbol cannot be studied in isolation. Just as often as with the concept of symbol, we shall be dealing, in the pages that follow, with sign and interpretation, use and enjoyment, tropes and figures, imitation and beauty, art and mythology, participation and resemblance, condensation and displacement, and many other terms as well.

If one gives the word "sign" a generic meaning through which it encompasses that of symbol (the symbol then becomes a special case of the sign), one may say that studies of the symbol belong to the general theory of signs, or semiotics, and that my book belongs to the history of semiotics. I must add at once that here too we are concerned with the thing itself and not with the word. Reflection on the sign has been undertaken in a number of disciplines that are distinct and even widely separated from one another, such as philosophy of language, logic, linguistics, semantics, hermeneutics, rhetoric, aesthetics, and poetics. The separation of these disciplines and their terminological inconsistencies have led us to ignore the unity of a tradition that is among the richest in Western history. I shall attempt to demonstrate the continuity of this tradition, and I shall be concerned only incidentally with authors who have used the term "semiotics."

Theory is to be taken in a loose sense; the word is opposed here to "practice," rather than to "nontheoretical reflection." In most cases, the theories in question did not fall within the framework of a science (no such framework existed at the time of their elaboration) and their formulation has none of the characteristics of a "theory" in the strict sense.

The plural ending of the word "theories" is essential. It signifies, first, that several concurrent descriptions of symbolic phenomena are in question. But in conjunction with the absence of the definite article it indicates, above all, the partial character of this research. Clearly this book is not to be a complete history of semiotics (nor even of one aspect of semiotics); we are not dealing with all the theories of the symbol nor even perhaps with the most important among them. This choice of the partial results from a material impossibility as well as from personal inclination: the tradition I am studying is so vast that as soon as one imagines extending it beyond the borders of a single country to the Western world as a whole, one realizes that it cannot be known in the course of a single human lifetime. At best I have written some few chapters in the history of Western semiotics.

A few chapters at random? It would be hypocritical, or naïve, to affirm that. In reality, this book is organized around a period of crisis which coincides with the end of the eighteenth century. A radical change in ways of thinking about the symbol occurred in this period (although the change had long been in preparation): a viewpoint that had been dominant for centuries in the West gave way to another that, I believe, still reigns today. It is thus possible, over the span of some fifty years, to grasp both the earlier viewpoint (which for convenience I often call "classic") and the new one (which I term "romantic"). This condensation of history over a relatively short period was decisive in determining my starting point.

This initial choice accounts for the organization of the book. The first chapter is situated outside the problematics I have just outlined; it is offered as a kind of brief handbook, summarizing the common stock of semiotic knowledge available to all. To this end I have started with another moment that I consider critical: the birth of semiotics in the work of Augustine.

The next four chapters explore various aspects of the "classic" doctrine in two particular areas, rhetoric and aesthetics (I have left aside the history of hermeneutics, which leads in much the same direction). The first of these four chapters includes a brief survey of the problematics of the entire book.

Chapter 6, the longest, presents yet another synthetic overview. Here I attempt to summarize and to systematize the new doctrine that gave rise to the crisis, describing the doctrine as it appears in what I take to be its locus of fullest development, German romanticism. Quotations are numerous in this chapter, as in the first; it seemed useful to provide the reader with the texts I was examining, since they have never been brought together and in many cases they have not even been translated. Without putting together an anthology, I wanted to make this book a useful source of documents.

The four chapters that follow deal essentially with authors who come after the romantic crisis. But in them we do not merely find diverse expressions of a common attitude. Chosen from among the most influential of our time, the authors examined here present new variations with respect to the great dichotomy between classics and romantics; they occupy positions that complicate the picture instead of clarifying it.

In each period I have chosen to study the area that seemed the most revealing; this choice doubtless accounts for the impression of discontinuity that may emerge from a reading of these chapters. The first chapter treats semiotics; the next two, rhetoric; then come three chapters devoted to aesthetics. The last four chapters deal with disciplines that in our time belong to the human sciences: anthropology, psychoanalysis, linguistics, poetics. But to reveal the unity of a problematics, a unity that has been dissimulated by diverse traditions and terminologies, is after all one of the chief tasks of this book.

The plurality of the theories examined gives this work its historical character. I would willingly regard it as a "history-fiction" if I did not suspect that this is the case for every history and that my feeling about it is shared by every historian. The historical fact, at first glance a pure given, proves to be wholly constructed. Two further choices have been made in the wake of this first and perhaps inevitable observation. On the one hand, I have sought to retrace the history of the advent of ideas and not that of their earliest formulation; I have attempted to grasp them at the moment of their reception rather than at that of their production. On the other hand, I do not believe that ideas alone generate other ideas: without venturing too far into unfamiliar areas, I have sought to suggest that the mutation in ideas can be seen in relation to the transformation of ideologies and societies.

I must add that I do not consider myself an impartial historian. I have confronted the earlier theories of the symbol in the course of my own work on linguistic symbolism, and have made their acquaintance in a totally interested fashion: I have looked to them for explanations of phenomena that I could perceive but not comprehend. I have thus chosen, in the authors of the past, what I have found best and most useful. I have doubtless betrayed them; I take comfort from the conviction that one can betray only the living.

I have not written this book for specialists (at least not for those who are *only* specialists), and for this reason I have sought to keep the apparatus of notes and references as simple as possible, even though such an apparatus is to some degree inevitable in a work of this sort. In this minimal form it nonetheless allows readers to locate the sources quoted or to consult other studies on a particular question. I have quoted, as often as possible, from existing translations of foreign-language texts, modifying them as needed in the direction of increased literalness or with a view to unifying the terminology.

Theories of the Symbol

1

The Birth of Western Semiotics

The ambitious title of this chapter obliges me to begin with a limitation. My starting point was a summary notion of semiotics, two components of which are important here: the fact that, with semiotics, we are dealing with a discourse whose objective is knowledge (not poetic beauty or pure speculation), and the fact that its object is constituted by signs of various types (not by words alone). These two conditions were fully met for the first time, it seems to me, by Augustine. But Augustine did not invent semiotics; it can even be said that, quite to the contrary, he invented virtually nothing, that he merely combined ideas and notions drawn from several horizons. Thus I had to go back to his "sources," as they are found in grammatical and rhetorical theory, in logic, and so forth. By no means, however, have I undertaken a complete historical survey of each of these disciplines up to Augustine's day—even though, at other times, they may have inspired new developments in semiotics. The pre-Augustinian tradition is thus taken into account here only to the extent that it seems to be encountered in Augustine's work, hence the impression (an illusory one) that all antiquity leads to Augustine. This is clearly false, and—to take but one example—if the Epicurean philosophy of language is not dealt with here, this is simply because its relationship to Augustinian semiotics is not particularly significant.

These factors account for the way the chapter is organized. One of its sections is devoted to Augustine's predecessors, who are grouped in categories chosen more because of their logical coherence than because they represent genuinely separate traditions. The other section focuses on Augustinian semiotics itself.

PRE-AUGUSTINIAN DISCIPLINES

Semantics

I trust I shall be forgiven for beginning this overview with Aristotle; he will reappear under several headings. For the moment, I shall limit myself to his theory of language as it appears in particular in the early chapters of *On Interpretation*. The key passage is the following:

> Spoken words are the symbols of mental experience and written words are the symbols of spoken words. Just as all men have not the same writing, so all men have not the same speech sounds, but the mental experiences, which these directly symbolize, are the same for all, as also are those things of which our experiences are the images. [16a][1]

If we juxtapose this short paragraph with other parallel developments, we can distinguish several assertions.

(1) Aristotle speaks of *symbols*, among which words are a special case. This term should be noted. It is important that the term "sign" does not figure in the initial definition. As we shall see in a moment, "sign" has for Aristotle another, technical sense.

(2) The sort of symbol immediately taken up as an example is made up of words; these are defined as a relation among three terms: sounds, states of mind, and things. The second term serves as intermediary between the first and the third, which are not in direct communication with each other; this intermediate term thus participates in two relations that are different in nature, as are the terms themselves. Things are identical to themselves, always and everywhere; so are states of mind; for they are independent of individuals. Thus things and states of mind are linked by a moti-

1. For information about editions cited, see the Bibliographical Notes at the end of the book.

vated relation in which, as Aristotle says, the one is the *image* of the other. On the other hand, sounds are not the same in different countries. Their relationship with states of mind is unmotivated: the one signifies the other, without being the image of it.

This argument draws us into the ancient controversy over the cognitive power of nouns, and, correlatively, over the origin of language (was it natural or conventional?), of which the most familiar discussion is found in Plato's *Cratylus*. This debate emphasizes problems of knowledge and origin that will not preoccupy us here, and it concerns only words, not all types of signs; we must, however, take note of its form, for it can (and will) be said that signs are either natural or conventional. This was already true of Aristotle, who adhered, in this controversy, to the conventionalist hypothesis. The affirmation recurs frequently in his work; it is used to justify, among other things, his distinction between language and animal cries, which are also vocal, also interpretable. "By noun we mean a sound significant by convention. . . . The limitation 'by convention' was introduced because nothing is by nature a noun or name—it is only so when it becomes a symbol; inarticulate sounds, such as those which brutes produce, are significant, yet none of these constitutes a noun" (*On Interpretation*, 16a). The symbols are thus subdivided into (conventional) "nouns" and (natural) "signs." Let us note in this regard that, in the *Poetics*, 1456b, Aristotle provides still another basis for the distinction between human and animal sound: the latter cannot combine into larger signifying units. This suggestion seems not to have been pursued further in classical thought; it leads, however, in the same direction as the present-day theory of the double articulation of language.

As a partisan of the unmotivated relation between sounds and meaning, Aristotle is well aware of the cases of polysemy and synonymy that illustrate this relation. He speaks of them at several points; for example, in *On Sophistical Refutations*, 165a, and in the *Rhetoric*, iii, 1405b. These discussions bring clearly to light the noncoincidence of meaning and referent. "The sophist Bryson [claimed] that there is no such thing as foul language, because in whatever words you put a given thing your meaning is the same. This is untrue. One term may describe a thing more truly than another, may be more like it, and set it more intimately before our eyes" (1405b; cf. another example in the *Physics*, 263b). In a more general but also a more complex way, in certain texts the term *logos* designates what the word signifies, as opposed to the thing itself; for example, in the *Metaphysics*, 1012a: "The form of words of which the word is a sign will be its definition."

(3) Although they are taken up immediately as the privileged example of a symbol, words are not the only case (it is precisely in this respect that Aristotle's text goes beyond the framework of a strictly linguistic semantics): the second example cited is that of letters. I shall not dwell here on the secondary role attributed to letters with respect to sounds; that has become a well-known theme through the work of Jacques Derrida. Let us note instead that it is hard to imagine how the tripartite division of the symbol (sounds/states of mind/things) would apply to these particular symbols (letters). Here we are speaking only of two elements, written words and spoken words.

(4) One further remark on the central concept of this description, the states of mind. First, we are concerned here with a psychic entity, with something that is not in the word but in the mind of the language user. Second, although it is a psychic phenomenon, this state of mind is in no way individual: it is identical for all. This entity thus stems from a "social" or even a universal psychology rather than from an individual one.

One problem remains that we shall do no more than formulate here: the problem of the relationship between "states of mind" and significance, or signifying capacity, such as the latter appears, for example, in the text of the *Poetics* (1457a), where the noun is defined as "a composite significant sound." It would seem (but I shall refrain from making any categorical affirmations) that it may be possible to speak of two language states: potential, as envisaged in the *Poetics*, where all psychological perspective is lacking; and actualized, as in *On Interpretation*, where meaning becomes an experienced meaning. Whatever the case, the existence of significance limits the psychic nature of meaning in general.

Such are the results of the earliest thinking on the subject to which we have access. We can scarcely speak, here, of a concept of semiotics: the symbol is defined as being broader than the word, but Aristotle does not seem seriously to have raised the question of nonlinguistic symbols, nor to have sought to describe the variety of linguistic symbols.

A second moment of reflection on the sign occurs in Stoic thought. This body of thought is, of course, very little known, for only fragmentary texts have been preserved (and these texts are found, moreover, in authors generally hostile to the Stoics). We must therefore make do with a few succinct remarks. The most important fragment is found in Sextus Empiricus, *Against the Logicians*, II, 11–12:

> [The Stoics say] that "three things are linked together, the thing signified and the thing signifying and the thing existing"; and of these the thing signifying is the sound ("Dion," for instance); and the thing signified is the actual thing indicated thereby, and which we apprehend as existing in dependence on our intellect, whereas the barbarians although hearing the sound do not understand it; and the thing existing is the external real object such as Dion himself. And of these, two are bodies—that is, the sound and the existing thing—and one is incorporeal, namely the thing signified and expressible [the *lekton*], and this too is true or false.

Again, let us look at some important points.

(1) The terms "signifier" and "signified" (in a sense that Saussure, by the way, will not maintain) make their appearance here while the term "sign" is not used. This absence, as we shall see shortly, is not accidental. The example given is a word, more precisely a proper noun, and nothing in the passage suggests that other sorts of symbols might exist.

(2) Here, as in Aristotle, three categories are posited simultaneously; in both texts, the object, although exterior to language, is necessary to the definition. And in both of these presentations, no notable difference separates the first and third elements, sound and object.

(3) If there is any difference, it is in the *lekton*, the "expressible" or signified. Modern literature offers numerous discussions concerning the nature of that entity; the inconclusiveness of the debates leads us to keep the Greek term. We must recall first that the *lekton*'s status as "incorporeal" is exceptional in the resolutely materialist philosophy of the Stoics. This means that it is impossible to conceive of the *lekton* as an impression in the mind, even a conventional one: such impressions (or "states of mind") are, for the Stoics, corporeal. "Objects," on the other hand, need not necessarily belong to the world that can be observed by the senses: they may be physical or psychic. The *lekton* is not located in speakers' minds but in language itself. The reference to barbarians is revealing. The latter hear the sound and see the man,

but they are unacquainted with the *lekton*, that is, with the fact that this sound evokes that object. The *lekton* is the capacity of the first element to designate the third; in this sense, the fact of having a proper name as an example is highly significant, since the proper name, unlike other words, has no meaning, but, like other words, has a capacity for designation. The *lekton* depends on thought but must not be confused with thought; it is not a concept, and still less—as some would have it—a Platonic idea. It is rather upon the *lekton* that thought operates. By the same token, the internal articulation of these three terms is not what it was for Aristotle: there are no longer two radically distinct relations (of meaning and image); the *lekton* is what allows sounds to be related to objects.

(4) Sextus's last words, according to which the *lekton* may be true or false, suggest that it may be equivalent to a proposition; the example cited, however, which is an isolated word, leads in a different direction. Here, other fragments, reported either by Sextus or by Diogenes Laertius, give us a clearer view of the question.

On the one hand, the *lekton* may be complete (a proposition) or incomplete (a word). Here is Diogenes' text: Speaking of *lekta*, "the Stoics say that some are complete in themselves and others defective. Those are defective the enunciation of which is unfinished, as *e.g.* 'writes,' for we inquire 'Who?' Whereas in those that are complete in themselves the enunciation is finished, as 'Socrates writes'" (*Life*, VII, 63). This distinction was already present in Aristotle, and it leads to the grammatical theory of parts of speech; we shall not be concerned with it here.

On the other hand, propositions are not necessarily true or false. Only assertions can be so evaluated, while imperatives, interrogatives, oaths, curses, hypotheses, vocatives, and so on are not subject to this criterion (ibid., 65). Here again is an argument that was commonplace in its day.

We cannot speak of an explicit semantic theory here, any more than we could in Aristotle's case. For the time being, only the linguistic sign is in question.

Logic

It is somewhat arbitrary to set up independent categories such as "semantics" and "logic" where the classical authors themselves made no such distinctions. By doing so, however, we can see more clearly the autonomous character of texts that, from the modern point of view, deal with related problems. I shall review the same authors considered before.

Aristotle's logical theory of the sign is presented in the *Prior Analytics* and in the *Rhetoric*. Here, to begin with, is the definition: "Anything such that when it is another thing is, or when it has come into being the other has come into being before or after, is a sign of the other's being or having come into being" (*Pr. an.*, 70a). Aristotle illustrates the concept with the following example (one destined to serve many times over): the fact that a woman has milk is a sign that she has given birth.

The concept of the sign has to be situated first in its own context. For Aristotle, the sign is a truncated syllogism, one that lacks a conclusion. One of its premises (the other may be lacking, too, as we shall see later on) serves as a sign; the referent is the (absent) conclusion. Here a first correction must be offered: for Aristotle, the syllogism illustrated by the preceding example is indistinguishable from conventional syllogisms of the type "If all men are mortal. . . ." We now know that the two must be distinguished: the traditional syllogism describes the relation of predicates within a given proposition (or in adjacent propositions), while the example cited derives from the logic of propositions, not that of predicates. The relations among predicates are not pertinent here; only the interpropositional relations count. In classical logic, this distinction is masked by the term used to describe such cases as we are considering here: "hypothetical syllogism."

The fact that we are moving from one proposition to another (from "this woman has milk" to "this woman has given birth") and not from one predicate to another (from "mortals" to "men") is crucial, for we are passing by the same token from substance to event, and this passage makes it much easier to take nonlinguistic symbolism into consideration. Moreover, we have seen that Aristotle's definition dealt with things and not with propositions (in other texts, the reverse is true). As a result, we are not surprised to note that Aristotle is now explicitly referring to nonlinguistic and, more specifically, to visual signs (70b). The example offered is the following: large extremities may be the sign of courage in lions. Aristotle's perspective here is more epistemological than semiotic: he is speculating about the possibility of acquiring knowledge on the basis of such signs. From this viewpoint, he moves on to distinguish the necessary sign (*tekmêrion*) from the

sign that is merely probable. We shall not explore this aspect of
Aristotle's thought any further.

Another system of classification deals with the content of the
predicates in each proposition: "Of signs, one kind bears the same
relation to the statement it supports as the particular bears to the
universal, the other the same as the universal bears to the particular" (Rhet. I, 1357b). The example of the woman who has given
birth illustrates the latter case; an example of the former type
would be: "A sign that the learned are just is that Socrates was
learned and just." Once again, we see the damage done by the
confusion between the logic of predicates and the logic of propositions. If Socrates is, in fact, the individual with respect to the universal (learned, just), on the other hand the fact that the woman
in question has milk and the fact that she has given birth are two
"particulars" with respect to the general law according to which
"if a woman has milk it is because she has given birth."

On the linguistic level, signs are implied propositions; but
Aristotle cautions that not every implied proposition is evoked by
a "sign." In fact, there exist implicit propositions that derive either
from collective memory or from the logic of the lexicon ("e.g. the
man who said 'X is a man' has also said that it is an animal and
that it is animate and a biped and capable of acquiring reason and
knowledge": Topics, 112a); in other words, there are synthetic
propositions and analytic propositions. In order for a sign to exist,
something more than the implicit meaning must be present; but
Aristotle does not say what this additional element is.

Nowhere is the theory of the logical sign articulated with that
of the linguistic symbol (nor, as we shall see later on, with that of
the rhetorical trope). Even the technical terms are different: here,
sign; there, symbol.

The same situation prevails with the Stoics. Here is a transcription from Sextus Empiricus:

> The Stoics . . . , in attempting to establish the conception of the
> sign, state that "A sign is an antecedent judgement in a valid
> hypothetical syllogism, which serves to reveal the consequent."
> . . . "Antecedent," they say, is "the precedent clause in a hypo-
> thetical syllogism which begins in truth and ends in truth."
> And it "serves to reveal the consequent," since in the syllogism
> "If this woman has milk, she has conceived," the clause "If this
> woman has milk" seems to be evidential of the clause "she has
> conceived." [Outlines of Pyrrhonism, II, xi, 104, 106]

Here we encounter several elements of the Aristotelian analysis, including the key example. Sign theory is linked to the theory of demonstration, and once again what interests its authors is the nature of the knowledge to be derived from it. The only difference—but it is an important one—is that the Stoics, who practice propositional rather than categorical logic, are conscious of the logical properties of this type of reasoning. This preferential attention to propositions has surprising consequences: it is because of such interest in propositions, as we have already noted in the case of Aristotle, that sustained attention begins to be paid to what we would call nonlinguistic signs. Aristotle's logic of classes "is suited to a philosophy of substance and of essence" (Blanché, p.9); propositional logic, for its part, grasps facts in their becoming, facts as events. Now it is precisely events (and not substances) that come to be treated as signs. This change in the object of knowledge (from classes to propositions) thus entails an extension of the material under consideration (the nonlinguistic is added to the linguistic).

The lack of articulation between this theory and the preceding one (that of language) is all the more blatant here because of the close proximity of the terms used in each case. We have observed that, in their semantic theory, the Stoics did not speak of signs, but only of signifiers and signifieds; the relationship is nonetheless striking, and the Skeptic Sextus did not fail to pick it up. His critique, which formally states the necessity of bringing together the various theories of the sign, represents another major step toward the constitution of a semiotics. Purporting to believe that one and the same "sign" is at work in the two cases, Sextus compares the signifier-signified pair with the antecedent-consequent pair and observes several differences. This leads him to formulate the following objections:

(1) The signifier and the signified are simultaneous, whereas the antecedent and the consequent are successive: how can the same name serve for these two relations? "The sign cannot serve to reveal the consequent, if the thing signified is relative to the sign and is, therefore, apprehended along with it. . . . And if the sign is not apprehended before the thing signified, neither can it really serve to reveal the actual thing which is apprehended along with itself and not after itself" (*Outlines of Pyrrhonism*, II, xi, 117–118).

(2) The signifier is "corporeal," whereas the antecedent, being a proposition, is "incorporeal." "Some things signify, others are

signified. Vocal sounds signify, but expressions are signified, and they include also propositions. And as propositions are signified, but not signifying, the sign will not be a proposition" (*Against the Logicians*, II, 264).

(3) The passage from antecedent to consequent is a logical operation. Now anyone at all, even animals, can interpret observed facts:

> If the sign is a judgement and an antecedent in a valid major premiss, those who have no conception at all of a judgement, and have made no study of logical technicalities, ought to have been wholly incapable of interpreting by signs. But this is not the case; for often illiterate pilots, and [often] farmers unskilled in logical theorems, interpret by signs excellently—the former on the sea prognosticating squalls and calms, stormy weather and fair, and the latter on the farm foretelling good crops and bad crops, droughts and rainfalls. Yet why do we talk of men, when some of the Stoics have endowed even irrational animals with understanding of the sign? For, in fact, the dog, when he tracks a beast by its footprints, is interpreting by signs; but he does not therefore derive an impression of the judgement "if this is a footprint, a beast is here." The horse, too, at the prod of a goad or the crack of a whip leaps forward and starts to run, but he does not frame a judgement logically in a premiss, such as this—"if a whip has cracked, I must run." Therefore the sign is not a judgement, which is the antecedent in a valid major premiss. [*Against the Logicians*, II, 269–271]

We have to admit that, although Sextus's criticisms are often purely formal quibbles, here they are not without substance. The assimilation of the two types of signs does pose problems. Let us imagine that Sextus was looking not for inconsistencies in the Stoic doctrine but for the point of articulation between the two theories. His objections then become constructive criticisms that may be reformulated as follows:

(1) Simultaneity and succession are the consequences of a more fundamental difference: in the case of the linguistic sign (word or proposition), the signifier evokes its signified directly; in the case of the logical sign, the antecedent, inasmuch as it is a linguistic segment, has its own meaning, which will be maintained; only secondarily does it evoke something else as well, that is, the consequent. We are dealing then with the difference between direct and indirect signs, or, in a terminology opposed to Aristotle's, with the difference between signs and symbols.

(2) Direct signs are composed of heterogeneous elements: sounds, incorporeal *lekton*, object; indirect symbols are made up of entities that are like in nature: one *lekton*, for example, evokes another.

(3) These indirect symbols may be either linguistic or nonlinguistic. In the first case, they take the form of two propositions; in the second, of two events. In this latter form, they are accessible not only to logicians but also to the uneducated and even to animals. The substance of the symbol does not dictate its structure. Moreover, no one will confuse the capacity to make inferences with the possibility of talking (as logicians do) about this capacity.

If we consider the classification of *lekta* into two groups, complete and incomplete, we note that it is possible to draw up a chart with a blank space.

	WORD	PROPOSITION
direct	incomplete *lekton*	complete *lekton*
indirect	?	sign

This gap is all the more puzzling (perhaps it may be attributed simply to the fragmentary state of the Stoic writings that have been preserved) in that the Stoics are the founders of a hermeneutic tradition based on the indirect meaning of *words*—on *allegory*. But this line of reasoning draws us into the framework of another discipline.

Before abandoning the logical theory of the Stoics, we must mention one more problem. Sextus reports that the Stoics divide signs into two classes: commemorative and revelatory. This subdivision results from an a priori classification of things according to whether they are clear or obscure, and, in the second case, whether they are always, occasionally, or naturally obscure. In the first two classes that result from this categorization, things that are clear and things that are always obscure, the sign has no role. It is in the latter two classes that the sign comes into play; these classes become the basis for two categories of signs:

> Such objects as are occasionally or naturally non-evident are apprehended by means of signs—not of course by the same signs, but by "suggestive" signs in the case of the occasionally non-evident and by "indicative" signs in the case of the natu-

rally non-evident. Of the signs, then, according to them, some are suggestive, some indicative. [The Stoics] term a sign "suggestive" when, being mentally associated with the thing signified, it by its clearness at the time of its perception, though the thing associated with it remains non-evident, suggests to us the thing associated with it, which is not clearly perceived at the moment—as for instance in the case of smoke and fire. An "indicative" sign, they say, is that which is not clearly associated with the thing signified, but signifies that whereof it is a sign by its own particular nature and constitution, just as, for instance, the bodily motions are signs of the soul. [*Outlines of Pyrrhonism*, ii, x, 99–101]

Among the commemorative signs, another example would be a scar for an injury, a stab-wound in the heart for death; among the revelatory signs, perspiration for the pores of the skin.

This distinction does not seem to bring into play the properly semiotic structure of signs, and the problem it poses is simply epistemological. In his critique of the distinction, however, Sextus brings the debate back to a terrain closer to our area of interest. For he does not believe in the existence of revelatory signs. Thus he modifies, first, the relation of these classes, by elevating the one—the class of commemorative signs—to the rank of genus, and relegating the other—the class of revelatory signs—to the rank of species, in whose existence, moreover, he does not believe (*Against the Logicians*, 143). From here on, his discussion brings into play two other oppositions: polysemic and monosemic signs, and natural and conventional signs. The debate may be summarized as follows. Sextus contests the existence of revelatory signs by affirming that they do not allow us to derive any certain knowledge, since one thing may symbolize, potentially, an infinite number of other things; such a thing is therefore not a sign. To which the Stoics retort: yes, but commemorative signs may be polysemic as well, and may evoke several things at once. Sextus admits that this is so, but shows that his argument has another basis: commemorative signs can only be polysemic through the power of a convention. Now revelatory signs are, by definition, natural (they exist as things before being interpreted). Commemorative signs are either natural (for example, smoke for fire)—in which case they are monosemic—or else conventional—in which case they may be either monosemic (for example, words) or polysemic (for example, the lighted torch that announces on one occasion the arrival of friends, on another that of enemies). Here is Sextus's text:

> In reply to those who draw inferences from the commemorative sign and quote the case of the torch, and also of the sound of the bell [which may announce the opening of the meat-market or the need to wet down the streets], we must declare that it is not paradoxical for such signs to be capable of announcing more things than one. For they are determined, as they say, by the lawgivers and lie in our power, whether we wish them to indicate one thing or to be capable of announcing several things. But as the indicative sign is supposed to be essentially suggestive of the thing signified, it must necessarily be indicative of one thing. [*Against the Logicians*, II, 200–201]

Sextus's critique, attesting to the idea that the perfect sign has only one meaning and also to Sextus's preference for conventional signs, is interesting for other reasons as well. We have seen that the natural/conventional opposition has been applied, up to this point, to the origin of words, and that it has been necessary to opt for one solution or the other (or for a compromise between the two). Sextus applies this opposition to signs in general (of which words are only a special case), and he conceives furthermore of the simultaneous existence of *both* types of signs, natural and conventional. In this he shares in a properly semiotic perspective. Is it an accident that this perspective needed a certain eclecticism (that of Sextus) in order to flourish?

Rhetoric

Although Aristotle dealt with the "sign," in his sense of the word, within the framework of rhetoric, he analyzed it in purely logical terms. Here we shall examine under the heading of rhetoric not the "sign" but indirect meanings, or *tropes*.

Once again we must begin with Aristotle, for the proper/transposed opposition—which is of primary interest—originated with him. However, the opposition is not, at the beginning, what it will later become. Not only is all semiotic perspective absent from its description, in Aristotle, but the opposition does not yet have the preponderant role that we are used to seeing it play. Transposition, or metaphor (for Aristotle, the term designates all tropes) is not a symbolic structure that possesses a linguistic manifestation among others. It is rather a type of word: one in which the signified is something other than the conventional signified.

This type of word appears within a list of lexical classes that includes, at least at first glance, eight terms; it is a complementary type of neologism, or innovation, in the signifier. To be sure, the existing definitions are a little more ambiguous. We read in the *Poetics*: "Metaphor consists in giving the thing a name that belongs to something else" (1457b). A parallel passage from the *Topics*—but in which the term "metaphor" (transposition) does not appear—states that "those who make false statements and say that an attribute belongs to a thing which does not belong to it, commit error; and those who call objects by the names of other objects (*e.g.* calling a plane-tree a 'man') transgress the established terminology" (109a). The *Rhetoric* speaks, with regard to the tropic operation, of "using metaphors to give names to nameless things" (III, 1405a). It is clear that Aristotle is hesitating between two definitions of metaphor, or else is defining metaphor by this doubleness itself: it is either the improper meaning of a word (transfer, transgression of conventional usage) or the improper expression used to evoke a meaning (a displaced noun, a naming that avoids proper naming). Be that as it may, metaphor remains a purely linguistic category; in fact, it is a subclass of words. The choice of a metaphor rather than a nonmetaphorical term stems from the same tendency that makes us choose one synonym rather than another: we are always seeking what is fitting and appropriate. Here is a passage that says something to this effect:

> If you wish to pay a compliment, you must take your metaphor from something better in the same line; if to disparage, from something worse. To illustrate my meaning: since opposites are in the same class, you do what I have suggested if you say that a man who begs "prays," and a man who prays "begs"; for praying and begging are both variants of asking. [*Rhet.* III, 1405a]

Transposition is but one stylistic device among others (even if it is the one Aristotle preferred), and not a mode of existence of meaning that would have to be articulated with direct signification. Proper meaning, in turn, is not direct meaning, but appropriate meaning. It is understandable that, under these conditions, the theory of transposition as yet shows no opening toward a typology of signs.

This situation does not remain static. As early as the period of Aristotle's disciples, such as Theophrastes, rhetorical figures begin to play a more and more important role; that movement ends only with the death of rhetoric, which comes about when rhetoric is transformed into a "figuratic." The very proliferation of terms is significant. Alongside "transposition," still used in the generic sense, the terms "trope" and "allegory," "irony" and "figure" appear. Their definitions do not diverge much from those Aristotle gives. For example, in the spurious Heraclitus we read: "The stylistic figure that says one thing but means another has its own name, allegory": and in Tryphon: "The trope is a way of speaking that deviates from proper meaning." Here the trope and its synonyms are defined as the appearance of a second meaning, not as the substitution of one signifier for another. But the position and the global role cf tropes are gradually modified: tropes tend increasingly to become one of the two possible poles of signification (the other being direct expression); the opposition is much stronger in Cicero, for example, than in Aristotle.

In the work of Quintilian, synthesizer of the tradition, we can rapidly examine the last link of the rhetorical chain in the classical world. We do not find in him, any more than we did in Aristotle, a semiotic analysis of tropes. Owing to the breadth of his treatise, Quintilian ends up incorporating into his discourse several suggestions leading in this direction, but his lack of rigor prevents him from formulating the problem explicitly. Whereas Aristotle classified indirect expression among numerous other lexical devices, Quintilian tends to present it as one of the two possible modes of language: We "regard allusion as better than directness of speech" (*Institutio Oratoria* [The Education of an Orator], VIII, Pr., 24). But his attempt to elaborate a theory that would account for the opposition between "to say" and "to imply," an opposition that functions through the categories of the proper and the transposed, does not bear fruit; in the last analysis, tropes are equally "proper": "Propriety is also made to include the appropriate use of words in metaphor" (VIII, 2, 11).

The presence of onomatopoeia among the tropes constitutes a curious phenomenon. It is difficult to understand this categorization if we limit ourselves to the definition of trope as change of meaning (or as choice of an improper signifier—for both notions are found in Quintilian). The only possible explanation lies precisely in a semiotic conception of the trope, namely, that it is a motivated sign: this is the only feature common to the metaphor and to onomatopoeia. But this idea is not formulated by

Quintilian; it must wait for Lessing to give it expression, in the eighteenth century.

Quintilian devotes lengthy discussions to allegory, but his quantitative emphasis has no theoretical counterpart. He defines allegory, just as Cicero did, as a series of metaphors, as an extended metaphor. This conception sometimes poses problems, which are rediscovered in the definition of the example; for an example, unlike metaphor, maintains the meaning of the initial assertion that contains it; and yet Quintilian links the example to allegory. The problem (of the subdivisions within the category of indirect signs) goes unnoticed, just as the frontier between tropes and figures of speech remains imprecise.

The domain of rhetoric itself contains no semiotic theories. Nonetheless, it prepares the way for the theories to come, by virtue of the attention it focuses on the phenomenon of indirect meaning. Thanks to rhetoric, the proper/transposed opposition is to become familiar to the classical world (even though there is some uncertainty as to its content).

Hermeneutics

The hermeneutic tradition is so extensive and diversified that it is particularly difficult to grasp. Its object seems to have been recognized very early, at least in the form of an opposition between two orders of language, direct and indirect, clear and obscure, *logos* and *muthos*, and, consequently, between two modes of reception, comprehension in the one case and interpretation in the other. As testimony to this we have the famous fragment in which Heraclitus describes the speech of the Delphian oracle: "The master whose oracle is at Delphi says nothing and hides nothing, but he signifies." The teaching of Pythagoras is evoked in similar terms: "When he spoke with his companions, he exhorted them either by pursuing his thought or by employing symbols" (Porphyry). This opposition is maintained in later writings, although it continues to appear without any attempt at justification. The following example is from Dionysius of Halicarnassus: "Some dare to claim that the figurative form is not permitted in discourse. According to them, one should either say a thing or refrain from saying it, but in every case simply, and should henceforth give up speaking by means of innuendo" (*Ars rhetorica*, ix).

Within this extremely general conceptual framework are located a very large number of exegetic practices. We shall be content to divide them into two widely separated groups: textual *commentary* (especially commentary on Homer and on the Bible) and *divination* in its various forms (mantics).

It may be surprising to find divination among hermeneutic practices. Yet here, too, we encounter an effort to discover meaning in objects that had had none, or to find secondary meanings where there had been but one before. As a first step toward a semiotic conception, let us consider the sheer variety of substances that could become the starting point for interpretation: from water to fire, from the flight of birds to animal entrails, everything seems capable of becoming a sign and thus of giving rise to interpretation. We can assert, furthermore, that this type of interpretation is related to the one imposed by the indirect modes of language, that is, to allegory. Two authors can attest here to an extremely heterogeneous tradition.

First, Plutarch, who, when he seeks to characterize the language of the oracles, relates it inevitably to indirect expression:

> The introduction of clearness was attended also by a revolution in belief, which underwent a change along with everything else. And this was the result: in days of old what was not familiar or common, but was expressed altogether indirectly and through circumlocution, the mass of people imputed to an assumed manifestation of divine power, and held it in awe and reverence; but in later times, being well satisfied to apprehend all these various things clearly and easily without the attendant grandiloquence and artificiality, they blamed the poetic language with which the oracles were clothed, not only for obstructing the understanding of these in their true meaning and for combining vagueness and obscurity with the communication, but already they were coming to look with suspicion upon metaphors, riddles, and ambiguous statements, feeling that these were secluded nooks of refuge devised for furtive withdrawal and retreat for him that should err in his prophecy.
> [*Moralia*, v: *The Oracles at Delphi*, 407]

Oracular language is assimilated here to the transposed and obscure language of the poets.

Our second witness is Artemidorus of Ephesus, author of the famous *Interpretation of Dreams*, which summarizes and systematizes an already rich tradition. At first, the interpretation of dreams is continually related to that of words; sometimes through resemblance: "School teachers, once they have taught their students the values of the letters, then show them how they are to use the letters together. So too will I add a few small, easy-to-follow guidelines to what has already been said, so that the books will be readily understood by everyone" [III, 66]—sometimes through contiguity: "One must also show some degree of independent skill in judging dreams which are mutilated and which do not, as it were, give one anything to hold on to, especially [in the case of very difficult ones] in which certain letters which do not contain a thought that is whole and entire in itself or a meaningless name are seen, sometimes by transposing, sometimes by changing, sometimes by adding letters and syllables to them" (I, 11).

Moreover, Artemidorus opens his book with a distinction between two types of dreams, and the distinction makes its own origin clear: "Some dreams, moreover, are *theorematic* (direct), while others are *allegorical*. Theorematic dreams are those which correspond exactly to their own dream-vision. . . . Allegorical dreams, on the other hand, are those which signify one thing by means of another" (I, 2; emphasis added). This opposition is probably modeled on that of two rhetorical categories, the proper and the transposed, but here it is applied to a nonlinguistic matter. Furthermore, we find a connection—perhaps an unintentional one—between dream images and rhetorical tropes in Aristotle himself; he affirms, on the one hand, that "a good metaphor implies an intuitive perception of the similarity in dissimilars" (*Poetics*, 1459a), and, on the other hand, that "the most skilful interpreter of dreams is he who has the faculty of observing resemblances" (*Parva Naturalia: On Prophesying by Dreams*, II, 464b). Artemidorus, too, wrote that "the interpretation of dreams is nothing other than the juxtaposition of similarities" (*Interpretation of Dreams*, II, 25).

Let us now return to the principal hermeneutic activity, that of textual exegesis. This is, in the beginning, a practice that implies no particular sign theory but rather what might be called a strategy of interpretation, one that varies from school to school. Not until Clement of Alexandria do we find, within the hermeneutic tradition itself, any effort in the direction of semiotics. First of all, Clement explicitly articulates the unity of the symbolic field; he underlines this unity, moreover, by his systematic use of the word "symbol"; he also speaks of "what is expressed in veiled terms" (*The Miscellanies*, v, ix). He enumerates the varieties of the symbolic, as for example in the following text:

The observances practised by the Romans in the case of wills have a place here; those balances and small coins to denote justice, and freeing of slaves, and rubbing of the ears. For these observances are, that things may be transacted with justice; and those for the dispensing of honour; and the last, that he who happens to be near, as if a burden were imposed on him, should stand and hear and take the post of mediator. [v, viii]

All of these devices are symbolic, as is, also, indirect language: "'Atœeas king of the Scythians to the people of Byzantium: Do not impair my revenues in case my mares drink your water;' for the Barbarian indicated symbolically that he would make war on them" (v, v).

If Clement fails to distinguish here between linguistic and non-linguistic symbolism, he maintains a clear distinction, in contrast, between symbolic and nonsymbolic (indirect and direct) language. Holy Scripture includes passages written in each style, but different specialists enable us to read both: Didascalus on the one hand, the Pedagogue on the other. This difference derives not only from the fact that *direct* language is opposed to *indirect* language (see for example v, viii), but also from the fact that the one is univocal whereas the other lends itself to multiple interpretations: "Things unconcealed are perceived in one way, [but] we may draw several meanings . . . from what is expressed in veiled form" (v, ix).

Clement is also the author of some reflections on Egyptian writing that profoundly influenced the interpretation of this corpus for centuries to come. These reflections provide a revealing example of his tendency to treat different substances in the same terms, and, more particularly, to apply rhetorical terminology to other types of symbolism (in this case, visual). Clement affirms the existence of several types of writings among the Egyptians, one of which is the hieroglyphic method. Its description follows:

Now those instructed among the Egyptians learned first of all that style of the Egyptian letters which is called Epistolographic; and second, the Hieratic, which the sacred scribes practise; and finally, and last of all, the Hieroglyphic, of which one kind which is by the first elements is literal (Kyriologic), and the other Symbolic. Of the Symbolic, one kind speaks literally by imitation, and another writes as it were figuratively; and another is quite allegorical, using certain enigmas.

Wishing to express Sun in writing, they make a circle; and Moon, a figure like the Moon, like its proper shape. But in using the figurative style, by transposing and transferring, by changing and by transforming in many ways as suits them, they draw characters. In relating the praises of the kings in theological myths, they write in anaglyphs. Let the following stand as a specimen of the third species—the Enigmatic. For the rest of the stars, on account of their oblique course, they have figures like the bodies of serpents; but the sun like that of a beetle, because it makes a round figure of ox-dung, and rolls it before its face. [v, iv]

In this well-known text several points stand out. First, the possibility of encountering the same structures through different substances: language (metaphors and enigmas), writing (hieroglyphics), painting (imitation). This type of unification constitutes one step toward the elaboration of a semiotic theory. Furthermore, Clement proposes a typology of the whole area of signs: the brevity of his proposition obliges us to make certain hypothetical reconstructions. We can summarize his classification as shown in the diagram.

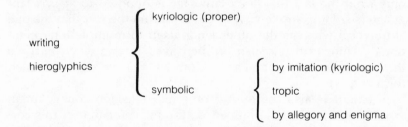

This distribution is obviously problematic in two respects: the fact that the kyriologic (proper) method appears in two different places in the chart, and the fact that allegory, considered a trope in rhetorical terms, here constitutes a separate class. In an attempt to preserve the coherence of the text, one might propose the following explanation, based on the examples quoted. First, the kyriologic genus and the kyriologic symbolic species have some common and some divergent features. They both denote a relation that is *direct*: a letter designates a sound as a circle designates the sun, in an immediate way; the letter and the circle possess no other, prior signification. However, the genus and the species differ as well: the relation between a letter and a sound is *unmotivated*, whereas that of the sun and a circle is *motivated*; this difference may in turn arise from other causes not mentioned here.

Thus the opposition between the kyriologic genus and the symbolic genus is the opposition between the unmotivated and the motivated, whereas the opposition within the symbolic genus between the kyriologic species and the other species is the opposition between the direct and the indirect (the transposed).

Furthermore, two steps are required to decipher tropic writing: the pictogram designates one object (by direct imitation); this object in turn evokes another, through resemblance, or participation, or opposition, and so on. What Clement calls enigma, or allegory, on the other hand, implies three relations: between the pictogram and the beetle, that of direct imitation; between the beetle and the piece of dung, a relation of contiguity (metonymic); finally, between the piece of dung and the sun, a relation of resemblance (metaphoric). The difference between trope and allegory lies thus in the length of the chain: in the first case there is a single link, in the second there are two. Allegory has already been defined, in rhetoric, as an extended metaphor; but for Clement, this prolongation does not follow the surface of the text—it occurs instead, as it were, on the spot, in depth.

If we accept the idea that the difference between tropic writing and allegorical writing is the difference between two relations and three, we find that the position of kyriologic symbolic writing is clarified: it takes first place, for it requires the constitution of a single relation, the one between the circle and the sun, between the image and its meaning; it does not depend on any other link. Such an interpretation would explain the classification Clement proposes, and would make manifest, at the same time, the sign theory underlying this system; this theory is plausible to the extent that the category of linkage is indeed present in Clement.

Even apart from this essential (but hypothetical) theoretical contribution, Clement remains a very important figure, for he prepares the way for Augustine on two critical points, by affirming (1) that the material variety of symbolism, which may be communicated by means of all the senses, and which may be linguistic or not, does not diminish its structural unity, and (2) that the symbol is articulated with the sign as transposed meaning is articulated with proper meaning, thus that rhetorical concepts can be applied to nonverbal signs. Finally, it is Clement who first spells out clearly the equivalence between the symbolic and the indirect.

THE AUGUSTINIAN SYNTHESIS

Definition and Description of the Sign

Augustine does not aspire to be a semiotician. His work is organized around a completely different objective, a religious one. It is only in passing, and in terms of this other objective, that he articulates a theory of signs. His interest in the problematics of semiotics, however, seems to be greater than he himself admits or even suspects; in fact, throughout his life he keeps coming back to the same semiotic questions. His thinking in this area does not remain constant; we shall need to examine the course of its evolution. The most important texts, from our point of view, are the following: a treatise of his youth, sometimes considered inauthentic, called *On Dialectics*, written in 387; *On Christian Doctrine*, a central text from every standpoint, of which at least the part that concerns us was written in 397; and *On the Trinity*, dating from 415. But many other texts also contain valuable information.

In *On Dialectics*, Augustine gives the following definition: "A sign is something which is itself sensed and which indicates to the mind something beyond the sign itself. To speak is to give a sign by means of an articulate utterance" (v). Several aspects of this definition merit our attention. First, one property of the sign that will play a major role later on makes its appearance here: a certain nonidentity of the sign with itself, a feature arising from the fact that the sign is originally double, is at once perceptible and intelligible (we found nothing of the sort in Aristotle's description of the symbol). Moreover, Augustine here affirms more strongly than earlier writers have done that words are merely one type of sign; this affirmation, which stands out with increasing sharpness in his later writings, is the cornerstone of the semiotic perspective.

The second important sentence is the one that opens the fifth chapter of *On Dialectics*: "A word is a sign of any sort of thing. It is spoken by a speaker and can be understood by a hearer" (v). This too is a definition, but a double one, for it brings to light two separate relations: first, the relation between sign and thing (this is the framework of designation and signification), second, the relation between speaker and hearer (this is the framework of communication). Augustine links the two in a couple of brief sentences, as if their coexistence posed no problem whatever. His insistence on the communicative dimension is new: that dimension is lacking in the work of the Stoics, who had a pure theory of signification, and it is much less strongly affirmed by Aristotle: he indeed refers to "states of mind," and thus to speakers, but he sheds no light at all on the communicative context. This passage from Augustine provides an early clue to the two major tendencies of his semiotics, its eclecticism and its psychologism.

The very ambiguity produced here by the juxtaposition of several perspectives appears again when the sign is broken down into its constituent elements (in a particularly obscure section of the treatise). "These four are to be kept distinct: the *verbum* [word], the *dicibile* [expressible], the *dictio* [expression], and the *res* [thing]" (v). In the explanation that follows (which is complicated by the fact that Augustine takes *words* as his example of *things*), two excerpts in particular help to clarify the difference between *dicibile* and *dictio*:

> Now that which the mind not the ears perceives from the word and which is held within the mind itself is called a *dicibile* [expressible]. When a word is spoken not for its own sake but for the sake of signifying something else, it is called a *dictio* [expression]. [v]

And:

> Let us take as an example a grammarian questioning a boy in this manner: "What part of speech is *'arma'*?" "*Arma*" is said for its own sake, the word for the sake of the word itself. The other words that he speaks, "what part of speech," whether or not they are understood by the mind or uttered by the voice, are not an end in themselves but concern the word "arma." Now when we consider words as perceived in the mind, prior to utterance they are *dicibilia*, but when they are uttered, as I have said, they become *dictiones*. As for "arma," in the context we supposed, it is a *verbum*, but when it was uttered by Vergil it was a *dictio*, for it was not said for its own sake but in order to signify either the wars which Aeneas waged, or his shield, or the other arms which Vulcan made for the hero. [v]

On the lexical level, this four-term series clearly has its origin in an amalgam. As Jean Pépin has shown, *dictio* translates *lexis*; *dicibile* is the exact equivalent of *lekton*, and *res* may replace *tughanon*; this would give a Latin version of the tripartite Stoic distribution among signifier, signified, and thing. From another standpoint, the opposition between *res* and *verba* is commonplace, as we shall see, in the rhetoric of Cicero and Quintilian. The merging of these two terminologies creates a problem, for it leaves us with two terms designating the signifier: *dictio* and *verbum*.

Augustine seems to resolve this terminological muddle by linking it with another ambiguity that we have encountered before: that of meaning as it belongs at one and the same time to the process of communication and to the process of designation. Thus on the one hand we have one term too many, and on the other hand a double concept: by the same token, *dicibile* is reserved for the experienced meaning (the Stoics used this term in another sense), and *dictio* is associated with referential meaning. *Dicibile* is experienced either by the person who speaks ("perceived in the mind, prior to utterance") or by the one who hears ("that which the mind . . . perceives"). *Dictio*, on the contrary, is a meaning that comes into play not between the interlocutors but (like the *lekton*) between sound and thing; it is what the word signifies independently of any user. By this token, *dicibile* takes its place in a sequence: first the speaker conceives a meaning, then utters sounds; next the hearer perceives the sounds, then perceives the meaning. *Dictio* functions in simultaneity: the referential meaning is realized at the same time the sounds are uttered: a word only becomes *dictio* if (and when) it is "uttered by the voice." Finally, *dicibile* is a property of propositions considered in the abstract, whereas *dictio* belongs to each particular utterance of a proposition (in the terminology of modern logic, reference occurs in propositions that are *tokens*, not *types*).

At the same time, *dictio* does not pertain simply to meaning: it is the word uttered, the signifier, endowed with its denotative capacity; it is "the word that comes out of the mouth," that which is "uttered by the voice." Conversely, *verbum* is not simple sonority, as we might be tempted to imagine, but it is the designation of the word as word, the metalinguistic use of language; it is the word that "is uttered for its own sake, that is, so that something is being asked or argued about the word itself. . . . '*Verbum*' both is a word and signifies a word" (v).

In *Divine Providence and the Problem of Evil* (*De Ordine*), written a few years later, the compromise is formulated differently. Designation becomes an instrument of communication:

> Now, that which is rational in us, that which uses reason and either produces or seeks after the things that are reasonable—saw that names, or meaningful sounds, had to be assigned to

things, so that men might use the sense almost as an interpreter to link them together, inasmuch as they could not perceive
one another's minds. . . . Men could not be most firmly associated unless they conversed and thus poured, so to speak, their
minds and thoughts back and forth to one another. [II, xii, 35]

In the seventh chapter of *On Dialectics*, Augustine provides
another example of his tendency to synthesize. Here he introduces a discussion of what he calls the forcefulness (*vis*) of a
word. Forcefulness is what is responsible for the quality of an expression as such, and what determines its perception by the person to whom it is addressed: A word "has efficacy to the extent to
which it is able to affect a hearer." Sometimes force and meaning
are conceived as two types of signification: "Our reflections give
rise to two ways of looking at the subject: partly through presenting truth, partly through observing propriety." We seem to
be dealing here with an integration of the rhetorical opposition
between clarity and beauty into a theory of signification (the integration is a problematic one, moreover, for the *significance* of a
word is not the same thing as its figural nature, or perceptibility).
The varieties of this "forcefulness" also bring to mind the rhetorical context: "forcefulness" is manifested by sound, by meaning,
or by harmony between the two.

The same theme is developed in *Concerning the Teacher*, written
in 389. Here the two types of signification seem to become properties either of the signifier or of the signified: the function of the
first is to act on the senses, that of the second is to assure interpretation. "Everything which is expressed by the articulate voice
with some signification both strikes the ear so that it can be sensed
and is committed to memory so that it can be known" (v, 12).
This relation is made explicit by means of a pseudo-etymological
argument. "What if words be called such because of one fact and
names be called names because of another, that is, words (*verba*]
from the striking [*a verberando*] and nouns from the knowing [*a
noscendo*]. As the first is called such with regard to the ears, should
not the second be called such in reference to the soul?" (*ibid.*) In
this dual process, perception is subject to intellection, for, as soon
as we understand it, the signifier becomes transparent for us:
"that law . . . by nature is very strong, namely, that when signs
are heard the attention is turned toward the things signified"
(VIII, 24). This second formulation, from the treatise *Concerning
the Teacher*, seems a step backward from the one in *On Dialectics*,

since here Augustine no longer imagines that the signified may have a perceptible form (a "forcefulness") that attracts attention.

Let us now move on to the central treatise, *On Christian Doctrine*. Given its importance in our context, we can justify a rapid glance at its overall plan. This is a work devoted to the theory of the interpretation—and, to a lesser degree, of the expression—of Christian texts. Its exposition is articulated around several oppositions: signs/things, interpretation/expression, difficulties arising from ambiguity or obscurity. Its outline can be presented in schematic form, with numbers designating the four parts of the treatise (the end of the third and the fourth were written in 427, thirty years after the first three).

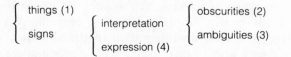

We shall not linger here to consider the tenor of Augustine's ideas about the way discourse is understood and uttered (H. I. Marrou has demonstrated their originality); the attempt at synthesis, apparent even in the outline, is what particularly concerns us. Augustine's project is hermeneutic at the outset; but he adds a section on production (the fourth part) which is to become the first Christian rhetoric. What is more, he inserts the whole into a general sign theory in which a properly semiotic undertaking encompasses what we distinguished earlier under the headings "logic" and "semantics." This text has a better claim than any other to be considered the first semiotic work.

Returning to the sign theory formulated in *On Christian Doctrine*: if we compare it to the one in *On Dialectics*, we observe that only the experienced meaning is preserved; thus the inconsistency of the schema is diminished. Even more surprising is the disappearance of the "thing," or referent. In fact, Augustine does speak of things and of signs in this treatise (and in this he is faithful to the rhetorical tradition handed down from Cicero's time), but he does not take the former to be referents of the latter. The world is divided into signs and things according to whether the perceived object has transitive value or not. Things participate in signs as signifiers, not as referents. Let us note before going any further that this sweeping affirmation is moderated by another assertion, one which, however, remains more an abstract principle than a characteristic of the sign: "Things are learned by signs" (ɪ, ii, 2).

The articulation between signs and things is further developed through the articulation between two basic processes, use and enjoyment. This second distinction is located in fact within the category of things; but things used are transitive, like signs, and things enjoyed are intransitive (here we have a category that allows us to oppose things to signs). "To enjoy something is to cling to it with love for its own sake. To use something, however, is to employ it in obtaining that which you love, provided that it is worthy of love" (ɪ, iv, 4).

This distinction has an important theological extension. In the last analysis, nothing other than God deserves to be enjoyed, to be cherished for itself alone. Augustine develops this idea when he speaks of the love that man can bear to man:

> It is to be asked whether man is to be loved by man for his own sake or for the sake of something else. If for his own sake, we enjoy him; if for the sake of something else, we use him. But I think that man is to be loved for the sake of something else. In that which is to be loved for its own sake the blessed life resides; and if we do not have it for the present, the hope for it now consoles us. But "cursed be the man that trusteth in man" [Jer. 17:5]. But no one ought to enjoy himself either, if you observe the matter closely, because he should not love himself on account of himself but on account of Him who is to be enjoyed. [ɪ, xxii, 20–21]

It follows that the only thing that is absolutely not a sign (because it is the object of enjoyment *par excellence*) is God. This fact, in our culture, imparts a reciprocal coloration of divinity to every ultimate signified (that is, to everything that is signified without signifying anything in turn).

The relation between signs and things having been articulated in this fashion, we now come to the definition of a sign: "A sign is a thing which causes us to think of something beyond the impression the thing itself makes upon the senses" (ɪɪ, i, 1). We are not far from the definition given in *On Dialectics*; "thought" has simply replaced "mind." Another formula is more explicit: "Nor is there any other reason for signifying, or for giving signs, except for bringing forth and transferring to another mind the action of the mind in the person who makes the sign" (ɪɪ, ii, 3). It is no longer a question of defining the sign, but of describing the reasons for the activity of signification. It is no less revealing to note that the relation of designation plays no part here; we are dealing only with the relation of communication. What signs bring to mind is the experienced meaning, the one the speaker has in mind. To signify is to externalize.

The schema of communication is spelled out and developed in certain later texts, for example, in *The First Catechetical Instructions* (405), in which Augustine mentions the problem of the temporal divergence between language and thought. Noting his own frequent dissatisfaction with the way a thought is expressed, he explains it as follows:

> This is so chiefly because intuition floods the mind, as it were, with a sudden flash of light, while the expression of it in speech is a slow, drawn-out, and far different process, and while speech is being formed, intellectual apprehension has already hidden itself in its secret recesses; nevertheless, because it has stamped in a wonderful way certain imprints upon the memory, these endure for the length of time it takes to pronounce the words; and from these imprints we construct those audible symbols which are called language, whether it be Latin, or Greek, or Hebrew, or any other tongue, whether these symbols exist in the mind or are actually uttered by the voice, though these marks are neither Latin, nor Greek, nor Hebrew, nor peculiar to any other race. [II, 3]

Thus Augustine imagines a state of meaning in which meaning does not yet belong to any language (it is not entirely clear whether or not there exists a Latin signified, a Greek signified, and so on, apart from the universal meaning; this would seem unlikely, since language is described exclusively in its phonetic dimension). The situation is not very different from the one Aristotle described; there, as here, states of mind are universal and languages are particular. But Aristotle accounts for this identity of psychic states by the identity with itself of the referent-object, while Augustine's text does not deal with objects at all. We must also note the instantaneous nature of the "intuition," and the inevitable duration of (linear) discourse; in more general terms, this passage points to the necessity of thinking of linguistic activity as endowed with a temporal dimension (a dimension undermined by the role of the imprints). All of these features are, once again, characteristic of the process of communication (the entire passage, moreover, reflects a highly nuanced psychological analysis).

The sign theory presented in *On the Trinity* is yet another extension of the one in *The First Catechetical Instructions* (as is the one appearing in the eleventh book of the *Confessions*). The schema here remains entirely within the realm of communication. "When we speak to others, we apply to the word, remaining within us, the ministry of the voice or of some bodily sign, that by some kind of sensible remembrance some similar thing may be wrought also in the mind of him that hears—similar, I say, to that which does not depart from the mind of him who speaks" (IX, vii, 12).

This description remains very close to that of the act of signification that we found in *On Christian Doctrine*. However, Augustine distinguishes still more clearly here between what he calls the *word* that precedes the division into languages, and the linguistic *signs* that make the word known to us.

> For those are called words in one way, which occupy spaces of time by their syllables, whether they are pronounced or only thought; and in another way, all that is known is called a word imprinted on the mind. [IX, x, 15]
>
> This [word] belongs to no tongue, to wit, of those which are called the tongues of nations, of which our Latin tongue is one. . . . The thought that is formed by the thing which we know, is the word which we speak in the heart: which word is neither Greek nor Latin, nor of any other tongue. But when it is needful to convey this to the knowledge of those to whom we speak, then some sign is assumed whereby to signify it. [xv, x, 19]

Words do not designate things directly; they merely express. What they express, however, is not the speaker's individuality, but an internal, prelinguistic word. This latter is determined in turn by other factors—two of them, it would seem. These are, on the one hand, the imprints left in the soul by the objects of knowledge, and, on the other hand, immanent knowledge whose source can only be God.

> We must go on, then, to that word of man . . . which is neither utterable in sound nor capable of being thought under the likeness of sound, such as must needs be with the word of any tongue; but which precedes all the signs by which it is signi-

fied, and is begotten from the knowledge that continues in the mind, when that same knowledge is spoken inwardly according as it really is. [xv, xi, 20]

This human process of expression and signification, taken as a whole, constitutes an analogue to the Word of God, whose outward sign is not the word but the world; the two sources of knowledge are in the last analysis but one, to the extent that the world is the divine language.

That which is uttered with the mouth of the flesh is the articulate sound of a word; and is itself also called a word, on account of that to make which outwardly apparent it is itself assumed. For our word is so made in some way into an articulate sound of the body, by assuming that articulate sound by which it may be manifested to men's senses, as the Word of God was made flesh, by assuming that flesh in which itself also might be manifested to men's senses. [xv, xi, 20].

The doctrine of universal symbolism, which is to dominate medieval tradition, can be observed in the process of formulation here.

In summary, we may establish a circuit (which is the same, in symmetrically inverse form, for speaker and hearer) as shown in the diagram.

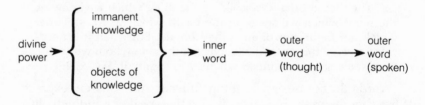

This schema makes it clear to what extent the word-thing relation in particular is the bearer of successive mediations.

It remains the case, so far as semiotic theory is concerned, that the materialist doctrine of the Stoics, which depends upon the analysis of designation, is progressively but decisively displaced in the work of Augustine by a doctrine of communication.

Classification of Signs

It is especially in *On Christian Doctrine* that Augustine concentrates on classifying the signs and thus on nuancing the very notion of sign; his other writings help to clarify certain details. In considering the Augustinian classifications, one is struck at once by their considerable number (even after attempting to group them together, we are left with at least five oppositions), as well as by the absence of real coordination among them: in this area, as elsewhere, Augustine displays a theoretical ecumenicalism by juxtaposing what might be articulated. Thus we shall examine his classifications, and the underlying oppositions, one at a time.

(1) *According to the mode of transmission.* This classification, destined to become canonical, in itself exemplifies Augustine's synthetic bent: since the signifier must be perceptible, all signifiers may be classified according to the sense by means of which they are perceived. Thus Aristotle's psychological theory converges with semiotic description. Two details warrant our attention here. First, the limited role of the signs that are transmitted by senses other than sight and hearing: Augustine conceives of their existence for obvious theoretical reasons, but he immediately limits their importance. "Among the signs by means of which men express their meanings to one another, some pertain to the sense of sight, more to the sense of hearing, and very few to the other senses" (II, iii, 4). A single example will suffice to illustrate the other channels of transmission: "Our Lord gave a sign with the odor of the ointment with which his feet were anointed [John 12:3–8]; and the taste of the sacrament of His body and blood signified what He wished [Luke 22:19–20]; and when the woman was healed by touching the hem of His garment, something was signified" [Matt. 9:20–22]. These examples emphasize the exceptional character of the signs that are based on smell, taste, or touch.

In *On the Trinity*, there remain only two modes of transmission of signs, sight and hearing. Augustine likes to stress their resemblance: "And generally a sound, sometimes a nod, is exhibited, the former to the ears, the latter to the eyes, that the word which we bear in our mind may become known also by bodily signs to the bodily senses. For what is to nod or beckon, except to speak in some way to the sight?" (xv, x, 19).

The opposition of sight and hearing allows us, in a first approximation, to situate words among the signs (and this is the second point that concerns us here). Indeed, for Augustine, language is phonic by nature (we shall return to his description of writing). Thus the immense majority of signs are phonic—for the immense majority are words. "A multitude of innumerable signs by means of which men express their thoughts is made up of words" (II, iii, 4). The advantage words enjoy is, apparently, only quantitative.

(2) *According to origin and use.* A new distinction produces two pairs of sign types, but it is possible to bring them together, as Augustine himself shows, in a single category. The way is paved for this distinction in the first book of *On Christian Doctrine*. This part of the work begins with a division between signs and things. No sooner is the distinction made than it is abolished, for signs, far from being opposed to things, are things themselves— "things" being understood in the broadest sense of everything that is. "Every sign is also a thing, for that which is not a thing is nothing at all" (I, ii, 2). The opposition can be reconstituted only at another level—at the level of function, not of substance. A sign indeed may be considered from two points of view: as thing or as sign (Augustine's discussion follows this order): "Just as I began, when I was writing about things, by warning that no one should consider them except as they are, without reference to what they signify beyond themselves, now when I am discussing signs I wish it understood that no one should consider them for what they are but rather for their value as signs which signify something else" (II, i, 1).

The opposition does not lie between things and signs, but between pure things and sign-things. Nevertheless, there are things that owe their existence entirely to the fact that they are used as signs; these are obviously the closest things to pure signs that can be found (since it is impossible to reach the limiting case). It is this capacity of signs to bracket, as it were, their nature as things, that opens the door to Augustine's new categorization.

Augustine in fact opposes natural signs to intentional signs (*data*). This opposition has often been misunderstood. It has been confused with another opposition, more common in the classical period, between natural and conventional; a study by J. Engels has shed useful light on this point. Augustine writes: "Among signs, some are natural and others are conventional. Those are natural which, without any desire or intention of signifying, make us aware of something beyond themselves" (II, i, 2). As examples of natural signs, he proposes smoke for fire, animal tracks, the human face. "Conventional signs are those which living creatures show to one another for the purpose of conveying, in so far as they are able, the motion of their spirits or something which they have sensed or understood" (ii, ii, 3). His examples of intentional signs are chiefly human (words), but he also mentions animal cries, which can indicate the presence of food or simply the presence of the sign-maker.

It is clear how the opposition between natural signs and intentional signs is related to the opposition between things and signs. Intentional signs are things that have been produced for the purpose of serving as signs (origin) and that serve only to this end (usage); in other words, they are things whose function as things is reduced to a minimum. These signs thus come as close as possible to being pure signs (given that pure signs do not exist). Intentional signs are not necessarily human, and there is no obligatory correlation between their natural or intentional character and their mode of transmission (the classification of these modes comes up with regard to the intentional signs, but it is hard to see why). Let us note also that words are intentional signs: this constitutes their second characteristic (phoneticism being the first).

We can discern, in this opposition, echos of another we have already found in Aristotle (*On Interpretation*, 16a). However, the example of animal cries, appearing in both texts but in opposing categories, allows us to clarify Aristotle's position. For Aristotle, the fact that these cries do not depend upon any convention suffices for them to be considered "natural." For Augustine, on the other hand, the intention to signify, once attested, justifies including animal cries among the intentional signs: Augustine does not equate intentional with conventional. We may suppose that this distinction is Augustine's own: based on the notion of intention, it squares well with his general project which, as we have seen, is psychological and oriented toward communication. It allows him to overcome the objection that Sextus addressed to the Stoics, namely, that the existence of signs does not necessarily imply a logical structure generating this existence: certain signs are given in nature. We may also note that here the two types of signs—which remained completely separate for Augustine's predecessors—are integrated: what was sign for Aristotle and the Stoics becomes "natural sign," Aristotle's symbol and the Stoics' combination of signifier and signified become "intentional signs" (moreover, the same examples are always used). The term "natural" is somewhat misleading: it would be clearer to oppose signs that *already exist* as things to those that are *deliberately created* for the purpose of signification.

(3) *According to social function.* Such a terminological precaution would be all the more desirable since, elsewhere in his text, Augustine introduces a subdivision—a much more familiar one, as we have seen—between natural (and universal) signs and institutional (or conventional) signs. The former are comprehensible in a spontaneous and immediate fashion; the latter have to be learned. In fact, in *On Christian Doctrine*, Augustine considers only the case of the institutional sign, and he does so by means of an example leading apparently in the opposite direction.

> If those signs which the actors make in their dances had a natural meaning and not a meaning dependent on the institution and consent of men, the public crier in early times would not have had to explain to the Carthaginian populace what the dancer wished to convey during the pantomime. Many old men still remember the custom, as we have heard them say. And they are to be believed, for even now if anyone unacquainted with such trifles goes to the theater and no one else explains to him what these motions signify, he watches the performance in vain. [II, xxv, 38]

Even pantomime, at first glance a natural sign, requires a convention, and thus needs to be learned. So Augustine reincorporates within his own topology the opposition customarily applied to the origin of language (as Sextus had done before him).

This opposition is no more explicitly connected to the others than its predecessors. We may suppose that if Augustine fails in this instance to provide any example of a natural sign (in the sense given above), it is because his treatise is explicitly concerned with the intentional signs. Now natural signs may be found only among already existing signs; the intentionally created sign implies learning and thus convention. But is every already existing sign natural, that is, capable of being grasped apart from any convention? Augustine does not make such an assertion, and counterexamples come readily to mind. Still, in *The First Catechetical Instructions* he describes as natural a sign that appears in *On Christian Doctrine* among the nonintentional signs.

[These imprints] are produced in the mind as is the expression of the face in the body. For instance, anger is designated by one word in Latin, by another in Greek, and by others again in the various other tongues; but the expression on the face of an angry man is neither Latin nor Greek. Thus it is that not all nations understand when a man says: *Iratus sum*, but Latins only; but if the feeling present in his mind as it kindles to white heat comes out upon his features and gives him a certain look, all who see him understand that he is angry. [II, 3]

The same affirmation appears in the *Confessions*:

The movements of their bodies [are] a kind of universal language, expressed by the face, the direction of the eye, gestures of the limbs and tones of the voice, all indicating the state of feeling in the mind as it seeks, enjoys, rejects or avoids various objects. [I, viii, 13]

Natural signs (although the example chosen seems questionable to us) here share the universality of the imprints of the soul whose properties we have already seen. Augustine, who is fairly close to Aristotle on this issue, sees the relation between words and things as arbitrary (conventional) and the relation between thoughts and things as universal, and thus natural.

This insistence on the necessarily conventional nature of language suggests how little stock Augustine places in motivation: in his view, motivation cannot be substituted for knowledge of the convention: "It is true that everyone seeks a certain verisimilitude in making signs so that these signs, in so far as is possible, may resemble the things that they signify. But since one thing may resemble another in a great variety of ways, signs are not valid among men except by common consent" (*On Christian Doctrine*, II, xxv, 38).

Motivation does not permit us to dispense with convention. The argument summarized here in one sentence is developed at length in *Concerning the Teacher*, in which Augustine shows that one can never be certain of the meaning of a gesture without the help of a linguistic commentary, that is, without the help of the institution that is language. By the same token, he refuses to concede any decisive importance to the natural/conventional (or natural/arbitrary) opposition; the eighteenth-century attempts, renewed by Hegel and Saussure, to found on that cornerstone the opposition between (arbitrary) signs and (natural) symbols, had already been outdistanced.

This "arbitrariness of the sign" leads naturally to polysemy.

> But since things are similar to other things in a great many ways, we must not think it to be prescribed that what a thing signifies by similitude in one place must always be signified by that thing. For the Lord used "leaven" in vituperation when He said, "Beware of the leaven of the Pharisees" [Matt. 16:11], and in praise when He said, "The kingdom of God . . . is like to leaven, which a woman took and hid in three measures of meal, till the whole was leavened" [Luke 13:20–21]. [*On Christian Doctrine*, III, xxv, 35]

(4) *According to the nature of the symbolic relation.* After classifying signs as intentional or nonintentional, and as conventional or natural, Augustine considers the same facts a third time and arrives at yet another articulation: that of *proper* signs and *transposed* signs (*translata*). The rhetorical origin of this opposition is obvious, but Augustine—like Clement before him, although more clearly—generalizes with regard to signs what rhetoric had to say about words.

The opposition is introduced in the following manner:

> Signs are either literal or figurative. They are called literal when they are used to designate those things on account of which they were instituted: thus we say *bos* [ox] when we mean an animal of a herd because all men using the Latin language call it by that name just as we do. Figurative signs occur when that thing which we designate by a literal sign is used to signify something else; thus we say "ox" and by that syllable understand the animal which is ordinarily designated by that word, but again by that animal we understand an evangelist, as is signified in the Scripture, according to the interpretation of the Apostle, when it says, "Thou shalt not muzzle the ox that treadeth out the corn" [1 Cor. 9:9]. [*On Christian Doctrine*, II, x, 15]

The proper signs are defined in the same way as the intentional signs; they have been created in view of their use as signs. But the definition of the transposed sign is not precisely parallel: these are not "natural" signs; that is, they are not among those whose existence precedes their use as signs. They are defined, more generally, by their secondary status: a sign is transposed when its signified becomes, in turn, a signifier; in other words, the proper sign is based on a single relation, the transposed sign on two successive operations (we have already seen this idea taking shape in the work of Clement).

In fact, we find ourselves from the outset within the category of intentional signs (since Augustine is exclusively preoccupied with these), and it is within this category that the operation that distinguished them from other signs is repeated: the proper signs are at once created expressly for the purpose of signification and used in accordance with this initial intention. The transposed signs are also intentional signs (words are the only examples given), but, instead of being used for their original purpose, they are redirected toward a second function, just as things were when they became signs.

This structural analogy—which is not identity—accounts for the affinity between transposed signs (which are linguistic nonetheless) and nonintentional signs ("natural" and nonlinguistic). It is not by chance that the two sets of examples overlap: the ox does not owe its existence to a semiotic intentionality, but it *can* signify; it is thus both a natural sign and a (possible ingredient of) a transposed sign. This third approach to the same phenomenon is, from the formal point of view, the most satisfying; we no longer depend upon empirical contingency to distinguish among signs (whether already existing or deliberately created, comprehensible directly or by means of a convention), but upon a difference in structure: the single or double symbolic relation. By this same token, language no longer forms a separate class among signs: one group of linguistic signs (indirect expressions) is found on the same side as the nonlinguistic signs. The formulation of this opposition, based upon an analysis of form and not of substance, represents in my view the most important theoretical acquisition of Augustinian semiotics; I can only regret the preference of the later tradition for the motivated/unmotivated, or natural/conventional, opposition (to the detriment of the opposition between indirect and direct). Let us note at the same time that this articulation itself contributes to the partial eradication of the difference between the two phenomena, which were much farther apart for Aristotle (symbol vs. sign), for the Stoics (signifier-signified vs. sign), and for Clement (direct language vs. indirect or symbolic language).

The proper/transposed opposition has its origin in rhetoric.

However, Augustine's departure from rhetorical tradition is not limited to his extension of it beyond the word to the sign. With Augustine the very definition of "transposed" is new: the term no longer refers to a word that changes meaning, but to a word that designates an object which in turn carries meaning. This description applies to the example cited, in fact (the evangelist, just like the ox . . .), an example which does not resemble a rhetorical trope. On the following page, however, Augustine gives another example of a transposed sign which conforms perfectly to the rhetorical definition. Rather than confusing two types of indirect meaning, Augustine is probably attempting here to broaden the category of transposed meaning so that it can include Christian allegory. Speaking of the difficulties that arise in the course of interpretation, he considers two sorts which correspond closely to the two forms of indirect meaning. The opposition is better formulated in *On the Trinity*, where Augustine conceives of two types of allegory (that is, of transposed signs), the one based on words, the other on things. This distinction may be derived from one of Clement's texts; Clement, however, believed that he was dealing with two alternative definitions of one and the same notion.

Another attempt at subdividing the category of transposed meaning leads, later on, to the well-known doctrine of the four meanings of Scripture. Whether this doctrine originated with Augustine remains subject to controversy; in our consideration of it we can draw upon several series of texts. In the first, represented by *On the Advantage of Believing*, 3, 5, and by a closely parallel but shorter passage from the *Unfinished Book on the Literal Meaning of Genesis*, 2, four terms are clearly distinguished: history, etiology, analogy, and allegory. But it is not certain that these are meanings, properly speaking; the terms may refer instead to the various operations carried out on the text that is being interpreted. Analogy in particular is a device that consists in drawing upon one text in order to explain another. Etiology has a problematic status: it consists in seeking the cause of the event evoked by the text. It constitutes an explanation, and thus a meaning, but this meaning does not seem to belong, in a strict sense, to the text under analysis: it is rather a supplement provided by the commentator. There remain, then, only two meanings: historical (literal) meaning and allegorical meaning. The examples Augustine gives of the latter indicate that he does not distinguish

between the various types of allegory in the way that a later
tradition would. These examples include the following: Jonah in
the whale representing Christ in the tomb (typology, in the later
tradition); the Jews' sufferings during the Exodus as an incita-
tion not to sin (tropology); the two women, symbol of the two
Churches (analogy). I must add here that Augustine does not
distinguish, either, between spiritual meaning and transposed
meaning (he attributes the same definition to both). If his approach is compared to the later tradition as codified by Thomas
Aquinas, we observe the redistribution as shown in the chart.

	PROPER MEANING	TRANSPOSED MEANING	SPIRITUAL MEANING
Augustine	proper meaning	transposed meaning	
Thomas	literal meaning		spiritual meaning

To summarize: only the proper/transposed dichotomy is essential to Augustine; the others are of little importance.

But one other text must be examined here. It is found in *On the
Literal Meaning of Genesis*, II, 1, where Augustine speaks of the
contents of the various books of the Bible. There are some, he
says, that evoke eternity, others that recount facts, others that
announce the future, still others that indicate rules of behavior.
He does not assert, here, that a single passage may have a qua-
druple meaning; the theory is nonetheless present in embryonic
form.

In his attempt to clarify the status of transposed signs, Augustine associates them with two related semantic phenomena: ambiguity and lies. Ambiguity is a long-term preoccupation, one
encountered in as early a work as *On Dialectics*, where difficulties
in communication are classified according to whether they can be
attributed to obscurities or to ambiguities (Aristotle had already
introduced this subdivision). Among its own subdivisions, the
category of ambiguity includes those arising from transposed
meaning. The same hierarchical articulation reappears in *On Christian Doctrine*: "The ambiguity of Scripture arises either from words
used literally or figuratively" (III, i, 1). An ambiguity due to proper (literal) meaning is an ambiguity in which semantics plays no
role: phonic, graphic, or syntactic ambiguity. Semantic ambiguities simply coincide with those that can be attributed to the pres-

ence of a transposed meaning. Augustine does not entertain the possibility of semantic ambiguities based on lexical polysemy.

Transposed signs, a species within the genus "ambiguity," must be sharply distinguished from lies, on the other hand—although neither transposed signs nor lies reveal the truth if taken literally.

> If we call "Jacob's deception of his father" a lie, then all parables and figures for signifying anything which are not to be taken literally, but in which one thing must be understood for another, will be called lies. A deplorable consequence! He who thinks this can bring this charge against all figurative expressions, be they ever so many. In this way even what is named a metaphor, that is, the so-called transfer of some word from its own object to an object not its own, could be called a lie. Thus, it will be considered a lie when we say that grain fields wave and the eyes sparkle or when we speak of the flower of youth and the autumn of life, because, undoubtedly, we do not find waves or sparks or flower or autumn in those objects to which we have transferred the words from another source. [*Against Lying*, x, 24]

This difference is explained soon afterward: it resides precisely in the existence of a transposed meaning, one absent in lies, which allows truth to be restored to the tropes. Such words or actions "should be judged as prophetic expressions and actions put for the understanding of those things which are true" (ibid.). Or again: "What is said or done figuratively is not a lie. Every pronouncement must be referred to that which it expresses. Everything said or done figuratively expresses what is signified to those to whom it was related" (*Lying*, v, 7). Lies are not true in the literal sense, nor do they have a transposed meaning.

(5) *According to the nature of the designatum, sign or thing.* Transposed signs are characterized by the fact that their "signifier" is already a full-fledged sign; we may now consider the complementary case, in which not the signifier but the signified is in its turn a complete sign. We shall in fact combine under this heading two cases that remain separate for Augustine: that of letters, signs of sounds, and that of the metalinguistic uses of language. In each of these cases, the sign is designated, but in the first instance we are concerned with its signifier, and in the second with its signified.

LETTERS. As far as letters are concerned, Augustine does not go beyond the Aristotelian adage according to which letters are the signs of sounds. Thus, in *On Dialectics*, he states: "Every word is a sound, for when it is written it is not a word but the sign of a word. When we read, the letters we see suggest to the mind the sounds of the utterance. For written letters indicate to the eyes something other than themselves and indicate to the mind utterances beyond themselves" (v). Similarly, in *Concerning the Teacher*: "What do we find about written words? Are they not better understood as signs of words than as words?" (IV, 8). Or in *On Christian Doctrine*: "Words are shown to the eyes, not in themselves but through certain signs which stand for them" (II, iv, 5). And in *On the Trinity*: "Letters . . . are signs of words, as words themselves are signs in our conversation of those things which we think" (xv, x, 19).

We discover, however, that Augustine has identified several additional characteristics of letters. The first one, noted in *On Dialectics*, constitutes a paradox: letters are signs of sounds, but not of just any sounds—they signify articulate sounds alone. Now articulate sounds are those that can be designated by a letter. "By an articulate sound I mean one which can be expressed in letters" (v). One might argue that letters are based on an implicit phonological analysis, since they represent only invariable elements. In a broader sense, "writing" appears equally indispensable to language: thus it is with the "imprints" that are mentioned in *The First Catechetical Instructions* and of which words are only the translation.

In *On Christian Doctrine*, Augustine insists on the durative nature of letters, as opposed to the punctual character of sounds: "Because vibrations in the air soon pass away and remain no longer than they sound, signs of words have been constructed by means of letters" (II, iv, 5). Thus letters permit an escape from the constraining "now" that weighs upon the spoken word. In *On the Trinity*, Augustine goes even further: writing makes it possible to envisage not only "once upon a time" but also "elsewhere." "Whereas we exhibit . . . bodily signs either to ears or eyes of persons present to whom we speak, letters have been invented that we might be able to converse also with the absent" (xv, x, 19). Writing is defined by its complicity with absence.

METALINGUISTIC USAGE. At no point does Augustine take into account the singular capacity of letters to designate other signs (sounds). This situation is nevertheless familiar to him, for he shows continuing interest in the problem of the metalinguistic use of words. In *On Dialectics,* he notes that words may be used either as signs of things or as names of words; the distinction persists throughout *Concerning the Teacher,* in which Augustine warns against the confusions that may result from these two quite separate uses of language.

Again, in *On Dialectics,* Augustine notes in passing: "We are unable to speak of words except by words" (v). This observation is generalized in *On Christian Doctrine*: "I could express the meaning of all signs of the type here touched upon in words, but I would not be able at all to make the meanings of words clear by these signs" (II, iii, 4). Thus words are not only available for metalinguistic use, but they are also uniquely capable of meta-semiotic use. Unfortunately, Augustine does not pursue this argument and subject it to theoretical development; nowhere does he try to articulate it with the other classifications he is outlining. One might wonder, for instance, whether all verbal signs (proper and transposed) possess this capacity to the same degree; or again, what property of words it is that fits them for assuming this role. Here again, Augustine is content to observe and to juxtapose, without advancing to a theoretical conclusion.

SOME CONCLUSIONS

Let me attempt to draw some conclusions concerning the dual object of this first chapter, Augustine and semiotics.

We have seen, first of all, how Augustine's own position is constituted. Throughout his semiotic work, he is guided by a tendency to inscribe the semiotic problem within the framework of a psychological theory of communication. This impetus is all the more striking in that it contrasts with his own point of departure, namely, Stoic sign theory. For all this, Augustine's approach is not entirely original: a psychological perspective was present in Aristotle's work. Still, Augustine developed this tendency further than any of his predecessors; we can account for this by the theological and exegetic use to which he sought to put sign theory.

Yet if Augustine's originality is limited in its detail, his synthetic "originality"—or rather his ecumenical capacity—is tremendous, and leads to the first construction in the history of Western thought that deserves to be called semiotic. Let us review the principal articulations of this ecumenicalism. A rhetorician by training, Augustine first applied his knowledge to the interpretation of particular texts (the Bible): thus hermeneutics absorbed rhetoric. Moreover, he also annexed to hermeneutics the logical theory of signs—at the price, to be sure, of a slide from structure to substance, since in the place of Aristotle's "symbol" and "sign" we discover intentional and natural signs. These two conglomerates converge in *On Christian Doctrine* to give rise to a general theory of signs, or semiotics, in which the "signs" that emerged from the rhetorical tradition (which has meanwhile become hermeneutics), that is, the "transposed signs," take their place. In modern terminology, signs (in the restricted sense) are opposed to symbols as the proper is opposed to the transposed, or, better yet, as the direct is to the indirect.

Augustine's extraordinary gift for synthesis (which is not diminished by the fact that he does have precursors on the path of eclecticism) is entirely consistent with his place in history: his work is a locus through which classical tradition will be transmitted to the Middle Ages. Augustine's synthesizing capacity is apparent in many other areas, which bear occasionally upon the one that concerns us: thus, for instance, in several passages of the treatise *On Dialectics* (in the section on etymology), we find that historical changes of meaning are described in terms of rhetorical tropes, and history appears as no more than a projection of the typology in time. An even more important instance: for the first time, the Aristotelian classification of associations, found in the second chapter of the treatise on memory (association by resemblance, by proximity, by opposition), is used to describe the variety of these synchronic and diachronic relations of meaning.

It is precisely at this point that we have to set aside the question of Augustine's personal destiny to consider at what cost to knowledge semiotics was born. Since language exists, the question that has empirical if not ontological priority for any semiotics must be: What is the place of linguistic signs among signs in general? So long as our consideration is limited to verbal language alone, we remain inside a science (or philosophy) of language; only the shattering of the linguistic framework justifies the establishment of a semiotics. And this is precisely the inaugural move that Augustine makes: what has been said of words, in the context of rhetoric or semantics, he transfers to the level of signs, where words occupy merely one place among others. But which place?

We may well ask, while seeking the answer to that last question, whether the price paid for the birth of semiotics is not too high. At the level of general utterances, Augustine locates words (linguistic signs) within only two classifications. Words belong on the one hand to the auditory realm, on the other to the intentional realm: the intersection of these two categories yields linguistic signs. In so stating, Augustine fails to observe that he is leaving himself no way to distinguish linguistic signs from other "intentional auditory signs," except for their frequency of use. His text is quite revealing on this point: "Most signs, as I have said, pertain to the ears, and most of these consist of words. But the trumpet, the flute, and the harp make sounds which are not only pleasing but also significant, although as compared with the number of verbal signs the number of signs of this kind are few" (*On Christian Doctrine*, ii, iii, 4). Between the trumpet announcing an attack (to take an example where intentionality is unmistakable) and words, the difference would lie only in the frequency of the latter? This is all that Augustine's semiotics offers us explicitly. We can see to what extent the phonetic prejudice, among others, is responsible for his blindness to the problem of the nature of language: the need to connect words with "meaning" conceals their specificity (a purely "visual" conception of language that identifies language with writing would invite the same reproach). Augustine's gift for synthesis works against him here: it is perhaps not by accident that the Stoics were no more prepared than Aristotle to give a single name to "natural" signs (associated, for them, with inference) and to words. Synthesis is fruitful only if it does not obliterate difference.

In fact, as we have also seen, Augustine identifies certain properties of language that cannot be explained by its intentional-auditory character: above all, its metasemiotic capacity. Yet he does not ask what property of language endows it with this capacity. Now, only a response to this fundamental question would make it possible to resolve another problem, one that grows out of the first: the problem of the "price" of instituting semiotics, the question whether it is useful to unify within a single notion—that of the sign—both what possesses this metasemiotic property and what lacks it (note that this new question contains, in circular fashion, the word "semiotics" itself). Such usefulness cannot be measured until we know what is at stake in the opposition between the linguistic and the nonlinguistic sign. It is thus in a context of ignorance—not to say repression—of the difference between words and other signs that Augustine's semiotics is born—just like Saussure's, fifteen centuries later. Which makes the very existence of semiotics problematic.

Still, Augustine had glimpsed a possible way out of this impasse (although he probably remained as unconscious of the possibility as of the impasse itself). The way out lay in his extension of the proper/transposed category from rhetoric to the domain of signs. For this category, transcending the substantive opposition between linguistic and nonlinguistic signs (since this opposition is found in both areas) as well as the pragmatic and contingent oppositions between intentional and natural signs or conventional and universal signs, allows for the articulation of two major modes of designation for which today one would be tempted to use two distinct terms: signification and symbolization. With this as our point of departure, we can inquire into the difference that underlies these two modes—the difference that explains, indirectly, the presence or absence of a metasemiotic capacity. In other words, semiotics deserves to exist only if, in the very move that inaugurates it, the semantic/symbolic articulation is present. That is what allows us to appreciate Augustine's groundbreaking work—sometimes in spite of itself.

2

The Splendor and Misery
of Rhetoric

═══════════

The first great crisis of rhetoric coincides approximately with the beginning of our era. Tacitus tells its story in his justly famous *Dialogue on Orators*. The very first sentence conveys an awareness of decline: "Our age above all, barren and stripped of the glory of eloquence, scarcely retains the very name of 'orator,' although earlier periods bloomed with the renowned talents of so many distinguished orators."[1]

It would be wrong to see in these words nothing more than a reformulation of the perennial nostalgic reference to the "good old days." Tacitus's own analyses and a study of the evolution of rhetoric in his day equally well demonstrate the reality of the change.

What was the rhetoric of "earlier periods"? In a well-known phrase, though one whose original impact is lost, it is the art of persuasion. Or, as Aristotle puts it at the beginning of his *Rhet-*

---

1. For editions cited, see the Bibliographical Note.

oric: "Rhetoric may be defined as the faculty of observing in any given case the available means of persuasion" (I, 2, 1355b). The object of rhetoric is eloquence, defined as effective speech that makes it possible to act on others. Rhetoric grasps language not as form—it is not concerned with utterances as such—but as action; the linguistic form becomes an ingredient of a global act of communication (of which persuasion is the most characteristic type). Rhetoric deals with the functions of speech, not its structure. Its one constant is the objective it seeks to achieve: to persuade (or, in the terminology of a later age, to instruct, to move, and to please). Linguistic means are taken into account to the extent that they may be used to reach this objective.

Rhetoric studies the means that allow a chosen end to be achieved. It is not surprising to discover that the metaphors used in rhetoric to designate rhetoric itself are always based on this relation of means to end. Rhetoric is sometimes compared to medical technique, sometimes to military strategy. Thus, in Aristotle:

> It is clear, then, that rhetoric . . . is useful. It is clear, further, that its function is not simply to succeed in persuading, but rather to discover the means of coming as near such success as the circumstances of each particular case allow. In this it resembles all other arts. For example, it is not the function of medicine simply to make a man quite healthy, but to put him as far as may be on the road to health; it is possible to give excellent treatment even to those who can never enjoy sound health. [*Rhet.*, I, 1, 1355b]

Or, in the *Rhetorica ad Herennium* (To Gaius Herennius on the Theory of Public Speaking), traditionally attributed to Cicero: "This arrangement of topics in speaking, like the arraying of soldiers in battle, can readily bring victory" (III, 10, 18).

It is clear that the spirit of rhetoric is pragmatic, and by that very token immoral: whatever the circumstances or the cause defended, one must be able to achieve one's end. The assorted declarations of principle clustered at the entrance or the exit of the rhetorical edifice hardly prevent the eloquent orator from using his art for purposes whose justice is apparent only to himself. Rhetoric does not valorize one type of speech over others; any means are good provided that the objective is attained. Any speech may be efficacious; it must simply be used toward an appropriate end. We may recall the "topical" enumerations that foresee all possible cases and find a solution for each:

> External Circumstances: Descent—in praise: the ancestors of whom he is sprung; if he is of illustrious descent, he has been their peer or superior; if of humble descent, he has had his support, not in the virtues of his ancestors, but in his own. In censure: if he is of illustrious descent, he has been a disgrace to his forebears; if of low descent, he is none the less a dishonour even to these. [*Rhet. ad Her.*, iii, 7, 13]

Rhetoric teaches its practitioners to use the type of discourse suited to each particular case.

The key notion of rhetoric is therefore the notion of suitability, appropriateness (*prépon, decorum*), as Albert Yon has pointed out ("an arbitrary simplification has made of suitability a component of elocution, whereas it is the guiding principle that governs the whole art of speaking"). Suitability is the basis of efficacity, thus of eloquence. As Cicero writes, in his *Orator*:

> This, indeed, is the form of wisdom that the orator must especially employ—to adapt himself to occasions and persons. In my opinion one must not speak in the same style at all times, nor before all people, nor against all opponents, nor in defence of all clients, nor in partnership with all advocates. He, therefore, will be eloquent who can adapt his speech to fit all conceivable circumstances. [xxxv–xxxvi, 123]

Speech is above all functional; to be functional is to be fitting.

Such was rhetoric before its crisis. Can we trace the path from this picture to the origin, the causes of the crisis? Yes, if we are willing to go along with the analyses of Tacitus, who links rhetoric directly to politics and society. In his view, eloquence progressed so long as it actually served some purpose, so long as it was an effective instrument. That was only possible, however, in a state in which speech had power: in other words, in a free and democratic state. "Great eloquence, like a flame, is fed by fuel, is excited by motion, and grows bright as it burns" (*Dialogue*, xxxvi).

Now this fuel is provided, in a democracy, by the destiny of a people: "In addition, there was the high rank of the defendants and the importance of the issues, which of themselves are in the highest degree conducive to eloquence. . . . For the power of genius grows with the importance of affairs, nor can anyone produce a speech that is brilliant and renowned unless he has found a case worthy of it" (xxxvii).

The requisite motion is assured by the freedom of citizens to speak of anything, without being inhibited by considerations of rank or person, with "the privilege that was granted of attacking the most powerful men" (XL). All that is possible only in a state where institutional constraints are weak and where the power of a deliberative assembly is very strong, these features being the basis of democracy. These are the terms in which Tacitus characterizes the preceding period: "When everything was in a state of confusion and lacked a single overseer, each orator was considered as wise as the errant people could be convinced that he was" (XXXVI). "Our state too, as long as it wandered aimlessly, . . . undoubtedly produced a more vigorous eloquence, just as an uncultivated field produces certain more luxuriant plants" (*Dialogue*, XL).

Democracy is the indispensable condition for the flowering of eloquence; conversely, eloquence is the highest quality of the individual belonging to a democracy: neither one can get along without the other. Eloquence is "necessary": this is its dominant feature, and at the same time this explains its success. The ancients "had convinced themselves that no one could rise in the state or could maintain a position of importance and prominence without oratorical ability" (XXXVI). "No one in those times attained great power without some eloquence or other" (XXXVII).

So eloquence sparkled in circumstances that were to change for reasons easy to surmise: in a word, lack of liberty, democracy ousted by a strong state with well-established laws and authoritarian leadership. Such is the particular case of Rome ("Gnaeus Pompey in his third consulship was the first to confine these [liberties] and, as it were, put reins upon eloquence" [XXXVIIII]); such is the general law, spelled out in detail by Tacitus: "We do not even know of eloquence among the Macedonians and Persians or any people who were satisfied with stable government" (XL). If democracy disappears, if it is replaced by a strong government that can dispense with public deliberations, of what use is eloquence? "What need is there for long expressions of opinion in the senate when *the best men* quickly come to an agreement? What is the need for many meetings before the people, when the ignorant masses are not deciding a matter of public policy but *the one individual who is the wisest*?" (XLI; emphasis added).

Furthermore, ought we to regret this state of affairs? Not if we are to believe Maternus, the interlocutor in the dialogue who establishes this diagnosis. For liberty and democracy threaten the peace and well-being of every individual: ought we to regret the absence of effective remedies when we can rejoice in the absence of illness? "If some state should be found in which no one did wrong, the orator would be unnecessary among guiltless people, as a doctor is among healthy ones" (XLI).

The eloquence of earlier times was too costly: its price was the insecurity of each citizen's life, this being the direct result of the democratic institution.

> That great and renowned eloquence is the offspring of license, which fools call liberty . . . , without respect, without dignity, violent, rash, arrogant, which does not appear in well-governed states. . . . Neither the eloquence of the Gracchi was of such great advantage to the state that the latter even put up with their laws nor did Cicero find that his oratorical renown was adequate compensation for his terrible death. [XL]

Tacitus's conclusion: "Since no one can attain great renown and great repose at the same time, let each one enjoy the blessing of his own age without detracting from the other" (XLI).

Let us leave this value judgment aside; the facts remain to be analyzed. The flowering of eloquence was linked to a certain form of government, democracy; with the disappearance of democracy, eloquence can only decline. Or even disappear? The rhetoric that taught how to be eloquent must meet the same fate. Unless eloquence were to change its meaning—and rhetoric were to change its object at the same time. And, as rhetoric is not dead in the Year One, far from it, that is what must have happened; that is, in fact, what did happen.

In a democracy, speech could be efficacious. In a monarchy (to leap quickly ahead), this is no longer possible (power belongs to institutions, not to assemblies); the ideal then necessarily changes. The best speech is now the one judged *beautiful*. Before the debate on the causes of the decadence of rhetoric, the same *Dialogue on Orators* contains another exchange in which Aper and Messala compare the relative merits of the old and the new eloquence. Aper, defending the latter, finds in it qualities that were not noticed at the time of eloquence-as-instrument: he likes recent speeches that are "brilliant," "striking," "beautiful"—and he is unconcerned with their efficacity. In the old speeches,

> just as in a rudely constructed building, the wall is certainly strong and going to last, yet it is inadequately polished and

shining. I, however, want an orator, just as a rich and tasteful head of a household, to be sheltered not only by the kind of home that keeps away the rain and wind, but even one that delights the eye; and I wish him to be possessed not only of furniture that is adequate for ordinary purposes, but gold and jewels should be among his belongings, so that he may more often get pleasure from handling and gazing upon them. [xxii; note the shift away from instrumental metaphors toward those that evoke ornament]

Cicero, last of the ancients and first of the moderns, belongs among the latter by virtue of certain qualities characteristic of his speeches: "He was the first one to apply a finish to a speech, the first one to follow a principle of selection in vocabulary and to produce skillful arrangement" (xxii). The inevitable consequence of this stylization is that speeches may grow more and more beautiful, but they are no more apt to fulfill their (former) function, which is to convince, to act. As Aper's interlocutor retorts: "We know by experience that care and concern for preparation are harmful" (xxxix).

The new eloquence differs from the old in that its ideal is the intrinsic quality of discourse rather than its aptitude for serving an external purpose. As a matter of fact, the earlier rhetoric included several notions that could have served from the beginning as the basis for this latter concept of eloquence; at the time of the crisis in question, these notions took on more precise meaning or a visibly expanded role. This is the case with the term *ornatio, ornare,* which becomes, as we shall see, the core of the new rhetorical edifice: "The proper meaning of *ornare* is 'furnish,' 'equip.' But 'adorn' is not far off, and it is in this sense that *ornatio* is the distinguishing feature of eloquence" (Albert Yon, pp. clxx–clxxi). We find examples of both meanings of the word in Cicero, who virtually embodies the transition. As it happens, these two meanings also correspond to the two conceptions of rhetoric, old and new, instrumental and ornamental.

More remarkable still is the case of the term "figure" (*skhéma, conformatio, forma, figura*). Not that its meaning varies, from Theophrastus or Demetrius to Quintilian. Each time, "figure" is defined by its synonym "form," or by a comparison with gestures and body postures: just as the body necessarily adopts postures, always holds itself in a certain way, so discourse always has a certain disposition, a way of being. Thus Cicero refers to "the embellishments that the Greeks call σχήματα, figures, as it were, of speech" (*Orator*, xxv, 83). One important consequence of this definition is that, if it is taken literally, all discourse is figurative. Quintilian does not fail to note this. He repeats the same defini- tion of the term "figure": "it is applied to any form in which thought is expressed, just as it is to bodies which, whatever their composition, must have some shape" (*Institutio Oratoria*, ix, 1, 10); "the name is to be applied to certain attitudes, or I might say gestures of language" (ix, 1, 13). He goes on to conclude: "In so doing we speak as if every kind of language possessed a *figure*. . . . Therefore in the first and common sense of the word everything is expressed by *figures*" (ix, 1, 12).

The figure is thus consistently defined as a discourse whose very form is perceived. But whereas, formerly, the figure was only one among countless manners of analyzing discourse, now this autotelic concept has become eminently appropriate—since entire speeches are beginning to be appreciated "in themselves"! The role of figures thus continues to grow in the rhetorical trea- tises of the period—and we know that the day is coming when rhetoric will be no more than an enumeration of figures.

But there is another, still more important change, from the old to the new rhetoric, before and after Cicero, that concerns the very organization of its conceptual field. It is well known that the rhetorical edifice is subdivided into five parts, of which two deal with enunciation and the other three—*inventio, dispositio, elocutio*—with utterances. In the old instrumental perspective, these five parts are in principle (despite the sometimes clear pref- erences of authors) on an equal footing: they correspond to five aspects of the linguistic act, which are *all* subject to an objective exterior to themselves, that of convincing the listener. Now that the exterior objective has disappeared, we find that elocution— that is figure, ornament—occupies an increasingly large place, since the new objective—that of speaking (or writing) artfully, of creating beautiful speeches—is best realized by this means. Cicero uses an etymological argument to support his observation of this shift:

> We must now turn to the task of portraying the perfect orator and the highest eloquence. The very word "eloquent" shows that he excels because of this one quality, that is, in the use of language, and that the other qualities are overshadowed by this. For the all-inclusive word is not "discoverer" (from *inven-*

tio), or "arranger" (from *dispositio*), or "actor" (from *actio*), but in Greek he is called *rhetor*, from the word "to speak," and in Latin he is said to be "eloquent." For everyone claims for himself some part of the other qualities that go to make up an orator, but the supreme power in speaking, that is eloquence, is granted to him alone. [*Orator*, XIX, 61]

Thus invention, or the search for ideas, is little by little eliminated from rhetoric, which becomes the province of elocution alone. The latter's victory, however, is ambiguous. Winning the battle within rhetoric itself, elocution nonetheless loses the war: just because of this victory, the entire discipline loses value to a very large degree. In this way the pairing of means and end is replaced by that of form and content. Rhetoric deals with form: "ideas," formerly means comparable to "words," now assume the external and dominating function of "ends."

Now discourse that could be appreciated for itself, for its intrinsic qualities, its form and beauty, already existed among the Romans, but such discourse had not previously been known as eloquence; it was rather what we would today call *literature*. Aper, in Tacitus's dialogue, is perfectly conscious of the shift: "For even the beauty of poetry is now required of the orator, a beauty not defiled by the old rot of Accius or Pacuvius but drawn from the shrine of Horace and Vergil and Lucan" (xx). In fact, that is how poetry was defined, in contrast with oratorical eloquence: the latter was dominated by a concern for transitive efficacity, whereas the former was admired for itself, because of the work which the very words of the speech had undergone. Thus when Cicero wanted to distinguish orators from poets, he said that the latter "pay more attention to sound than to sense" (*Orator*, xx, 68).

The new eloquence in no way differs from literature; the new object of rhetoric coincides with literature. And if eloquent speech was once defined by its efficacity, now, quite to the contrary, it is useless speech, speech without purpose, that draws praise. Let us return one last time to Tacitus's dialogue. It opens with a discussion, not yet mentioned here, between Aper and Maternus on the respective value of eloquence and poetry. Although they defend opposing opinions, the two orators agree on one point: that eloquence can be used and that poetry is useless. Their disagreement thus hinges entirely on the value they attribute to usefulness. According to its champion, eloquence enables a speaker to "produce and preserve friendships, acquire connections, and become the patron of provinces" (v); according to its opponent, it puts orators in the position of being asked for favors daily and of angering those who ask (xiii). Conversely, speaking of literature, Aper holds that "poetry and versification . . . do not win any honor for their authors nor do they produce any tangible benefits . . . Maternus, who gets any benefit if Agamemnon or Jason speaks with skill in your plays? Who for this reason goes home obligated to you because of a successful defense?" (ix). Maternus, on the other hand, says: "Indeed, let 'the sweet Muses,' as Vergil says, carry me off to those sacred places and those fountains, after I have been released from worries and cares and the necessity of doing something daily against my inclination; nor let me any more experience with dread the mad and dangerous forum and the glory that brings on paleness" (xiii).

The one reproaches poetry for its uselessness, the other rejoices in it. Poets have no contact with the world; should we applaud this or deplore it? Here is Aper's position: "Poets have to leave the acquaintance of friends and the charm of the city, if they wish to work out and produce anything worthy, that they must disregard other duties, and, as they themselves say, they must go off into meadows and groves, that is, into solitude" (ix).

But one man's poison is another man's meat. Maternus says: "Indeed the meadows and groves and the very solitude which Aper chided afford me so much pleasure that I rank them among the outstanding rewards of poetry, because it is not composed in hustle and bustle nor with a litigant sitting before one's door nor in the midst of the mourning clothes and tears of those who are being prosecuted, but the mind goes off into pure and unsoiled locales and enjoys holy surroundings" (xii).

Whatever attitude one may take toward literature, there is general agreement that it is defined by its uselessness. Quintilian's view is the same: "Perhaps the highest of all pleasures is that which we derive from private study, and the only circumstances under which the delights of literature are unalloyed are when it withdraws from action, that is to say from toil, and can enjoy the pleasure of self-contemplation" (Institutio Oratoria, ii, 18, 4). Poets "aim solely at pleasing their readers" (viii, 6, 17).

Thus useless, inefficacious speech is to become the object of rhetoric, and rhetoric itself becomes the theory of language admired in and for itself. To be sure, certain voices will be heard demanding a return to efficacity; thus Augustine will want Christian preachers to possess an eloquence at least as effective as that of their adversaries:

> Who would dare to say that truth should stand in the person of its defenders unarmed against lying, so that they who wish to urge falsehoods may know how to make their listeners benevolent, or attentive, or docile in their presentation, while the defenders of truth are ignorant of that art? . . . While the faculty of eloquence, which is of great value in urging either evil or justice, is in itself indifferent, why should it not be obtained for the uses of the good in the service of truth if the evil usurp it for the winning of perverse and vain causes in defense of iniquity and error? [On Christian Doctrine, iv, ii, 3]

But he forgets what Tacitus's characters knew: eloquence needs freedom. It does not flourish when its aim is prescribed by dogma, whether political or religious, nor when it is asked to join in the service of *the* truth. Eloquence prospers only in the search for truth, not in the mere illustration of a particular truth.

The second great period of rhetoric, from Quintilian to Pierre Fontanier in the early nineteenth century (it is a discipline in which such shortcuts are possible and even legitimate, so slow is its evolution: Quintilian and Fontanier, had they been able to communicate with each other across the centuries, would have understood each other perfectly), is thus characterized by one essential feature: the function of discourse is forgotten. Thus it is the poetic text that becomes the privileged example. In the *Rhetorica ad Herennium*, in a naive way perhaps, the description of each figure was followed by that of its effects; in later rhetorics, function is first treated separately, then unified for all figures, and relegated to the last chapter; finally it is forgotten. When someone like Fontanier speculates on the effects of figures and tropes, he no longer considers the effect on other people, but only the relation between expression and thought, form and content—an internal function of language: "We shall be asked whether it is useful to study figures, to know them. Yes, we shall answer, nothing is more useful, more necessary even, for those who seek to penetrate the genius of the language, to master the secrets of style, and who wish to be able to grasp, in everything, the true relation between expression and idea or thought" (*Les Figures du discours*, p. 67; cf. p. 167).

Of the three functions of figures—to instruct, to move and to please—only the latter remains, with an illusory extension: "The general effects [of figures] must be: (1) to embellish language; (2) to please by this embellishment" (ibid., p. 464).

Rhetoric's first great crisis thus seems harmoniously resolved. Since it is no longer possible to use speech freely, it is appropriate to draw back, like Maternus, into "pure and unsoiled locales." Since it is useless to know the secrets of efficacious discourse (in any case, such discourse no longer serves any purpose), rhetoric will be turned into knowledge of language for language's sake, language offering itself up as a spectacle, allowing itself to be savored for itself, apart from any of the offensive services to which it was formerly subjected. Rhetoric becomes a celebration, a festival of language.

All appears to be well; and yet the celebration is not to be. Between Quintilian and Fontanier, fortune does not smile upon a single rhetorician, and this longest period in the history of rhetoric—lasting nearly 1800 years—turns out to be, at least in its broad outlines, a period of slow decadence and degradation, suffocation and bad conscience. Rhetoric embraces its new object, poetry—language as such—but it does so reluctantly. Before trying to comprehend this guilty conscience, let us attempt to gather some evidence of it.

We first find testimony to it in the very segmentation of the phenomenon of rhetoric. Take Quintilian: for him the whole set of rhetorical categories is based on the opposition between *res* and *verba*, thoughts (or things) and words: the opposition is banal, but its interest lies in the fact that it does not valorize the two terms equally. Let us look a little more closely. First, here is the opposition, explicitly stated: "Every speech however consists at once of that which is expressed and that which expresses, that is to say of matter and words" (*Institutio Oratoria*, III, 5, 1). Onto this are grafted several articulations, first of all that of the components of rhetoric: "As regards matter, we must study invention, as regards words, style, and as regards both, arrangement" (VIII, Pr., 6). These components are related to the functions of discourse: instructing and moving depend heavily upon invention and arrangement, but pleasing depends upon style alone.

> The duty of the orator is composed of instructing, moving and delighting his hearers, statement of facts and argument falling under the head of instruction, while emotional appeals are concerned with moving the audience and, although they may be

employed throughout the case, are most effective at the beginning and end. As to the element of charm, . . . though it may reside both in facts and words, its special sphere is that of style. [VIII, Pr., 7]

(In spite of their apparently exclusive attachment to the addressee, these functions of discourse clearly recall the basic functions described by Karl Bühler and Roman Jakobson: "instructing" is oriented toward the referent, "moving" toward the receiver, and "delighting," or pleasing, toward the utterance itself. Significantly, the expressive function, oriented toward the speaker, is missing: discourse does not begin to *express* a subject—in a systematic way, in any case—until the romantic era.) The celebrated theory of the three styles conforms to these same oppositions: the low style serves to instruct, the middle style to please, the high style to move (XII, 10, 58–59).

This tripartite division is based on a dichotomy (words/thoughts) plus a compromise term (disposition), or else on the same dichotomy paired with a second: ideas/feelings (this latter dichotomy is the basis for the instructing/touching subdivision and all that rests upon it). But Quintilian does not limit himself to this simple juxtaposition; implicitly and explicitly, he valorizes the term *res*; by the same token, the term *verba*, with all its correlatives, is subject to a new analysis that is organized, once again, around the *res verba* axis. Elocution ("style"), which depends, as we have seen, on words, will be the province of stylistic qualities. The list of these qualities varies from one account to another, but their systematic presentation in Book VIII reduces them to two major ones: discourses must be clear (*perspicua*) and ornate, embellished (*ornata*). Now words are clear when they make us see things clearly, and they are beautiful when we admire them for themselves: clarity is to beauty as things are to words. This opposition in turn governs others. For example, the opposition between proper meaning and transposed meaning: "The canon, that clearness mainly requires propriety of language and ornament the skilful use of metaphor (*translatis*), is perfectly sound" (VIII, 3, 15). From here we move on to the opposition of historical styles or even of languages; we find this, for example, in the dichotomy between Atticism and Asianism: "As Greek gradually extended its range into the neighboring cities of Asia, there arose a class of men who desired to distinguish themselves as orators before they had acquired sufficient command of the lan-

guage, and who consequently began to express by periphrases
what could have been expressed directly, until finally this practice
became an ingrained habit" (xii, 10, 16). Greek and Latin are contrasted in the same way: "A still stronger indication of the inferiority of Latin is to be found in the fact that there are many things
which have no Latin names, so that it is necessary to express
them by metaphor or periphrasis" (xii, 10, 34).

Finally, if in an ultimate repetition of the same gesture we
analyze the term now linked to *verba*, that is, transposed meaning, we discover within it once again the opposition between
words and things. In fact, among the tropes, "some . . . are
employed to help out our meaning and others to adorn our style"
(viii, 6, 2). Thus in the very way tropes are used we find yet again
the familiar dichotomy between those that serve mainly to reveal
thought and things, and those that are there to be appreciated for
themselves. The path we have taken can be summarized as in the
diagram.

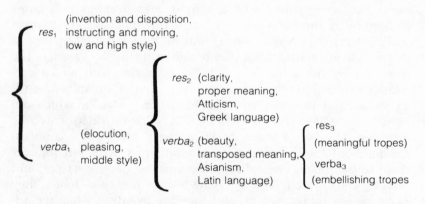

Such an articulation has a paradoxical aspect: like a shrinking
skin, the domain of *verba* is continually reduced when confronted
with the rhetorician's desire, whereas the proper object of rhetoric, even for Quintilian, is located much nearer to *verba* than to
res. Rhetoric, which ought to have been privileged work with
words, is constantly cut back in scope, since rhetoricians claim in
effect to value only discourse that serves to inform, discourse
unadorned with useless embellishments, discourse, in the extreme case, that goes unnoticed—in short, discourse that does not
derive from rhetoric. The demands are contradictory, and the contradiction has an inevitable consequence: the rhetorician does not

change his trade, but practices it henceforth with a guilty conscience.

Moreover, Quintilian does not limit himself to this implicit condemnation; he formulates it openly, asserting confidently that he prefers Greek to Latin, Atticism to Asianism, in short, meaning to beauty. "When a speech is praised for its words, it implies that its sense is inadequate" (VIII, Pr., 31). "For my own part, I regard clearness as the first essential of a good style" (VIII, 2, 22). "These critics would show finer feeling and better judgement if they took the view that Attic eloquence meant perfect eloquence" (X, 10, 26); and so on.

Quintilian cannot draw rhetoric into the celebration of language, for he sees not a celebration but an orgy. His thesis will be confirmed and amplified by another analysis of the tropes used by rhetoricians to designate rhetoric,—or rather, more specifically, of the particular trope, which is located, as we have just seen, at the very heart of rhetoric. Let us recall that the metaphors of the earlier rhetoric (from Aristotle to Cicero) referred to a relation of the means/end type. Now things are different; the means/end relation has been replaced by the form/content pair, or rather— and this is where the door is opened to devalorization—by the outside/inside pair. Thoughts or things are the interior, which is only covered over by a rhetorical wrapping. And, since language, as we have seen, is endlessly compared to the human body, with its gestures and its postures, rhetorical ornaments are the adornments of the body.

Such an identification implies two complementary positions: to use metaphors oneself is to cover the body; to understand them is to unveil it. Examples of each are easy to find. The interior/ exterior relation is posited in Cicero, although it turns out to be slightly dislocated, as it were: the body itself is merely an exterior envelope for something else: "To discover and decide what to say is important . . . and is to eloquence what the mind is to the body" (*Orator*, XIV, 44). Aper, who describes the new eloquence in Tacitus's dialogue, also invokes the body, but in a more material sense: "Just as a man's body, so precisely is that speech beautiful in which the veins do not stick out and the bones cannot be counted but rather temperate and healthy blood fills the limbs and swells in the muscles and a glow coats the sinews themselves and an elegance graces them" (XXI). Ideas are like bones and veins; words, like flesh, fluids, and skin.

One step further and we come to the body's covering: adornment or clothing. This comparison is canonical: Aristotle, speaking of metaphors, had already stated that "it is like having to ask ourselves what dress will suit an old man; certainly not the crimson cloak that suits a young man" (*Rhet.*, III, 1405a). As for Cicero:

> Just as some women are said to be handsomer when unadorned—this very lack of ornament becomes them—so this plain style gives pleasure even when unembellished: there is something in both cases which lends greater charm, but without showing itself. Also all noticeable ornament, pearls as it were, will be excluded; not even curling-irons will be used; all cosmetics, artificial white and red, will be rejected; only elegance and neatness will remain. [*Orator*, XXIII, 78–79]

One of Tacitus's characters chooses among several types of clothing: "it is so much better to clothe a speech even in a rough toga than to make it stand out with the colored clothes of a courtesan" (XXVI).

Clearly, these comparisons are permeated with moral condemnations: ornate discourse is like an easy woman, with glaring makeup; how much more highly must one value natural beauty, the pure body, and thus the absence of rhetoric! Right up to Kant we continue to find traces of these assimilations: pleasing, the rhetorical function par excellence, as we have seen, is women's business (the function of touching, moving, belongs to men . . .); beauty is the province of women, intelligence of men (*Observations on the Feeling of the Beautiful and Sublime*).

This moral condemnation reaches a kind of pinnacle in Quintilian, for whom discourse is masculine, from which it follows that ornamented discourse is the male courtesan: the vice of homosexuality is superimposed upon lust. It is hard to believe that these invectives have to do with anything but a clean-shaven transvestite:

> There are even some who are captured by the shams of artifice and think that there is more beauty in those who pluck out superfluous hair or use depilatories, who dress their locks by scorching them with the curling iron and glow with a complexion that is not their own, than can ever be conferred by nature pure and simple, so that it really seems as if physical beauty depended entirely on moral hideousness. [*Institutio Oratoria*, II, v, 12]

The same theme appears elsewhere:

Healthy bodies, enjoying a good circulation and strengthened by exercise, acquire grace from the same source that gives them strength, for they have a healthy complexion, firm flesh and shapely thews. But, on the other hand, the man who attempts to enhance these physical graces by the effeminate use of depilatories and cosmetics, succeeds merely in defacing them by the very care which he bestows on them. . . . Similarly, a translucent and iridescent style merely serves to emasculate the subject which it arrays with such pomp of words. [VIII, Pr., 19–20]

And again:

But such ornament must, as I have already said, be bold, manly and chaste, free from all effeminate smoothness and the false hues derived from artificial dyes, and must glow with health and vigor. [VIII, 3, 6]

Cicero, accused of stylistic Asianism, became immediately suspect in terms of his sexual mores: he was reproached with the charge that he was "bombastic, Asiatic, redundant, given to excessive repetition, liable at times to be pointless in his witticism, sensuous, extravagant and (an outrageous accusation!) almost effeminate in his rhythm" (XII, 10, 12). Such an elimination of masculine characteristics leads to monstrosity: "We see that some people place a higher value on figures which are in any way monstrous or distorted than they do on those who have not lost any of the advantages of the normal form of man" (II, 5, 11).

Discourse must both "give pleasure and awaken admiration; and the admiration will be of a kind far other than that which we bestow on portents, while the pleasure evoked by the charm will have nothing morbid about it, but will be praiseworthy and dignified" (VIII, Pr., 33).

Rhetorical ornamentation changes the sex of discourse. And we need not be unusually perceptive to see that Quintilian is not a partisan of sex changes. Nor are we astonished to see that, although he had been able to transmit the definition of the figure as an attitude of language, a definition that implied a valorization of language for its own sake, he himself could not stop there; he abandoned that definition in favor of another which was to become canonical in European rhetorical tradition. Quintilian judged the earlier definition of the figure too vague, and proposed the following: "In the second and special sense, in which it is called a *schema*, it means a rational change in meaning or language from the ordinary and simple form" (IX, 1, 11); and again, "we must interpret *schema* in the sense of that which is poetically or rhetorically altered from the simple and obvious method of expression" (IX, 1, 13). It is here that the figure is defined for the first time as divergence. This definition will come to dominate the entire Western tradition; and yet it contains something very close to a condemnation.

If rhetorical production stems from adornment and clothing, then interpreting texts that use these devices is, as Jean Pépin leads us to observe, an activity akin to undressing them—with all that may be pleasurable in such an activity. For in classical hermeneutics, as in the stripteases of Pigalle, the duration of the process and even its difficulty augment its value—so long as one is certain to arrive in the end at the body itself. The writings of Augustine, an author who transforms rhetoric into hermeneutics, are particularly revealing on this point. That a conscious principle is indeed involved can be shown by doctrinal affirmations of the following sort: Christ "did not hide [truths] in order to prevent them from being communicated, but in order to provoke desire for them by this very concealment" (*Sermons*, 51, 4, 5); or: "No one doubts that things are perceived more readily through similitudes and that what is sought with difficulty is discovered with more pleasure. Those who do not find what they seek directly stated labor in hunger; those who do not seek because they have what they wish at once frequently become indolent in disdain" (*On Christian Doctrine*, II, vi, 8).

At the end of this same period, in the eighteenth century, we encounter these comparisons once again, modulated by the Swiss writer Johann Jakob Breitinger: "Metaphors and the other figures are like salt and spices: too skimpy a dose leaves the dish tasteless; too heavy a sprinkling makes the dish inedible. Such inopportune and disproportionate prodigality with spices in the preparation of food testifies to the wealth and generosity of the master of the house; but it betrays, at the same time, his corrupted taste" (*Kritische Abhandlung*, p. 162).

Ordinarily, however, what is in question is not a carefully cultivated hunger, but libido. Here are a few of the many connections made—these, again, by Augustine: "The more these things seem to be obscured by figurative words, the sweeter they become when they are explained" (*On Christian Doctrine*, IV, vii, 15). "All these truths slipped to us in figures serve to feed the fire of love . . . ; for they inspire and inflame love more than if they were

presented in their nakedness devoid of any signifying imagery"
(*Letters*, 55, xi, 21). "But in order that manifest truths should not
become tiring, they have been covered with a veil, while remaining unchanged, and thus they become the object of desire; being
desired, they are in a way made young again; with their youth
restored, they enter the spirit gently (*suaviter*)" (ibid., 137, v, 18).
"These things are veiled in figures, in garments as it were, in
order that they may exercise the mind of the pious inquirer, and
not become cheap for being bare and obvious. . . . For being
remote, they are more ardently desired (*desiderantur ardentius*), and
for being desired they are more joyfully discovered (*lucundius*)"
(*Against Lying*, x, 24).

We may well rejoice in Augustine's secret sensuality (which is
all the more flavorful, I dare say, in that it is supposed to help
transcend the primary sense, the material and sensual one, in
favor of a secondary spiritual sense), but it remains no less true
that for him, just as for the other rhetoricians and exegetes, clothing is of less value than the body; clothing is an external envelope
that must be removed (even though this operation can be pleasurable). Further evidence for this position is found in the frequent comparison of a metaphor to a prostitute—a comparison
now oriented in the inverse direction (when all the veils have
been removed, the woman finds herself naked and there is only
one profession left for her to practice). Thus Macrobius relates
the misadventures of the neo-Pythagorean philosopher Numenius
(*Commentary on the Dream of Scipio*, i, ii, 19):

> Indeed, Numenius, a philosopher with a curiosity for occult
> things, had revealed to him in a dream the outrage he had
> committed against the gods by proclaiming his interpretation
> of the Eleusinian mysteries. The Eleusinian goddesses them-
> selves, dressed in the garments of courtesans, appeared to him
> standing before an open brothel, and when in his astonishment
> he asked the reason for this shocking conduct, they angrily
> replied that he had driven them from their sanctuary of mod-
> esty and had prostituted them to every passer-by.

Such comparisons, and the value judgments they imply, are
passed along throughout the second period of the history of
rhetoric, from Cicero to Fontanier. They become the defining feature of a civilization which, under the influence of the Christian
religion, consistently values thought above words, so sure is it
that "the letter kills, and the spirit brings life." Let us recall here

one last piece of evidence, one that is particularly eloquent owing to the fame of its author. It is found in Locke's *Essay Concerning Human Understanding*. Locke condemns rhetoric (and therefore eloquence, and therefore speech) as a travesty of thought.

> I confess, in discourses where we seek rather pleasure and delight than information and improvement, such ornaments as are borrowed from them can scarce pass for faults. But yet if we would speak of things as they are, we must allow that all the art of rhetoric, besides order and clearness; all the artificial and figurative application of words eloquence hath invented, are for nothing else but to insinuate wrong ideas, move the passions, and thereby mislead the judgment; and so indeed are perfect cheats: and therefore, however laudable or allowable oratory may render them in harangues and popular addresses, they are certainly, in all discourses that pretend to inform or instruct, wholly to be avoided; and where truth and knowledge are concerned, cannot but be thought a great fault, either of the language or person that makes use of them. . . . I cannot but observe how little the preservation and improvement of truth and knowledge is the care and concern of mankind; since the arts of fallacy are endowed and preferred. It is evident how much men love to deceive and be deceived, since rhetoric, that powerful instrument of error and deceit, has its established professors, is publicly taught, and has always been had in great reputation: and I doubt not but it will be thought great boldness, if not brutality, in me to have said thus much against it. Eloquence, like the fair sex, has too prevailing beauties in it to suffer itself ever to be spoken against. And it is in vain to find fault with those arts of deceiving, wherein men find pleasure to be deceived. [III, x, 34]

We can now return to causal analysis and once again raise the question, why? Why is an acceptable rhetoric impossible during this period? Why is it impossible to appreciate language for itself? Why does the celebration fail to occur?

A satisfactory rhetoric would have been possible if the disappearance of political, and thus verbal, liberties had been accompanied by a disappearance of all social morality: that would have legitimized the solitary admiration, on individualist principles, of each linguistic utterance for itself. Yet the opposite is the case. Whether we look at the Roman Empire or at later Christian states, we are far from finding individual pleasure, and the value of self-satisfaction, set up as a model. We see this with Augustine: *the* truth is believed known, more and more surely; there is no question of allowing each individual to appreciate his own truth and to love objects (in this case, linguistic ones) simply for the sake of their harmony and beauty. Thus poetic pleasure, inasmuch as it consists in an appreciation of useless language, is unacceptable in this social order.

But if the ideal of the new rhetoric is impossible, why does it manage to subsist during nearly two millennia? It is because there is no question, either, of abandoning the regimentation of discourse. The very principle that is responsible for the disappearance of the old form of rhetoric—efficacious eloquence—keeps rhetoric alive as a body of rules. The value system that is obligatory for the whole society suppresses free speech, but maintians regimentation. The principle that condemns eloquence (and, with it, rhetoric) to decadence, contributes at the same time to keeping it alive. In the face of this contradictory requirement—that rhetoric be concerned exclusively with the beauty of discourse but at the same time that it must not valorize this beauty—there remains only one possible attitude: that of bad conscience (one is tempted to say of mental illness). Rhetoric goes about its business reluctantly.

This state of affairs finds a kind of confirmation in the subsequent history of rhetoric—a history that we shall here only skim over rapidly. History indeed does not stop with Fontanier, or rather, only the history of rhetoric stops there—that of society and of civilizations continues. At the end of the eighteenth century a mutation occurs that will set in motion the second crisis of rhetoric, one that will prove to be more serious than the first. And just as, during the first crisis, one and the same gesture condemned it and kept it alive, so now at a single stroke it will be acquitted, liberated, and put to death.

The eighteenth century is the first to endorse what had been in preparation, within rhetoric, since Tacitus's day: the enjoyment of language as such. This same century is the first to value imitation—a relation of submission to the external world—less highly than beauty, which is now defined as a harmonious combination of the elements of an object among themselves, as an accomplishment in itself. This is in fact an era in which everyone claims to have the same rights as everyone else, and to possess in him or herself the standard for measuring beauty and value. "We no longer live at the time when universally accepted forms were dominant," wrote Novalis. Farewell to religion, the norm common to all; farewell to the aristocracy, a caste with preestablished privileges. The useful need no longer be admired, for there is no longer a common goal to serve, and each separate goal seeks priority. Moritz, Kant, Novalis, Schelling will define the beautiful, art, poetry as that which suffices unto itself; they will not be the first to do so, as we have seen, but they will be the first to be heard: their message falls upon well-disposed ears.

And rhetoric? Here it is, we might think, freed from its bad conscience, becoming this time, in truth, the celebration of language. But the romantic wave that suppressed the reasons for bad conscience had far deeper consequences: it also suppressed the necessity for regimenting discourse, since now everyone, by drawing upon personal inspiration, without technique or rules, can produce admirable works of art. Thought is no longer divorced—or even distinguished—from expression; there is no longer, in a word, any need for rhetoric. Poetry can do without it.

This second crisis can be diagnosed simply on the basis of the material disappearance of rhetorical texts, the shadow into which a whole problematics will plunge. Moreover, we can turn to some eloquent testimonials, such as the one Kant left us in his *Critique of Judgement*. Compared to poetry, which finds its justification in itself, rhetoric—subjugated speech—is not only inferior, it is unworthy even to exist. As for the former: "In poetry everything is straight and above board. It shows its hand: it desires to carry on a mere entertaining play with the imagination, and one consonant, in respect of form, with the laws of understanding, and it does not seek to steal upon and ensnare the understanding with a sensuous presentation" (§53, p. 535). (We might be listening to Maternus, at the beginning of Tacitus's dialogue.) And as for the latter:

> Rhetoric, so far as this is taken to mean the art of persuasion, i.e., the art of deluding by means of a fair semblance (as *ars oratoria*), and not merely excellence of speech (eloquence and style), is a dialectic, which borrows from poetry only so much as is necessary to win over men's minds to the side of the speaker before they have weighed the matter, and to rob their verdict of its freedom. [Ibid.]

Kant thus takes great care to establish two series: on one side there is poetry, purely a formal game, and eloquence properly so called, that is, the art of saying well and with style; and on the other, there is oratorical art, which submits these same linguistic means to an external goal, whose diabolical kinship is immediately apparent: "subjugate," "bewitch," "deceive," "win minds." The rhetoric criticized by Kant, clearly, is the rhetoric of the time before Cicero, that which sought to persuade and not to say well. And he spells out his hostility to traditional eloquence in a note:

> I must confess to the pure delight which I have ever been afforded by a beautiful poem; whereas the reading of the best speech of a Roman forensic orator, a modern parliamentary debater, or a preacher, has invariably been mingled with an unpleasant sense of disapproval of an insidious art that knows how, in matters of moment, to move men like machines to a judgement that must lose all its weight with them upon calm reflection. Force and elegance of speech (which together constitute rhetoric) belong to fine art; but oratory (*ars oratoria*), being the art of playing for one's own purpose upon the weaknesses of men (let this purpose be ever so good in intention or even in fact) merits no *respect* whatever. Besides, both at Athens and at Rome, it only attained its greatest height at a time when the state was hastening to its decay, and genuine patriotic sentiment was a thing of the past. [I, ii, 53]

In this text, alongside the dichotomy already evoked between the useful, which is impure, and the useless, object of unreserved admiration, one should note the surfacing of typically bourgeois values: individual independence, national autonomy (patriotism). Subjugated discourse is no longer worthy of esteem; neither is rhetoric. There is no room for rhetoric in a universe dominated by romantic values.[2]

If one abandons history altogether and turns to the problematics of today, one may wonder to what extent things have changed, to what extent we still live in Kant's era. If, on the one hand, social morality is still lacking in our day, as it was in Kant's, speech has perhaps increased in importance. Tacitus reported, as a distant memory, that the ancient orators "had convinced themselves that no one could rise in the state or maintain a position of

2. Is it by chance that Goethe, that other romantic, valued above all else in Kant's work this condemnation of rhetoric? "If you wish, by and by, to read something of his [Kant's], I recommend to you his *Critique on the Power of Judgment*, in which he has written admirably upon rhetoric, tolerably upon poetry, but unsatisfactorily on plastic art" (*Conversations with Eckermann* [New York and London, 1901], p. 196; April 11, 1827).

importance and prominence without oratorical ability" (*Dialogue*, xxxvi); but in our day, when the words and acts of public figures are transmitted directly to the most distant corners of the state, thanks to the mass media and above all television, is it still conceivable that "without eloquence" one can hold on to an important position? Two recent facts, among hundreds, prove the contrary. A president of the United States appeared less contemptible in the eyes of his fellow citizens when on numerous occasions he transgressed the laws of his country than when he revealed his linguistic deficiencies: the publication of his private conversations, intended to prove his legal innocence, had an overwhelmingly negative effect, when it became clear that Nixon spoke badly, as badly as the average American; that he swore in every sentence; that his remarks were studded with slang. Do we dare affirm, after that, that "eloquence" is no longer required of the statesman? Another example comes from French political life. In the opinion of the experts, the choice of a new president in 1974 was in large part decided during a television debate in which the two candidates confronted each other for an hour and a half; are we to believe that their rhetorical skills, their ability to manipulate speech in order to instruct, to move, and to please, had no effect on the spectators? A public figure cannot allow himself to speak badly. Power today is at the tip of the tongue; speech—as transmitted by telecasts rather than as heard in deliberative assemblies—has once again become an effective weapon.

We are perhaps at the beginning of a fourth era of rhetoric, in which eloquence will lack neither the "matter" nor the "movement" it needs in order to shine; will this power of speech be able to conquer that of institutions? I shall not take up the game of divination, but I shall note what is perhaps only a coincidence, after all: the awakening of rhetorical studies in Western Europe over roughly the past twenty years—since mass communications began to dominate our world.

Will fortune come to smile on rhetoricians once again, as in the early days in Greece and Rome? One dares not affirm it; one must be content to note—sadly—their absence during the two thousand years our world has just lived through.

Unless we have the wrong history. Unless all these characters I have been referring to, Cicero, Quintilian, Fontanier, and the rest, are fictitious beings, and their writings mere jokes. Unless the true history is the one told one day in the seventh century by a citizen of Toulouse known as Virgil the Grammarian. His story goes like this:

> The first, then, was a certain Donatus at Troy, who is said to have lived a thousand years. He came to Romulus, by whom Rome was founded, and was received by him with many honors. He spent four years there, building a school, and he left behind countless little texts in which he set forth questions for solution, such as: "Who is it, my son, who extends her breasts to children beyond number, and who provides as much nourishment as they can take?" This was wisdom. . . .
>
> There was also, at Troy, a certain Virgil, a disciple of that same Donatus, who was most diligent in classifying verses; he wrote seventy books on metrics, and a letter to Virgil Assianus about the explanation of the word.
>
> As for the third Virgil, it is I. . . .
>
> Then there was Gregorius, in Egypt, greatly devoted to Greek studies, who composed three thousand texts on Greek history. At Nicomedia, there was the late Balapsidus, who at my request translated books of our laws into Latin—books which I read, for my part, in the Greek. . . .

There was also Virgil of Asia, who claimed that each word had twelve Latin names that could be used on appropriate occasions.

There was also Aeneas, the third Virgil's professor, who taught him the noble and useful art of breaking up words, of grouping letters according to their similarities, of composing new words from old ones by taking a single syllable from each.

There was. . . .

There have been fortunate rhetoricians.

3

The End of Rhetoric

Classical rhetoric has not existed since the nineteenth century. But before it disappeared, it produced—through a final effort more powerful than any that had gone before it, as if to try to stave off imminent extinction—a body of reflections whose quality is unmatched. This swan song deserves to be examined from two viewpoints: theoretical—for the body of thought in question is not yet outdated—and historical—the form taken by this climax is highly significant.

We are in France, and the period in question covers exactly one hundred years. It begins in 1730, when Du Marsais published a rhetorical treatise destined to stir up more interest in its own country than any of its predecessors; the period ends in 1830, when Fontanier put the finishing touches to the last edition of his *Manuel classique*, prefacing it with these words, whose prophetic import he could not have realized: "This work has been improved as much as possible; doubtless not in its own terms, but with respect to the limited capacity of its author, who declares that he has done his utmost and that nothing remains for him to do but recommend the faithful execution of his work to the printers charged with reproducing it."

The rhetorical body is thoroughly embalmed; nothing is left but to bury it.

Let us meet the authors of this rhetorical rhapsody. They span one hundred years and three generations.

To the first generation belongs only César Chesneau Du Marsais (1676–1756). His *Tropes* was among his earlier works although it was by no means a production of his youth. Poor throughout his life, a tutor who authored a new method of teaching Latin that meant more to him than anything else, he received, at the age of seventy-five, his first prestigious assignment: he was made responsible for the grammatical and rhetorical sections of the *Encyclopedia*. The task suited him very well, moreover: Du Marsais was endowed above all with the attributes of a writer—not to say a popularizer; beyond that, he was unencumbered with original ideas. A great eclectic, he had read widely, he had the "philosophical" spirit; nevertheless, his indifference to all system and coherence was his undoing on more than one occasion. Furthermore, his collaboration on the *Encyclopedia* was brief: when he died, he had only just completed the "Grammarian" article.

The second generation consists, in our account, of two rather dissimilar individuals. The first is Du Marsais's heir as head of the grammatical and rhetorical sections of the *Encyclopedia*: Nicolas Beauzée (1717–1789), a professor at the Ecole Militaire. He continued to contribute to the *Encyclopedia* until its completion in 1772; during the same period, in 1767, he published a synthetic work, his two-volume *Grammaire générale*, which included some excerpts from his *Encyclopedia* articles. At the opposite pole from Du Marsais, Beauzée had a particularly systematic cast of mind. His principal interest was grammar, not rhetoric. But the one goes with the other, and his *Grammaire* also included some decisive pages devoted to rhetorical figures. Between 1782 and 1786, finally, the three volumes of the *Encyclopédie méthodique* appeared, containing all the articles of the *Encyclopedia* dealing with "grammar and literature." To Beauzée, too, fell the task of revising the sections on rhetoric in the *Encyclopedia*, a task that gave him the opportunity to comment on, criticize, and complete the articles by Du Marsais.

The second representative of this generation is too well known for us to linger over the biographical facts. Etienne Bonnot, Abbé of Condillac (1714–1780), was a tutor like Du Marsais; between 1758 and 1780 he composed a rhetoric that was published in his *Cours d'études pour l'instruction du prince de Parme* (1775). A friend of Du Marsais and of the Encyclopedists, Condillac nonetheless, occupied a position apart from theirs, and in his treatise *De l'art d'écrire* he was satisfied to participate in the prevailing atmosphere rather than to begin an open debate with his predecessors and his contemporaries. These rhetoricians had in common the fact that they were all also grammarians, this at a time when grammar was "philosophical"; it follows that their rhetorical treatises were likewise "general and reasoned."

The third generation appeared after a considerable lapse of time (the direct line of descent is broken): it is represented by Pierre Fontanier, about whom, oddly enough, virtually nothing is known. He must have taught rhetoric in a lycée, using Du Marsais's manual; dissatisfied with the incoherence of many passages in that work, he decided to replace it with one he had written himself. But Du Marsais's prestige was such that Fontanier opted for a very complex strategy: he first published, in 1818, a new edition of the *Tropes*, along with an equally thick volume which contained his own *Commentaire raisonné*. This commentary went beyond its original objective, however: not only Du Marsais but also Beauzée, Condillac, and others are invoked in a debate that no longer focuses on eloquence—and therein lies its originality—but rather on rhetoric (Fontanier's *Commentaire* is a work of metarhetoric). Having thus laid the groundwork, Fontanier published his *Manuel classique pour l'étude des tropes* in 1821 (the definitive fourth edition appeared, as we have seen, in 1830); the second part, the *Traité général des figures du discours autres que les tropes*, followed in 1827.

Reading these treatises and articles today, one is in no way impressed by the genius of their authors; it would not be going too far to say that genius is purely and simply lacking here. Every page, taken by itself, reeks of mediocrity. We are dealing with an elderly gentleman (rhetoric): he never dares to stray very far from the ideal of his youth (exemplified by Cicero and Quintilian—although they were elderly gentlemen themselves, in their way); he does not notice the transformations of the world around him (Fontanier came *after* romanticism, in its German manifestation at least). And yet there is something splendid about this old age: the old man has forgotten nothing of the two-thousand-year history of his life. Better still, in a debate animated by many voices, notions, definitions, and relations are refined and crystallized as never before. Here then is the paradox: this sequence of lusterless pages, when taken as a whole, produces a dazzling impression indeed.

Let us now try to listen to a fragment of this many-voiced rhapsody.[1]

THE FIGURE: THEORY AND CLASSIFICATIONS

Du Marsais begins his treatise with a distinction between two definitions of the figure that we can summarize as follows: figure as deviation, and figure as form. In fact, these two definitions had already been recorded by Quintilian: instead of opposing the one to the other, he presented the second as a restriction and clarification of the first. To say that a figure is the form of an utterance is, for Quintilian, insufficient, for in that case all language would be figurative; thus we must complete the assertion by adding that a figure is a manner of speaking that is removed from the simple, common manner.

Du Marsais's preferences lie in the opposite direction: he chooses the broad as opposed to the narrow definition. His arguments against the idea of the figure as deviation are well known ("More figures are produced in a single market day at the Halles than in several days of academic meetings"): "Figures do not deviate from the ordinary language of men, far from it; on the contrary, speech without figures would be deviant, if it were possible to construct a discourse that contained only nonfigurative speech" (*DT*, p. 3).

Consequently, he chooses to define the figure as form, and does so, moreover, by way of the comparison—already a canonical one in Latin rhetoric—between language and the body. "*Figure*, in the proper sense, is the exterior form of a body. All bodies have extension; but beyond that general property of extension,

1. The French version of this book presents the rhetorical theories considered here in greater detail (pp. 88–113). These theories have also been dealt with briefly in the following studies (generally without regard to their historical context or to their mutual relationships): Gérard Genette, *Figures* (Paris, 1966), pp. 205–222; Todorov, *Littérature et signification* (Paris, 1967), pp. 91–118; Genette, preface to the 1967 edition of the *Tropes*; also "Introduction, la rhétorique des figures," in the 1968 edition of *Figures du discours*, pp. 5–17; J. Cohen, "Théorie de la figure," *Communications* 16 (1970), 3–25; Genette, *Figures III* (Paris, 1972), pp. 21–40; M. Charles, "Le discours des figures," *Poétique*, 4 (1973), 340–364; Paul Ricoeur, *La métaphore vive*, Paris, 1975, pp. 63–86. G. Sahlin's solid study, *C. C. Du Marsais . . .* (Paris, 1928), deals very little with Du Marsais's rhetorical work.

each one still has its figure and its specific form, which make each body appear different from others in our eyes: the same holds true for figurative expressions" (*DT*, p. 7). An utterance may change its figure, but it can never avoid having one: "When a word is taken in another sense, it then appears, as it were, in a borrowed form, in a figure that is not its natural one" (*DT*, p. 27).

All bodies have form; does it follow, as Quintilian had seen, that all language is figurative? Du Marsais never raises this question openly, and its suppression leads him to a whole series of inconsistencies and evasions. His initial reaction is to reject the reproach, affirming that there are indeed nonfigurative expressions; but he does not equip himself with the means to establish the distinction. This deficiency is veiled by the word "modification": figures are those expressions that have undergone a modification; but Du Marsais does not specify the nature of the material modified. And if the figure is defined, in relation to the nonfigure, as a modification imposed on a primary expression, have we not returned, minus the pejorative nuance, to the definition of figure as deviation? Here is Du Marsais's text:

> [Figurative expressions] first reveal what one thinks; they have first of all that general property belonging to all sentences and all word groups, which consists in signifying something by virtue of a grammatical construction; but beyond this the figurative expressions also have a specific modification peculiar to themselves, and it is by virtue of this specific modification that each type of figure becomes a species apart. . . . The ways of speaking in which [grammarians and rhetoricians] have observed no other property but that of revealing thought are called simply sentences, expressions, periods; but those that express not merely thoughts, but thoughts uttered in a particular manner which gives them a characteristic feature, these, I am saying, are called *figures,* because they appear, so to speak, in a specific form, and with that characteristic feature that distinguishes them from each other and from what are merely sentences or expressions. [*DT*, pp. 7–9]

Du Marsais formulates his definition at the end of this same chapter:

> *Figures* are ways of speaking distinctly of others by means of a specific modification, which means that each one is reduced to a separate type and rendered either livelier, or nobler, or more agreeable than the ways of speaking that express the same basic

thought without having any particular modification. [*DT*, pp. 13–14]

Not all language is figurative: some sentences merely signify, merely transmit thought; others add to this general property their own modification, or specific manner. But when he has to explain the precise nature of this modification, Du Marsais hides behind a finalist argument, abandoning the structural terrain that was his until then: the figural modification is the one that improves nonfigurative expressions.

Perhaps Du Marsais does not mean to imply that nonfigurative expressions are "simpler and more common," nor that they are preferable to figures; however, the dichotomy that he has established, with the figure coming to modify an expression deriving from pure thought, draws him inevitably along this path. For he is incapable of surmounting one of the most persistent paradigms of classical Western culture, the one according to which thought is more important than its expression, as the spirit is more important than matter, the inside more important than the outside. It is no accident that Du Marsais declares that the differentiating feature of the trope "consists in the way a word *deviates* from its proper signification" (*DT*, p. 18; emphasis added). It is not without reason that he situates the clarity of discourse above all other considerations (for what could be clearer than discourse that "makes known what one thinks"?): "Today . . . people love what is true, what teaches, enlightens, interests, has a reasonable object; they no longer look at words except as signs over which one does not linger except to go straight to what they signify" (*DT*, pp. 326–327). But if signs must be transparent, how shall we discover the "characteristic feature" that sets apart tropic constructions? And how could we appreciate such a feature, if the ideal of discourse is that transparent clarity? "One cannot repeat too often to young people that they must speak and write only to be understood, and that clarity is the first and foremost quality of discourse" ("Amphibologie," *Encyclopédie, Oeuvres*, iv, 137).

The figure's exteriority—and therefore its inferiority—are best revealed in the comparisons and tropes that are used to talk about it. Du Marsais passes without difficulty from the first image—the figure as body—to another, which draws attention to its superficial and unnecessary character—that of the figure as cloak, a comparison that, as we know, has accompanied rhetoric since its birth, and one that Du Marsais seems to discover in his turn with a disconcerting freshness. Figures "lend nobler dress, as it were, to these common ideas" (*DT*, p. 34). He even constructs a veritable "apologue" on this point:

> Imagine for a moment a crowd of soldiers in which some are wearing only the ordinary clothes that they had before joining up, and the others are in the uniform of their regiment: the latter all have clothes that set them apart, and that reveal what regiment they belong to; some are dressed in red, others in blue, white, yellow, and so on. It is the same with groups of words that make up discourse: an informed reader can relate a certain word or phrase to a given type of figure, assuming that he recognizes in it the form, the sign, the distinguishing characteristic of that figure; sentences and words that lack the mark of some specific figure are like the soldiers that lack the uniform of a particular regiment: they have no modifications except those that are necessary for revealing thought. [*DT*, pp. 10–11]

And a few lines further on Du Marsais adds, "Aside from the properties of expressing thought, shared with all word groups, they also have, so to speak, the advantage of their dress, by which I mean their particular modification, which serves to arouse attention, to please, or to move" (*DT*, p. 11).

This passage deserves attention on more than one account. In the first place, it bears witness to the fact that Du Marsais shares in the traditional ideology of rhetoric, and, what is more, does so without noticing it. At the same time—and this again illustrates the fecund inconsistency so characteristic of Du Marsais—he manages to subvert this tradition from within: everything is cloaked (figurative and nonfigurative expressions alike); moreover, the cloak no longer serves to embellish, as it always did in the past, but rather to indicate belonging; the cloak is functional, and no longer ornamental. It is not entirely clear whether Du Marsais is subverting tradition or vice versa, in this conflict of which doubtless neither side is aware.

For no matter how Du Marsais manipulates the comparison, it has, in itself, a meaning it has carried for some two thousand years, one that gives primacy to the essentially ornamental function of figures. We shall not be astonished to see poetry, a favored locus for figures, defined as discourse that says "the same thing" as nonpoetic discourse, but in a more ornate way. "The genius of poetry consists in amusing the imagination by images which in the last analysis are often reduced to a thought that ordinary discourse would express with more simplicity, but in a manner that is either too dry or too lowly" (*DT*, pp. 222–223). Without being actually denigrated here, figures are pulling away from the simple manner of speaking.

These contradictions and uncertainties bring about the only notable evolution in Du Marsais's work, between his treatise *Des tropes* and his presentation of rhetorical doctrine in the *Encyclopedia* articles. In the article entitled "Figure," he no longer presents as his own the idea according to which every expression has a figure (form), but limits himself to the notion of figure as deviation from the simple expression, a more consistent but less ambitious concept.

> *Figure.*   This word comes from *fingere*, in the sense of *efformare*, *componere*, to form, to dispose, to arrange. It is in this sense that Scaliger says that a figure is nothing but a particular arrangement of one or several words. . . . To which we may add . . . that this particular disposition is relative to the primitive and, as it were, fundamental state of the words or phrases. The various deviations brought about in this primitive state and the various alterations effected in it create the various figures of words and thoughts. [*Oeuvres*, v, 262]

Thus figures are now nothing more than deviations and alterations; not, to be sure, with respect to the most common, most frequent manner of expressing oneself, but with respect to a "fundamental" state of discourse, about which Du Marsais has very little to say. The direction in which his thought is inclined can, however, be inferred from the article "Construction," which contains the essence of his thought on grammatical questions. Construction, or the syntactic structure of particular sentences, may itself be proper or figurative:

> This second sort of construction is called *figurative construction*, because in fact it takes a figure, a form, which is not that of the *simple construction*. The figurative construction is, in truth, authorized by a particular usage; but it is no longer in conformity with the most regular way of speaking, that is, with that complete and orderly construction of which we spoke first. [*Oeuvres*, v, 17]

Here "simple" is interpreted as *regular*: the figure is opposed to a rule, which may also produce results that are "complete" (otherwise there is *ellipsis*) and "orderly" (otherwise there is *inversion*). The figure, like the nonfigure, is "authorized by usage": it is opposed not to usage (as Quintilian's definition would have it) but to the rule, thus to the norm.

The definition of figure proposed by Du Marsais, brought to its own logical conclusion, is no longer opposed to the idea of figure as deviation, it is merely a variant of this idea (even though Du Marsais never succeeds in formulating it with precision). This retraction and this relative failure result from Du Marsais's inability to systematize his own ideas.

Still, in the formulations found in the *Tropes*, there remain several that point toward another solution of the initial difficulty as it had already been formulated by Quintilian (since every utterance has a particular form, each is a figure, therefore nothing is a figure). Thus at the very beginning of his work Du Marsais quotes several examples of figures: "Antithesis, for example, is distinguished from other forms of speech in that, in the group of words that constitutes antithesis, the words are opposed to each other. . . . Apostrophe is different from other enunciations because it is only in apostrophe that one suddenly addresses one's speech to some present or absent person . . ." (*DT*, p. 8).

We perceive all the sentences, and each sentence has a form; however, we discern the "characteristic feature," that is, the quality of figure, only in certain ones: as in those in which someone is addressed *suddenly*, and not slowly and after some preparation; or in those in which the words are *opposed* to one another, and not in those in which they are alike or simply different. Why? What accounts for the fact that certain forms are perceptible while others are not? the fact that we "recognize" the figures in one case but not in another? Du Marsais seems to return to this question much later on: "As figures are only ways of speaking that have a particular character to which a name has been given, and moreover since each type of figure may be varied in several different ways, it is obvious that, if we are going to observe each of these manners and give them specific names, we will create a certain number of figures" (*DT*, p. 253).

This sentence is important. The figure is not a property that belongs, intrinsically and out of all context, to sentences: every sentence is potentially figurative, thus no discriminatory criterion is to be found here. But we know how to "observe" the form of certain utterances, and not that of others. Du Marsais does not question the origins of this difference (which resides then in our attitude toward the sentences rather than in the sentences themselves), but he provides us with a cue for recognizing it: the fact that certain figures have names while others do not. By giving a name to a figure, we institutionalize it; but the institution, incarnated here in the existence of the name, obliges us to perceive certain linguistic forms and allows us to ignore the others. Thus in Du Marsais's presentation there is the basis for a second interpretation of the figure as form: it does not deviate from the rule, but obeys another rule, not a linguistic one this time but a meta-linguistic—and thus a cultural—rule. An expression is figurative when we know how to perceive its form; now this knowledge is imposed on us by a social norm, incarnated in the existence of a name for the figure. Jean Paulhan, in a commentary on Du Marsais, has noted this paradoxical consequence: "This is to say that figures have as their single characteristic the reflections and the inquiry that rhetoricians pursue with regard to them" (*Oeuvres complètes*, II, "Traité des figures," p. 229). All language is potentially figurative, for it is theoretically possible to perceive the form of every utterance; however, it is not an omnipresent and thus nondistinctive property; to say that an expression is figurative is not tautological, because at any given instant we are capable of perceiving the form only of certain utterances and not of all. The notion of figure is not distinctive at the linguistic level, but it regains its full meaning at the level of our perception of language. An utterance becomes figurative as soon as we perceive it in itself.

Let us try to summarize this line of thought. Du Marsais rejects the idea of the figure as deviation, substituting for it that of the figure as form. But in the face of the difficulties to which this definition gives rise, unwilling to confront them directly, he lays the groundwork for two interpretations of his initial position, without managing, however, to formulate either one: (1) the figure is indeed a deviation, with respect this time not to usage but to an abstract rule; (2) the figure is a form, but not just any form: it is only that form which, owing to a social convention, is incarnated in the existence of a name and is perceptible as form by the users of a given language.

Of these two possible ways out of an initial impasse, Beauzée, Du Marsais's direct heir, resolutely chooses the first, formulating it with a clarity entirely absent in Du Marsais's writing, and giving it wider extension. Just as meaning was derived from signification through the figure, the empirical form being opposed to the abstract idea, so any construction or observable grammatical structure is produced by means of a figure on the basis of an abstract and universal syntax. Each individual sentence is figurative precisely in that it is individual; only the abstract structure common to several related sentences is figureless. In the language of transformational grammar, which seems to fit here, "figure" would be replaced by "transformation"; every sentence in surface structure is derived through a transformation (through a figure) from a deep structure. Here is the way this idea is expressed in Beauzée's language:

> Just as the figure, in the primitive and proper sense, is the individual determination of a body by the set of perceptible parts of its contour, so the linguistic figure is the individual determination of a body by the specific turn of phrase that distinguishes it from other analogous expressions. In each language, usage and analogy have established the material of diction, the primitive meaning and the accidental forms of the parts of a prayer, the rules of syntax appropriate to this basic stock prepared by the genius of the language; that is, so to speak, the universal form of language, which is found unchanged in all discourse, but which nevertheless receives various specific modifications in discourse; owing to these modifications, the primitive form never appears in the same aspect. Thus it is that all men have a form common to the whole species, and resemble each other through this general conformation: but when we compare individuals, what variety! what differences! not one resembles another; the form is always the same, but all the figures are different. It is the same with the expressions of a language: all are subject to the same general, inalterable form, yet each one has its own physiognomy, so to speak, which results from the difference between the modifying figures and the common form; these figures are like those that characterize individuals among men, they announce the soul and depict it. ["Figure," *EM*, ii, 108]

The "general" and abstract "form" necessarily manifests itself in a figurative state. Beauzée's position is extreme, and perfectly consistent: unlike Du Marsais, he does not envisage the existence of nonfigurative "constructions" whose manifest structure would be a faithful reflection of the underlying structure; this leads him to ask: "Is there a way to speak without figures?" (ibid., p. 111). In his *Grammaire générale* he draws closer to his predecessor nonetheless. In the course of a debate with the Abbé Batteux, according to whom a figure in one language may not be a figure in another, Beauzée replies as follows: there exists a general form common to all languages, which deserves on that account to be called "natural"; an actual sentence may embody that general form without modification; but as soon as there is modification, there is a figure, whatever the language in question, and whatever the customary usage may be. "A *figure*, in language, is thus an expression that is removed not from the ordinary and time-honored way of speaking but from the natural manner of rendering the same ideas in any idiom whatever; so that ordinarily what is a figure in one language will be a figure in another" (p. 546).

Of the two directions suggested but not formulated by Du Marsais, Beauzée chooses, in theory, the former. And yet once again, when he gives examples of figures, or attempts to classify them, like all of his predecessors he considers only the figures in the existing repertory of rhetorical tradition—only the figures that already have names. Might this not be proof in itself that the second response would have been more efficacious? Beauzée's theory is irreproachable from within, except for the fact that he applies the label "figure" to a much broader set of phenomena than are ordinarily called by that name (to the linguistic manifestation, as opposed to the abstract and universal form); this extension of the name is so little justified that Beauzée himself does not succeed in holding himself to it.

For Beauzée, the need for a notion of the figure disappears, since figures are identified with manifest linguistic form. It is a case of disappearance by overextension: every signifier is figurative. With Condillac, we observe a comparable but distinct disappearance, this one obtained through an operation on the signified. Let us recall one last time that, for traditional rhetoric, there exists a nonfigurative way of speaking, in which one merely communicates thought; and then figures, which add to this thought some heterogeneous material—feelings, images, ornaments. The existence of the figure rests on the conviction that two expressions, one with and one without images (feeling and so on) express, as Du Marsais put it, "the same store of thought." It suffices then to abolish the qualitative difference between thought and feeling, for the difference between the expression of thoughts and the expression of feelings to disappear in its turn. This is precisely the line of reasoning (already outlined in the Port-Royal *Logic* and by Father Bernard Lamy) that Condillac will follow. More precisely, without eliminating the distinction between thoughts and feelings, he will do without the distinction between proper and figurative expression, in that each will be the proper expression of a different signifier: feelings are no longer an appendix to thoughts but a source of signification in their own right.

Condillac sets forth at the outset a distinction which Beauzée also made but which for the latter lacked doctrinal significance: the distinction between proper meaning and proper word.

> Just as rhetoricians call "tropes" words taken in a borrowed meaning, they call "proper names" words taken in the primitive meaning; and we must observe that there is a difference between "proper name" and "proper word." When we say that a writer always has the proper word, we do not mean that he always uses words in their primitive signification, we mean that the words he uses convey all his ideas perfectly; the proper word is always the best expression. [*AE*, p. 560]

What interests Condillac is thus not the literal, as opposed to the figurative, but rather the appropriate, which encompasses the figurative. The notion of appropriateness is hardly foreign to classical rhetoric; it is even this meaning of the term "proper" that Quintilian retains for his own use—without failing, however, to draw the self-evident conclusion, namely, that the figurative is not opposed to the "proper" (and thus cannot be defined through it): "*Propriety* is also made to include the appropriate use of words in metaphor" (*Institutio Oratoria*, VIII, ii, 10). Yet if Quintilian had applied this principle consistently, his whole study of ornamentation could not have come about. This is just what happens with Condillac: consistent with himself, he ends up eliminating the notion of figure.

What is sought, then, is "the best expression": whatever the nature of the meaning intended, there is always one expression that is better than all the others. Condillac says so again, very explicitly, in the introduction to *La Langue des calculs* (II, 419): "Different expressions represent the same thing in different aspects, and the viewpoints of the mind, that is, the aspects according to which we consider a thing, determine the choice we have to make. Then the expression chosen is what we call the

proper term. Among several, there is thus always one that deserves preference."

Conversely, an expression—figurative or otherwise—can never
be translated without loss: it states its signified better than any
other expression can. There is no longer variation, as there was
for Du Marsais, among several expressions of a single thought,
but variation among the thoughts themselves: to each signified
corresponds, ideally, a single signifier; thus one can neither translate nor reduce figures. But if the difference lies in the signified
alone, the figure is nothing but a reflection of a conflict that occurs elsewhere; it loses all importance and does not deserve to be
singled out. Condillac thus moves from an ornamental conception
of rhetoric back to a functional one—whether he returns to the
one that preceded Quintilian or the one that followed Fontanier is
difficult to say. It is nonetheless the case that, chronologically
situated within the classical period, Condillac's work is, in certain
respects at least, conceptually foreign to it.

Let us look at some examples of the treatment to which he
subjects figures:

> There is, for each sentiment, a proper word to arouse its idea.
> . . . A sentiment is better expressed when we stress forcefully
> the reasons that produce it in us. . . . The details of all the ef-
> fects of a passion are also the expression of the sentiment. . . .
> Interrogation also contributes to the expression of sentiments; it
> appears to be the turn of phrase most appropriate to reproaches.
> [AE, pp. 572–573]

The figure is the proper (and unique, irreplaceable) expression
of a given sentiment. Interrogations are appropriate to reproaches;
for passion in general, the whole for the part (synecdoche) or the
cause for the effect (metonymy). Or, again:

> To write clearly, it is often necessary to turn away from the
> subordination to which direct order subjects ideas. . . . The law
> that prescribes clarity is also dictated by the chararacteristics to
> be given to the style, according to the sentiments of the speaker.
> A man who is upset and a man who is calm do not arrange
> their ideas in the same order. . . . Both make the greatest
> possible connection among their ideas, and yet each one fol-
> lows a different construction. [AE, p. 576]

In traditional rhetoric, one would have said that direct order
serves to instruct, and favors clarity, whereas inversion serves to
move and to please, and contributes to beauty. The whole scheme

is disrupted in Condillac: inversion may serve clarity if the person being described (or the one who is speaking) is upset. Words no longer have three functions, but only one: instead of instructing, moving, and pleasing, they only signify; only the things signified vary. The absolute norm of ornamental rhetoric is replaced by the relativism of "what is appropriate": there are as many truths as individuals and particular cases.

It is worth noting here that this rhetorical relativism leads Condillac to formulate a literary aesthetic that is just as relativistic, in which the classical and unifying notion of *nature* is replaced by the plural notion of *genres* (this is the famous Chapter v of the fourth part of the *Art d'écrire*). "We suppose that the natural is always the same. . . . [As a matter of fact], every time there is a difference in genre we are differently disposed, and consequently we judge according to different rules" (p. 602). "Naturalness thus consists in the ease with which a thing can be done" (p. 603). "In general, it suffices to observe that in poetry as in prose there are as many ways of being natural as there are genres. . . . Thus it appears demonstrably clear to me that the naturalness proper to poetry and to each type of poem is a conventional naturalness that varies too much to be defined" (p. 611).

This rejection of the universal norm, of absolute truth, is applied to the notion of literature itself: literature does not exist, or rather exists only within specific historical contexts. "To try to discover the essence of poetic style would be a vain effort: there is none" (p. 606). It is decidedly to Condillac's era, rather than to the one that preceded Quintilian, that Fontanier belongs after all.

The latter's theory of the figure remains to be examined: this takes us backward in conceptual history, but not in analytical refinement. Like Du Marsais, but more clearly, Fontanier presents a double definition, structural and functional: the figure is defined at once by what it is and by what it does. And if Fontanier does not innovate so far as the effects of figures are concerned, he moves away from Du Marsais in his structural definition, by choosing the second of the well-traveled paths, that of deviation, while trying to give it a precision that it did not have before. Refuting Du Marsais's objection, according to which figures are as common as nonfigures, he writes: "That does not prevent figures from *deviating*, in a sense, *from the simple manner, from the ordinary and common manner* of speaking. They deviate from it in the sense that one could substitute something more ordinary and more common for them; in the sense that they present something loftier, nobler, more outstanding, more picturesque; something stronger, more energetic, or more gracious, more agreeable" (CR, pp. 3–4).

The same double definition is formulated in his own treatise: "The figures of discourse are the features, the forms or the turns of phrase that are more or less remarkable and more or less privileged in their effect, and through which, in the expression of ideas, thoughts, and feelings, discourse deviates more or less from what would have been the simple and common expression" (FD, p. 64).

The duplicity of structure and function—of which Fontanier takes skillful advantage—is not the only one present in this definition: there is another, at the heart of the structural element itself, and it is embodied in the two terms "simple" (or ordinary) and "common." The two do not necessarily coincide: the simple derives from a qualitative criterion, the common from a quantitative one. This ambiguity has led in our day to controversy among Fontanier's interpreters. In fact, Fontanier's text is sufficiently clear: the expressions that one "could substitute" for figures must be above all simpler, more direct; frequency does not play a discriminatory role here. Even though the formula "more or less" appears three times in the definition of the figure, the difference between the latter and the nonfigure is the difference between all and nothing, not the difference between more and less: either the simple and direct expression exists or else it does not, and if it did not exist, the figure would no longer result from a choice. Now, for Fontanier, no necessary figure exists: "The figures . . . , however common they may be and however familiar they may have become through usage, can only deserve and keep their title of *figure* inasmuch as they are in free usage, and are not in some way imposed by the language" (FD, p. 64).

The figure is based on the existence or nonexistence of a direct expression. This alternative is best conveyed by Fontanier in an opposition that he finds among the tropes: the opposition between catachresis and figures. We must remember that, even for Beauzée, catachresis was not a trope like the others, but a way of using any of the tropes. Fontanier now names the other, complementary aspect of tropes: it is, in fact, the figure. The tropes are defined by change in meaning; this in itself does not make a figure. But they may, in addition, be used in two ways: to compensate for the deficiencies of the language (the catachretic use) or to replace already existing direct expressions: and this second use alone gives rise to figures. The trope is a signifier with two signifieds, one primitive and the other tropic; the figure presupposes a signified that can be designated by two signifiers, one proper and the other figurative. The difference between these relationships, and the complex nature of the trope-figure, may be schematized as shown.

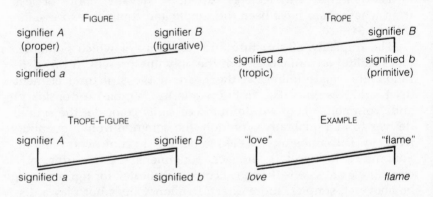

The trope becomes a figure owing to the relation established between signified *a* and signifier *B*; meaning *a* of word *B* must have its direct name *A*, and word *B* must have a proper meaning *b* in order for *B* to be a trope-figure (metaphor, synecdoche, and so on); tropes and figures are intersecting sets.

Another way to represent this relationship would be through the following diagram (in which we are no longer concerned with relations among signifiers and signifieds but with subdivisions within these classes).

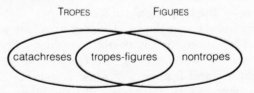

Fontanier formulates these two distinctions in separate passages of his argument. Here he deals with the subdivision of tropes. "Either tropes consisting of a single word offer a figurative meaning, or else they offer only a purely extensive meaning. In the first case, they are true figures. . . . In the second case they can be called *catachreses*" (FD, p. 77).

And here is the other subdivision, among nontropic figures and tropes: "In word figures . . . , either the words are taken in some *proper meaning*, that is, in one of their usual and ordinary significations, whether primitive or not; or they are taken in a *divergent* meaning, not a proper meaning, that is, in a signification that is purely a temporary borrowing" (*FD*, p. 66).

In this passage, we note that the trope-figure exists only in discourse, within a particular utterance (moreover, Fontanier insists on this: "the *figurative meaning* is never present except on loan, and is attached to the word only by the very circumstance that led to its borrowing" [*CR*, p. 385]).

Thus it is indeed a relationship of all-or-nothing that grounds the figure, and not one of greater or lesser frequency, as Fontanier reminds us in connection with several examples: "This synecdoche, in losing the boldness that it had in its novelty, has nevertheless not lost all of its figurative character, and it must not be regarded as a *catachresis*, since the idea that is its object could always be expressed by the proper and specific sign to which it was originally attached" (*CR*, p. 54).

To be sure, one passage of the *Commentaire* presents an interpretation of the figure that seems to go in the opposite direction: "One could prove by a thousand examples that the figures that appear boldest at the beginning stop being regarded as figures when they become quite common and ordinary" (pp. 5–6). But we should probably be more attentive to the expression Fontanier uses: "stop being *regarded* as figures," and not "stop being figures." Familiarity and frequency of occurrence cause us to stop noticing the figurative character of the figure—but do not thereby eliminate it.

Even if his definition of the figure is qualitative, Fontanier is not indifferent to the problem of greater or lesser frequency. The proof lies in the fact that he takes up again entirely on his own account the distinction proposed by the Abbé de Radonvilliers between tropes of usage and tropes of invention (the same subdivision could be applied to the figure):

Some, in reality, and even most, as they are generally accepted, having no novelty whatsoever, are part of the language at its very root, whereas others, fewer in number, are not part of the language at all, either because they are too new, or because the only authority they have in their favor is the writer who gave them the light of day. Now is that difference between them not essential enough for us to make it the subject and the basis for a distinction? Let us call the first type *tropes of usage* or *tropes of the language*, and the second type *tropes of invention* or *tropes of the writer*. [*FD*, p. 164]

The difference is thus "essential enough," but nevertheless subordinate to the difference between figure and nonfigure.

The absence of the proper word to evoke the meaning of catachresis obscures the possibility of measuring the gap between the proper word and the figurative word, and thus it annihilates the figure. The same is true of another group of figures, ordinarily classified among the figures of thought, and which are not true figures, according to Fontanier, for no literal expression exists (none more "proper" than they are themselves) to which they might be compared. "Would it therefore be the particular object of language, or the feeling, the passion that language expresses, that would make the figure here? But then [there would be] as many new figures as there are diverse feelings or passions, or as there are diverse manners in which feelings and passions can burst forth" (*FD*, pp. 434–435).

If it sufficed, for a figure to exist, that the signified be a feeling or a passion, the notion of figure would lose its interest. Both Condillac and Fontanier use this argument, but they base opposing positions on it: the former abolishes the figure, the latter attempts to stabilize it. "Shall we say that these are *figures of thought*?" But for there to be a figure, there must be deviation: here, for example, a gap between what words seem to say and what they really say, between their truth and their falsehood—which would be the improper expression of a signified that is always identical to itself. Now the same cannot be said of the pseudofigures, which Fontanier eliminates for that reason. "Is it possible that these sentiments uttered with so much force and energy may not be sincere and genuine?" (*FD*, p. 435).

Such is Fontanier's theory; we still have to ask whether his own practice conforms to his theory, whether figures are always identified through their opposition to a simple and direct expression. Here we must review the various classes of figures that Fontanier established, whose articulation we shall examine shortly. The anticipated comparison between "proper" and "figurative" forms is relatively easy to make (even if it is not always very revealing) for some of them: for example, the tropes, properly and improperly so-called, and the figures of diction, in which the phonic form of words is altered, or the figures of construction, in which the syntax of the language is not always respected. It must be noted at the outset that these latter two cases are not entirely alike: only tropes and figures of diction deviate from another expression that is as specific and concrete as the figurative expression; figures of construction deviate not from another expression but from a rule of the language (these are figures in Beauzée's sense). Fontanier is aware of this: "The utterance of what grammar and logic would seem to reject as superfluous, the omission of what they would seem to demand as necessary, or finally the ordering of an utterance in a way entirely different from the one grammar and logic would seem to prescribe—that is what gives rise to these figures" (FD, p. 453).

But it is in the three remaining classes of figures that a real difference emerges: here Fontanier completely abandons his definition of the figure as a deviation from a literal expression, and has to call upon the second half of his initial definition, the functional half. Figures belonging to these classes are figures because they improve discourse!

> It is the choice, the arrangement of words and their more or less felicitous use in the sentence that give rise to *figures of elocution*. [FD, p. 224]
>
> *Figures of style* differ from figures of elocution in that they extend to the expression of a complete thought, and they consist of a group of words that constitutes if not a whole sentence at least a good part of one, and an essential part. They are characterized by a certain liveliness, nobility, or attractiveness that they impart to any expression, whatever its meaning, whether it be figurative or nonfigurative. [p. 226]
>
> Authentic *figures of thought* consist to such an extent in the cast of the imagination and in the specific manner of thinking or feeling that even if the words used to express them were to change, they would remain essentially the same nonetheless. [p. 228]

And again:

> Whether the meaning is borrowed or not, whether it is single or double, direct or indirect, observe in the total expression of the thought how striking and out of the ordinary it is in its beauty, grace, or forcefulness! *Figures of style*. [p. 280]

If functional justifications (the felicity and the elegance, the beauty and grace of the discourse . . .), are set aside here, the definitions that remain can in no way be connected with the general principle. For from what does one deviate in *choosing* words? The definition of figures of thought proposed here brings us directly back to Du Marsais's point of departure: figures are "manners" or particular "turns." If we insist at all cost that the figure continue to be opposed to some other expression, we might say that it deviates from another utterance in which, all else being equal, this figure would be absent. But this is obviously a false solution: the two oppositions have different meanings, we have moved from a relation of contraries to a relation of contradictories. In the figurative trope, one expression diverges from another; in the elocutionary trope (such as repetition, gradation, or polyptoton), an expression diverges from its own absence, from anything that is not itself. But there is nothing in the world, and certainly no linguistic expression, that cannot be opposed to its own absence: such a definition of the figure is meaningless.

Thus we must bow to the facts: we cannot accept at one and the same time Fontanier's theory and his practice, his definition of the figure and his list of figures. The situation, in short, is quite like the one we encountered with Beauzée. Both theories are perfectly consistent in themselves (unlike Du Marsais's); but neither creator succeeds in using his own theory, and each resorts, in practice, to another definition of the figure—without ever formulating it—which leads him finally to deal with a never-changing list of figures—precisely the one bequeathed to him by tradition. As if, to return to Du Marsais, the figures were nothing other than what is called figure. . . .

It is time now to say a few words about the *classifications* of figures. Du Marsais proposes the ordering shown in the diagram.

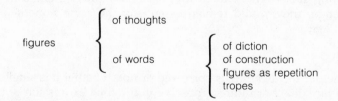

The first opposition is a commonplace of rhetorical tradition; the subsequent distribution is ill defended and presented with little explanation. The third category is particularly odd; about it Du Marsais says only that, in it, "words keep their proper signification" (*DT*, p. 16)—a feature, however, that characterizes all figures that are not tropes. He was no clearer in the "Figure" article he prepared for the *Encyclopedia*. Here is his description of that same mysterious class:

> The fourth sort of figures of words are those that cannot be included in the class of tropes, since in this sort of figure words keep their first signification: nor can one call them figures of thought, since they are figures by virtue of words and syllables alone, and not by virtue of thought; they are figures, that is, they have that particular conformation which distinguishes them from other ways of speaking. [*Oeuvres*, vi, 266]

Given such a "definition," one may prefer Condillac's more honest approach. He is not concerned with classifying the figures nor even with enumerating them—even less so, in fact, then he had been for the tropes: "The rhetoricians have indeed identified various sorts of figures, but nothing is more useless, your Lordship, and I have not bothered to go into such details" (*AE*, p. 579).

Beauzée divides the figures into five groups (in the article entitled "Figure," *EM*, ii and in the "Tableau méthodique," at the end of the third volume).

$$\text{figures} \begin{cases} \text{of diction} \\ \text{of syntax} \\ \text{of oration (tropes)} \\ \text{of elocution} \\ \text{of style} \end{cases}$$

He has the same number of groups as Du Marsais, and approximately the same categories (his "style" corresponds to Du Marsais's "thoughts," and "elocution" is the name of Du Marsais's anonymous class). We must add, first, that Beauzée tries to couple an affective or aesthetic realm (euphony, energy, imagination, harmony, and feeling respectively) with each of these linguistic forms, and, second, that within each of these groups, he proceeds to make further subdivisions, according to more obvious principles: it is ordinarily a matter of binary pairs such as "addition/subtraction" or "unity/disunity" and so on.

Fontanier devotes more space to classifications, and modifies them slightly from one discussion to another. The classifications are his real pride and joy, as we can judge from the falsely modest declaration that follows the presentation of some other efforts: "It is thus more appropriate to stay with the entirely simple, natural, precise, clear, and complete classification that we have adopted. Does it not surpass all the others? and, after the indirect comparison that we have just made of it with the others, do its advantages not appear the more clearly?" (*FD*, p. 459). The classification so highly praised is shown in the diagram.

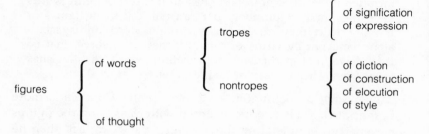

This chart is obviously more complex than the preceding ones. Beauzée's five classes reappear here, but the tropes are subdivided into two groups, and the figures of thought are again detached from the figures of style. Furthermore, a certain hierarchy is introduced, as we can see by the intermediate categories, words/thoughts and tropes/nontropes. Finally, and most important, Fontanier is the first to seek to justify his classification, to explain why there are so many classes and not more, and to account for their mutual relations. Yet even he does not go very far in this direction. One of the categories he uses in this schematization is the dimension of the distinctive linguistic segment: this is what allows him to oppose figures of signification (words) to figures of expression (propositions), figures of elocution to figures of style (the same criterion), and finally, figures of diction to figures of construction. Another opposition, between signifier and signified, seems to come into play at several points. The figures of diction and construction have to do with the *materiality* of language (see *FD*, p. 453); in this they are opposed to the other nontrope figures. That would make it possible to organize the different classes of word-figures that are not tropes in a logical matrix.

But the same category comes into play in yet another fashion: in order for a figure to exist, the signified alone may be necessary, or the signified and the signifier may both be required (this is the

	WORD	PROPOSITION
signifier	diction	construction
signified	elocution	style

traditional opposition between thought-figures and word-figures). This would allow us to articulate the relationships among the three remaining classes of figures.

	WORD	PROPOSITION
signifier and signified	signification	expression
signified alone		thought

We need to recognize that this schema remains embryonic and inexplicit. The rhetoricians never cease to classify, but they classify badly, or rather they are unable to account for their classifications.

HISTORICAL PERSPECTIVE

We can now return to the second of the perspectives announced at the beginning of this analysis: after our look at the theoretical issues, we need to examine their historical significance.

First, we are dealing here with two separate traditions, not just one. The first is embodied by Du Marsais, Beauzée, and Fontanier (even though there are important differences among them); the second by Condillac alone—but he is linked to certain manifestations of rhetorical thought at the end of the seventeenth century, most notably in the *Logique ou l'art de penser,* by Antoine Arnauld and Pierre Nicole, and in the *Rhétorique ou l'art de parler* by Bernard Lamy. The differences appear most clearly on two points: the object of rhetoric and the definition of the figure. A rhetoric such as Condillac's grants an important place to the study of figures (or "turns"), but does not eliminate all the rest (that is, considerations regarding the construction of discourse in general). A rhetoric such as Du Marsais's, on the other hand, amounts to a simple study of figures (or even, in Du Marsais's particular case, of tropes alone). Moreover, in the Du Marsais-Beauzée-Fontanier tradition, the figure is defined through the signifier: it is a means of expressing oneself (a less simple, less attractive means) that differs from some other expression with the same meaning. It is defined through the signified in the tradition represented by Condillac: figures are expressions that designate sentiments or emotions, as opposed to those that designate pure thoughts. One might also say that the first definition is ornamental, the second affective.

These differences are important. And yet they pale in the face of the resemblances—which establish that both traditions belong to the broader tradition of rhetoric, and more particularly to the last centuries of rhetorical activity in France. Even if Condillac's rhetoric cannot be reduced to the description of figures alone, the dominant place given them bears witness to this same tendency that we have seen in the other tradition. Even if Condillac's rhetoric does not describe a figurative expression that diverges from another, proper expression, the divergence between thought and feeling, idea and emotion, is maintained. The Du Marsais-Beauzée-Fontanier variant takes to the extreme a tendency that is likewise present in "affective" rhetoric. And it is this common bond that explains the disappearance of rhetoric from the beginning of the nineteenth century on—not only in its extreme form, that is, in the variant represented by Du Marsais and his successors, but also in its moderate—and, in the last analysis, its modern—form, embodied for us by Condillac.

The disappearance of rhetoric may indeed seem perplexing. The quality of the work we have just surveyed is undeniable. Even if on a given point the description of the linguistic facts that these treatises propose has been surpassed today (and that is not often the case, precisely because of the abrupt interruption of all work in this area), the whole is impressive: for accuracy of observation, for precision of formulation, for the abundance of phenomena considered (and I have left the treatments accorded each separate figure completely aside). How can one account for this aberration in the evolution of knowledge, which leads to the abandonment of such a rich, well-surveyed field?

The answer lies in the fact that the turning points in the history of science (perhaps, more modestly, of rhetoric) are not determined by internal conditions of maturity or fecundity. At the root of all the specific rhetorical research we find a few general principles that would have to be discussed under the heading not of rhetoric but of ideology. When a radical change occurs in the ideological arena, in the values and premises that are generally taken for granted, the quality of observation and explanation of detail counts for little: these are swept away along with the principles that they imply. And no one worries about the baby being thrown out with the bath water.

Now it is precisely a rupture of this sort that we witness in the period we are looking at here, a break whose way was prepared in the eighteenth century and whose full consequences appear in the century that follows. The cause—remote but unmistakable—of

THE END OF RHETORIC

this disruption is the rise of the bourgeoisie, and of the ideological values that the bourgeoisie brings along. In the area that concerns us here, this break consists in the abolition of a world-view that possessed absolute and universal vaues, or, to take only the most eloquent example, the loss of prestige suffered by Christianity; and in the replacement of this world-view by another that refuses to assign a unique place to each value, one that recognizes and accepts the existence of individual facts—the latter no longer being considered merely as imperfect examples of an absolute norm.

The ideological basis that is suddenly revealed to be so fragile, through which the whole edifice can be attacked and shattered, coincides, in the domain of rhetoric, with the notion of figure. All of rhetoric, or nearly all, boils down, in this period, to a theory of figures. Now this notion (like any other) is doubly determined: by an empirical consideration—the theory of figures corresponds to the observable linguistic facts—and by a theoretical considera-tion—it can be integrated into a coherent system characterizing a particular world-view. It is in this last respect that the figure—and with it all of rhetoric—errs in the eyes of the advocates of the new ideology. For the entire rhetorical tradition from Quintilian to Fontanier, the figure is something subordinate, superimposed, ornamental (and it matters little whether or not the ornaments themselves are admired); the figure is, as we have just seen, a deviation with respect to the norm. Rhetoric is no longer possible in a world that takes the plurality of norms as a norm in itself; and the quality of a Fontanier's observations counts for little, as does even the fact that his practice—by virtue of the place that it allots to all the phenomena of language—may well contradict his theory.

If we confine ourselves for the moment to observing the inter-nal evolution of the discipline, we note that rhetoric disappears for two principal reasons—reasons whose autonomy, moreover, is more apparent than real.

(1) *The abolition of the privilege granted to certain (linguistic) forms as opposed to others.*   The figure could be defined only as a devia-tion: deviation in the signifier (an indirect, or uncommon, way of expressing oneself); deviation in the signified (feelings as opposed to thoughts). But to perceive figures as deviations implies a belief in the existence of a norm, of a general and absolute ideal. In a world without God, in which each individual is deemed to con-stitute his own norm, there is no longer any room for the consid-

eration of deviant expressions. Equality reigns among expressions as among men. Hugo, a romantic, knew this well when he declared "war on rhetoric" in the name of equality.

> And I said: not a word on which the idea in pure flight
> Cannot alight, all moist with azure;
> [. . .] I declared words equal, free, adult.

Rhetoric is from this perspective a victim of that same French Revolution which, paradoxically, breathed new life into eloquence.

(2) *The expulsion of rationalism by empiricism, and of speculative constructions by historical study.* Here, rhetoric—which we have seen to be "general and reasoned"—shares the fate of (philosophical) grammar. General grammar aimed to construct a single model, the universal structure of language; the same is true of rhetoric, whose object is not synchronic but rather panchronic: it seeks to establish the system of expressive devices in all periods, in all languages; hence the continuing pertinence of Ciceronian rhetoric, even though it deals with Latin and is eighteen hundred years old; hence, too, the explicit debate between Beauzée and Batteux.

These two movements, rejection of the norm/deviance pairing and rejection of panchronic constructions in favor of history, have a common source, as it is easy to see: the disappearance of absolute and transcendental values, with which one could confront (and boil down) individual facts. In a world without God, every man is God. So, too, sentences are no longer measured against an ideal sentence, nor are languages compared with an abstract "deep" structure.

The entire debate on the contemporary value of rhetoric, on the signification of this old doctrine for us today, thus depends on the way we respond to the following questions: To what extent is a body of knowledge reducible to its ideological premises? To what extent can a discipline built on a foundation that we ourselves—inheritors of bourgeois and romantic ideology—reject, nonetheless include notions and ideas that we are still prepared to accept today?

But perhaps the romantics are only our fathers, and perhaps people are sometimes prepared to sacrifice their fathers to their grandfathers?

4

The Misfortunes of Imitation

Aesthetics begins precisely where rhetoric ends. The two realms do not coincide completely; nevertheless, they have enough in common to prevent them from existing simultaneously. The reality of a succession that was not only historical but conceptual was perceived by contemporary observers of the change: the first *aesthetic* project, A. G. Baumgarten's, was modeled on rhetoric. An interpolated remark by F. A. Wolf provides additional testimony: "Rhetoric, or, as we say among ourselves, aesthetics, . . ."[1] The substitution of aesthetics for rhetoric coincides, by and large, with the passage from classical to romantic ideology. In fact, it could be said that in classical doctrine art and discourse are subordinated to an external objective, whereas for the romantics they constitute an autonomous realm. Now we have seen that rhetoric could not endorse the idea that discourse might find its justification in itself; aesthetics, in turn, cannot come into being until its object, the beautiful, is recognized as having autonomous existence, and until this object is judged ir-

1. F. A. Wolf, "Darstellung der Altertumwissenschaft nach Begriff, Umfang, Zweck und Wert," in F. A. Wolf and P. Buttmann, eds., *Museum der Altertumwissenschaft* (Berlin, 1807), i, 38–39.

reducible to neighboring categories such as the true, the good, the useful, and so on. If the terms could be used in this strict sense, this book could have been called *Rhetoric and Aesthetics*.

This historical distribution, however, is only approximate. In fact, the end of rhetoric is already romantic, while aesthetics in its early stages remains attached to classical doctrine. We have seen that, with Condillac, rhetoric abolished the difference between proper expression and figurative expression, thereby establishing equality among all expressions. In the nascent aesthetic theory of the arts, on the other hand, allegiance to the classical framework manifests itself through submission to the principle of imitation. This principle, which had been present in the theory of the arts from the beginning (but especially since the Renaissance) and which had undergone numerous transformations in the course of history, will be examined here only for the period during which the end of its reign is announced; it is incompatible with the romantic outlook, in that it subjects works of art to a consideration that is external (anterior, superior) to them, namely, nature. At the same time, imitation or representation makes common cause with signification: thus we shall rediscover, in a different guise, the problematics of the symbol.

The principle of imitation reigns uncontested over the theory of art during the first three quarters of the eighteenth century. To borrow the formula of a modern historian, "all these partial laws must fit into and be subordinate to one simple principle, an axiom of imitation in general."[2] No aesthetic writings of the period fail to refer to this principle: no art escapes it: music and dance "imitate" as much as painting and poetry do. Even if the principle of imitation is perfectly well established, however, it leaves some gaps in the body of reflection on the theory of art. For quite obviously, this principle in and of itself does not suffice to explain *all* the properties of a work of art. Artistic imitation is, as it happens, a paradoxical notion: it disappears at the very moment that it achieves perfection. As Johann Elias Schlegel was already pointing out, no one would claim that one egg imitates another egg, even though the two resemble each other: an egg simply *is* an egg (this argument goes back to Augustine's theory of images).

2. Ernst Cassirer, *The Philosophy of the Enlightenment*, trans. F. C. A. Kuelln and J. P. Pettegrove (Princeton, 1951), p. 280.

If imitation were the only law of art, it ought to bring about the disappearance of art: the latter would differ in no way from "imitated" nature. For art to endure, the imitation must be imperfect. But can one be content with negative recourse to a necessarily imperfect imitation? Might one not discover, alongside imitation, another constituent principle of art? Might not deviations from imitation find a positive justification in the appeal to a law other than that of imitation? Another historian summarizes the situation as follows: "All in all, we can see that everyone in the eighteenth century has something critical to say about the principle of imitation. Obviously this is something that people would like to get around, get away from, and they go about trying to do so in all sorts of ways, for want of finding a good one."[3] These efforts at getting around the problem are the ones I shall attempt to spell out now, dwelling as much on the content of the notion as on its place within a global conceptual system.[4]

In order to present the different variants of the mimetic doctrine and its development, I propose to distinguish several degrees of adhesion to the principle of imitation. A compiler of the period, Friedrich Justus Riedel, did just this, isolating as many as four degrees of distance from the model object.[5] I shall limit myself to three; and among these, the one I shall call *zero degree* is only the standard against which the others can be measured: this is the affirmation according to which works of art are the product of imitation, and of imitation alone.

Thus I shall begin my overview with the *first degree*, a minimal deviation with respect to the zero degree. Adherents of this view believe exclusively in the principle of imitation of nature, but they add that this imitation need not be perfect. Having recourse to

3. Wladyslaw Folkierski, *Entre le classicisme et le romantisme* (Paris-Krakow, 1925), p. 117.
4. In addition to Folkierski's history, that of A. Nivelle can also be consulted: *Les Theories esthétiques en Allemagne de Baumgarten à Kant* (Paris, 1955). Several studies have been specifically devoted to the fortunes of imitation in this period, for example, A. Tumarkin, "Die Überwindung der Mimesislehre in der Kunsttheorie des XVIII. Jhdts," in *Festgabe für S. Singer* (Tübingen, 1930); W. Preisendanz, "Zur Poetik der deutschen Romantik. I. Die Abkehr vom Grundsatz der Naturnachahmung," in H. Steffen, ed., *Die deutsche Romantik* (Göttingen, 1967), pp. 54–74; and Herbert Dieckmann, "Die Wandlung des Nachahmungsbegriffes in der französischen Ästhetik des XVIII. Jhdts," in H. R. Jauss, ed., *Nachahmung und Illusion*, 2d ed. (Munich, 1969), pp. 28–59. But it must be added that none of these studies adopts the position that I take in this chapter.
5. *Theorie der schönen Künste und Wissenschaften* (Jena, 1767), p. 146.

grammatical terminology, we might say that the verb "to imitate" is qualified here by an *adverb*: "imperfectly." This is close to the title of a treatise of the period by J. E. Schlegel, uncle of the romantic brothers: "How Imitation Must Sometimes Be Unlike the Original."[6] Schlegel's argument is that certain aspects of nature do not give us pleasure; now art is supposed to induce pleasure; consequently, those unpleasing aspects of nature must be omitted. "If more pleasure can be obtained thereby, it is not an error but a feat of skill to introduce dissimilarity into imitation" (p. 101). Lessing occasionally draws upon the same sort of argument. In the fragments of the *Laocoön* (and in the *Hamburg Dramaturgy*), he refers in passing to "necessary defects." This is the term used for deviations with respect to the rules of imitation, deviations required by the harmony of the whole. Milton's Adam speaks in an implausible way, but the author was right to depict him as he did: "It is undeniable that the poet's higher plan consists in gratifying the reader's fancy with big, beautiful tableaux rather than in attempting to be faithful in every detail."[7] But what is it that "gratifies the reader's fancy?" What is it that determines the poet's "higher plan?" Lessing says nothing about this here, any more than Schlegel did, and we are left with a negative formulation of imperfect imitation.

The most common answer to our initial question consists in a modification not of the nature of the operation—that is, the action of imitating itself—but of the object on which it bears. This is a *second degree* of divergence with respect to imitation pure and simple; we no longer have an adverb that qualifies and restricts the verb "imitate," but an *object complement*. One no longer simply imitates nature, one imitates "beautiful nature," that is, nature that is "selected," "corrected" on the basis of an invisible ideal. This version has numerous variations. A certain Jonathan Richardson, an English aesthetician, asks that a dominant place be granted, in the work of art, to the "characteristic features" of the object being imitated, to the detriment of its other features. He also writes that the principal goal of painting is to elevate and improve nature. The same ideas are widespread in France, as early as the end of the seventeenth century, in the writings of De

6. *Abhandlung dass die Nachahmung der Sache der man nachahmet, zuweilen unähnlich werden müsse* (1745), included in *J. E. Schlegels aesthetische und dramaturgische Schriften* (Heilbronn, 1887); the same idea is summed up in his *Abhandlung von der Nachahmung*, ibid., trans. as *On Imitation* by E. A. McCormick (Indianapolis, 1965).
7. Lessing, *Laocoön*, ed. Blümner (Berlin, 1880), p. 454.

Piles, Fénelon, and La Motte. The last writes, for example, that "by imitation is meant skillful imitation, that is, the art of taking from things only what is suitable to produce the intended effect" (*Réflexions sur la critique*, 1715). The Abbé Batteux becomes the uncontested champion of this idea, which is the basis for his book, *Les Beaux-Arts réduits à un même principe* (1746), one of the most admired books of the period. Batteux complains about the lack of a unifying aesthetic perspective, and, with touching in-genuousness, rediscovers the theory of imitation in art. But his rule is the imitation of beautiful nature:

> On this principle, we must conclude that if the arts imitate Nature, it must be a wise and enlightened imitation that does not copy Nature with servility, but that chooses its objects and its features and presents them with all the perfection they are capable of manifesting: in a word, an imitation in which we see Nature not as it is in itself, but as it can be, and as it can be conceived by the mind. [P. 45][8]

Beautiful nature is thus derived from ordinary nature through the choice of its best parts: "All efforts necessarily came down to choosing the best parts of Nature, in order to form an exquisite whole that was more perfect than Nature itself, without for all that ceasing to be natural" (p. 29).

Batteux's reasoning is remarkable in its blindness. He affirms at one and the same time that imitation is the sole constituent principle of art, and that imitation is subject, through the inter-mediary of the object being imitated, to a prejudgment—whose reasons, however, are unknown. Here is another passage that shares the same confusion (it comes from a comparison between poet and historian):

> As the individual fact is no longer in the hands of history but in the power of the artist, who may take any sort of liberty to reach his goal, the fact is molded anew, so to speak, and given a new form: things are added, subtracted, transposed. . . . If [all that] is not [in history], then art enjoys all of its rights to the fullest extent, it creates everything it needs. Art is granted this privilege because it is obliged to please. [P. 50]

The imprecision of his vocabulary does Batteux a disservice. For example, he writes: "Imitation, to be as perfect as it can be, must have two qualities: exactitude and liberty" (p. 114). But is

8. I am quoting from the edition of 1773.

"liberty" anything other than a euphemism for inexactitude? Or, as Batteux himself puts it on the following page: "Liberty . . . is all the more difficult to achieve in that it appears to be opposed to exactitude. Often the one can excel only at the expense of the other" (p. 115). Are we to understand then that imitation has been adequately characterized when it has been asked to be both exact and inexact? It is here that Batteux, having failed to explain what he means by "beautiful nature," goes back in effect to our "first degree." It is for this, moreover, that Diderot criticizes him, in his *Lettre sur les sourds et muets* (1748): "And, furthermore, do not neglect to insert at the beginning of that work a chapter on what you mean by 'beautiful nature,' for I know there are people who agree with me that without the second of these two things, your treatise lacks a foundation" (Crocker, pp. 38–39).[9] But neither Batteux nor any other defender of "beautiful nature" can come up with a response.

What about Diderot himself? It is well known that his formulations on this subject are often contradictory.

Certain of these formulations would allow him to be taken for a defender of imitation-with-no exceptions, an extreme position, and an indefensible one. In the *Pensées detachées sur la peinture* (c. 1773), he writes: "Every composition worthy of praise is entirely and in every respect in harmony with nature; I have to be able to say: 'I have not seen this phenomenon, but it exists'" (*OE*, p. 773). Twenty-five years earlier, in *Les Bijoux indiscrets* (1748), he invoked the same maxim, insisting on the spectator's experience: "The perfection of a spectacle consists in such an exact imitation of an action that the spectator, uninterruptedly deceived, imagines that he is present at the action itself" (*OR*, p. 142). The same thing holds true for the author: "If observation of nature is not the dominant passion of the writer or artist, we can expect nothing worthwhile from him" (*OE*, p. 758). There is no use looking for anything but the imitation of nature, even in the name of a more beautiful nature: "How many paintings have been ruined by the precept that one should embellish nature! Do not attempt, then, to embellish nature. Use good judgment in choosing the nature that suits you, and portray it with scrupulous respect" (*OC*, 14, 201–202). Imitation and nothing else (we shall leave aside here the

9. For editions of Diderot's writings, see the Bibliographical Notes.

question as to whether this praise or imitation benefits art or nature).

On other occasions, Diderot recognizes the impossibility of a perfect imitation, but he settles for the following negative statement ("first degree"):

But, nature being one, how do you suppose, my friend, that there are so many different ways of imitating it, all acceptable? Might that not stem from the fact that, given the recognized and perhaps fortunate impossibility of portraying it with absolute precision, there is a conventional borderline on which art is allowed to tread; from the fact that, in all poetic production, there is always an element of untruth whose limit is not and can never be determined? Leave to art the freedom of a deviation approved by some and forbidden by others. Once we have admitted that the painter's sun is not that of the universe and could not be, are we not forced to make another avowal that has infinite consequences? [OC, 11, 185–186]

These are, however, only incidental formulations which Diderot is defending on the occasion of some particular development; in principle, he is a partisan of imitation not of nature but of the *ideal* (thus of our "second degree").

This opposition between ideal and nature is often modeled on Aristotle's distinction between the historian, who copies the particular, and the poet, who paints the general. Let us consider a famous passage:

The distinction between the historian and poet is not in the one writing prose and the other verse . . . ; it consists really in this, that the one describes the thing that has been, and the other a kind of thing that might be. Hence poetry is something more philosophic and of graver import than history, since its statements are of the nature rather of universals, whereas those of history are singulars. [*Poetics*, 1451b].

Batteux had already been inspired by this text; Diderot does not stray far from it when he distinguishes two types of imitation: "Imitation is either strict or free. He who imitates nature strictly is its historian. He who composes it, exaggerates it, weakens it, embellishes it, disposes of it as he likes, is its poet" (OC, 15, 158–169); or when he calls upon that same definition in discussing Richardson's work: "I would dare affirm that the most accurate history is full of lies, and that your novel is full of truths. History delineates a few characters, but you paint the human race" (*OE*, pp. 39–40; in Tollemache, p. 280; note that Diderot praises Richardson for what is, in Aristotle's view, a property of all poetry). Likewise, in painting, Diderot opposes the portrait artist, faithful copyist, to the painter of genius whom he addresses as follows: "What is a portrait, if not the representation of some individual being? . . . You have felt the difference between the general idea and the individual object even in the smallest details, since you would not dare to affirm to me that, from the moment you took up painting until now, you have been subjecting yourself to the strict imitation of a hair" (*OC*, 11, 8–9).

The poet and the artist are opposed to the historian; or again, once more in Aristotelian terms, the lifelike is opposed to the true: "The poet . . . is less true and more lifelike than the historian" (*OE*, p. 214). But Diderot's favorite formulation seems to be the one that opposes genuine nature to the ideal model (a formulation that closely resembles that of Shaftesbury, whom Diderot admired—the idea is widespread in the whole neo-Platonic tradition). In the view of the aestheticians of the day, this position amounted to abandoning Aristotle in favor of Plato (it scarcely matters now whether these proper names were used correctly or not). This is what Diderot wrote in the introduction to the *Salon de 1767*:

> Admit then that there is and can be neither an entire existing animal nor any part of the existing animal that you could take in the last analysis as a primary model. Admit then that this model is purely ideal, and that it is directly borrowed from no individual image of Nature, whose scrupulous copy would have remained in your imagination as one that you could summon back, hold before your eyes and copy slavishly, unless you wanted to be a portraitist. Admit then that when you make something beautiful, you make nothing that is, nothing even that can be. [*OC*, 11, 11]

The same doctrine is defended in the *Paradoxe sur le comédien* (1773). It is interesting to see that the doctrine of spontaneous and sincere expression is challenged in this text precisely by arguments drawn from the principle of imitation. "The actor . . . is still listening to himself at the moment when he disturbs your heart; and . . . his whole talent consists not in feeling, as you suppose, but in re-creating the external signs of feeling with such scrupulous accuracy that you are taken in by them" (*OE*, p. 312; in Crocker, p. 322). Imitation above all, but imitation of an ideal model and not of nature:

> Reflect for a moment on what is called "being true" in the theater. Does it mean presenting things as they are in nature? Not at all. The true, in that sense, would be merely the commonplace. What is truth on the stage, then? It is the conformity of action, speech, facial expression, voice, movements, and gestures with an ideal model imagined by the author and often exaggerated by the actor. [*OE*, p. 317; in Crocker, pp. 323–324]

The reasons why Diderot prefers imitation of the model to imitation of nature are equally Platonic: nature itself is already an imitation—but an imperfect one—of its own ideal model. The artist should avoid an unnecessary transition, an awkward intermediate degree, and should imitate the original (the model) rather than the copy (nature). So Diderot calls upon the artist of genius:

> You have added to it, you have subtracted from it, otherwise you would not have made a primary image, a copy of the truth, but a portrait or a copy of a copy (*fantasmatos ouk alètheias*), *the phantom and not the thing*; and you would have been only third-rate, since between the truth and your work, there would have been the truth or the prototype, its lingering phantom that serves as your model, and the copy that you make of this badly-finished shadow of that phantom. . . . You come in third, after the beautiful woman and beauty; . . . between truth and its image, there is the individual beautiful woman that [the portraitist] has taken as his model. Admit then that the difference between the portraitist and yourself, a man of genius, consists essentially in the fact that the portraitist portrays Nature faithfully as it is, and establishes himself in the third rank by taste; and that you who seek the truth, the first model, make a continuous effort to raise yourself to the second rank. [*OC*, 11, 8–11]

Thus everything that cannot be explained by the imitation of perceived objects is attributed to imitation of an invisible model that is held in the mind of the artist. The expedient is effective, but to what extent is it satisfying? What has been done but to give a name ("ideal model") to what was incomprehensible in the process of imitation—a name that, far from revealing anything, by its very existence blocks the way to exploration of the problem, making it appear to have been resolved? The "ideal model" does not coincide perfectly with "beautiful nature"—the latter is situated at the same level as nature, the former is the prototype of nature—but they converge in their inability to designate in any positive way everything that, in the work of art, cannot be explained by the principle of imitation.

Imitation of the model would have meaning only if rules were provided for its construction, only if the ideal were described in itself. Diderot hesitates on this issue. Sometimes he suggests seeking the common denominator of several individuals who might be, for example, miserly, in order to create the type of the miser—in this he is close to the "choice" advocated by Batteux; but at other times he rejects this device, insisting that no part of the ideal can exist in nature. At still other times he describes a process of slow and inductive perfecting on the basis of observed examples; but he is unable to explain the criteria of perfection. The following formulation is more concrete than most: "In a real action, in which several people are involved, each one will of his own accord adopt the most authentic manner; but this manner is not always the most advantageous one for the painter, nor the most striking for the onlooker. Hence the necessity for the painter to alter the natural state and reduce it to an artificial one; and will it not be the same on stage?" (OE, p. 277).

Here we are back again at the idea of "alterations" within imitation. But how are we to decide what way is "most advantageous" and "most striking"? Diderot does not tell us, and we are justified in turning his criticism of Batteux against its author: for want of a definition of the ideal model, his doctrine of imitation belongs among all those it claims to surpass.

The expression "beautiful nature" could nonetheless have become the starting point of a more productive reflection on imitation, if anyone had seriously questioned the meaning of the adjective "beautiful" in that context. It is time to consider that notion more closely. Here is how Erwin Panofsky summarizes classical thinking on beauty:

> "Beauty is the harmony of the parts in relation to each other and to the whole." . . . This concept—developed by the Stoics, unquestioningly accepted by a host of followers from Vitruvius and Cicero to Lucian and Galen, surviving in medieval Scholasticism and ultimately established as an axiom by Alberti who

does not hesitate to term it the "absolute and primary law of nature"—was the principle called συμμετρία or ἁρμονία in Greek, "symmetria," "concinnitas" or "consensus partium" in Latin, "convenienza," "concordanza" or "conformità" in Italian. . . . It meant, to quote Lucian, the "equality and harmony of all parts in relation to the whole."[10]

Such are the eighteenth-century associations of the word. Let us recall the interpretation of Diderot himself. In one of his quips, Rameau's nephew sums up the attitude that is as much Diderot's own as that of his contemporaries: "Truth, which is the father, begets goodness, which is the son, whence proceeds the beautiful, which is the holy ghost" (OR, p. 467; in Tancock, p. 101).[11] But even if he does subordinate beauty to truth, Diderot affirms as early as 1748, in his Mémoires sur différents sujets de mathématiques:

Pleasure, in general, consists in the perception of relationships. This principle holds true in poetry, in painting, in architecture, in morals, in all the arts and all the sciences. A fine machine, a beautiful painting, a lovely portico please us only through the relationships that we observe in them. . . . The perception of relationships is the unique basis for our admiration and our pleasures. [OE, p. 387]

This assertion is developed at length in the article on the "Beautiful" in the Encyclopedia:

I therefore term "beautiful," independently of my existence, everything that contains the power of awakening the notion of relation in my mind; and I term "beautiful" in direct relation to myself everything that does awaken that notion. . . . [In order to appreciate beauty,] it is enough for [the spectator] to perceive and sense that the various parts of the building or the sounds of the piece of music are in fact related, either among themselves or with other objects. [OE, pp. 418–419; in Crocker, pp. 54, 55]

10. Erwin Panofsky, The Life and Art of Albrecht Dürer, 4th ed. (Princeton, 1955), pp. 261 and 276. For another enumeration, somewhat caricatural, of similar opinions, see L. Tatarkiewicz, "Les deux concepts de la beauté," Cahiers romains d'études littéraires, 4 (1974), 62. The quotation from Alberti is from De Re aedificatoria, book IX, chapter 5. Another of Panofsky's works, Idea (Leipzig, 1924), is equally pertinent for the history of the concepts discussed here.

11. This solidarity, not to say indistinguishability, of the three categories is characteristic of the period. Did not Shaftesbury write: "What is Beautiful is Harmonious and Proportionable: What is Harmonious and Proportionable is TRUE; and what is at once both Beautiful and True is, of consequence, Agreeable and GOOD?" (Characteristics of Men, Matters, Opinions, Times [London, 1711], 3, 182–183.)

A famous example follows:

I shall content myself with one example, taken from literature. Everyone knows that sublime phrase from the tragedy *Horace*: "*Qu'il mourût.*" ["He should have died."] Suppose I ask someone who is unacquainted with Corneille's play, and who has no notion of what old Horatius' answer means, what he thinks of this phrase. It is obvious that since he does not know what this "*Qu'il mourût*" is, since he cannot tell whether it is a complete sentence or merely a fragment of one, and since he can only with difficulty make out any grammatical relation between the separate words, the person of whom I ask this question will reply that to him the phrase appears neither *beautiful* nor *ugly*. But if I tell him that it is the reply of a man who has been consulted on what another man should do in combat, then he will begin to apprehend a kind of courage in the speaker, one that will not allow him to believe it is always better to go on living than to die, and this "*Qu'il mourût*" begins to interest him. If I add that this combat involves a nation's honor, that the combatant is the son of the person being questioned, that he is his last remaining son, that the young man was confronting three foes who had already taken the lives of his two brothers, that the old man is talking to his daughter, and that he is a Roman, then the reply "*Qu'il mourût,*" at first neither *beautiful* nor *ugly*, acquires beauty in proportion as I develop its relation to the circumstances and eventually becomes sublime. [*OE*, pp. 422–423; in Crocker, p. 57]

Qu'il mourût is not beautiful in terms of what it imitates, but rather by the position it occupies in a network of relations.

But then should we not postulate that the work of art is subject to *two* concurrent principles: that of *imitation* (in the case of the representative arts, but not in that of music, nor—we would add, nowadays—of abstract painting), which links it with what is external to it; and that of the *beautiful*, concerning the relations established within the work itself (or within art in general), and which are independent of imitation? Or, as Diderot himself says in passing, the work is created "out of symmetry and imitation" (*OE*, p. 427).

As strange as it may seem, the "beautiful" is only rarely evoked in connection with imitation, even if it is *beautiful* nature that is being imitated. Those who do make the association, moreover, do so either in order to assimilate the one to the other (always the beautiful to imitation) or else to subordinate the one to the other (again, the beautiful to imitation).

This view had already been adopted by the Abbé Dubos, in his *Critical Reflections on Poetry, Painting, and Music* (1719). Describing imitation in music—in which he firmly believes, along with everyone else of his day—he adds that music is subject to other principles as well, namely, harmony and rhythm. But there is no doubt as to the hierarchy: "The concords in which harmony consists . . . contribute also to the expression of the sound the musician intends to imitate. . . . The *rhythmus* throws a new likeness into the imitation arising from a musical composition, because it produces also an imitation of the progression and movement of the natural sounds already imitated by the modulation and harmony."[12]

The same relation is found in the other arts:

> The richness and variety of concords, the charms and novelty of modulations should be applied to no other use in music but that of drawing and imbellishing the imitation of the language and passions of nature. That which is called the knowledge of composition is a handmaid (to make use of this expression) which a musical genius ought to entertain in his service, in the same manner as a poet's genius should keep the knack of rhiming. He is undone (to continue the figure) if the maid makes herself the mistress of the house, and has liberty to dispose of it according to her own fancy and pleasure. [i, 374]

As in so many other areas, the slave has become the mistress: Dubos did not know how well he was putting it. Still, are we to conclude that all is *lost*?

Harmony is to be the slave of imitation. J. E. Schlegel, in Germany, is less categorical, not because he sees harmony in a better light, but because he does not even notice a possible conflict between master and slave. A conceptual shift facilitates his pacific world view. Imitation, in poetry, is of two types: dramatic, in which words imitate words, or narrative ("historical"). Here Schlegel maintains only the relations of *resemblance*, as they can be observed in metaphor, comparison, or parallelism. Thus, in this latter case, what imitates and what is imitated are both found within the work. Now the presence within the work of two similar elements leads us to observe the *order* that reigns there.

Through the intermediary of resemblance, "imitation" and "order" become virtually synonymous, and Schlegel can calmly

12. From the English translation by Thomas Nugent, *Critical Reflections on Poetry, Painting and Music* (New York, 1978), reprint of the 5th ed., 3 vols. (London, 1748), i, 361 and 363.

write: "Imitation whose aim is pleasure attains its end when similarity and, hence, also the order that creates it are perceived" (*On Imitation*, p. 30). Imitation, therefore order. . . . Batteux, for his part, introduces considerations of harmony without worrying about how they fit in with the rest of his doctrine: "The arts . . . must not use color or sound indiscriminately: a judicious choice must be made, an exquisite blend achieved. Colors and sounds must be allied, blended proportionately, nuanced, harmonized. Colors and sounds have their own sympathies and repulsions among themselves" (*Les Beaux-Arts*, p. 61).

The question arises for Diderot again in relation to music, the imitative nature of which is especially problematic. In his "Lettre à Mlle de la Chaux," an appendix to the *Lettre sur les sourds et muets*, he replies to the objection according to which music procures pleasure without necessarily imitating anything:

> I recognize this phenomenon; but I beg you to consider that these pieces of music that affect you agreeably without awakening in you either the painting or the direct perception of relationships only gratify your ear as the rainbow pleases your eyes, with the pleasure of a sense impression pure and simple; and that they fall far short of the perfection that you could require, and that they would have, if the truth of imitation were joined to the charms of harmony. [*Lettre*, p. 101]

This sentence deserves some attention. Diderot is identifying three, and not just two, sources of pleasure: the pleasure that comes purely from the senses, the pleasure that derives from the perception of relationships, and the pleasure that comes from imitation. The distinctions are not sharp, and he visibly hesitates in attempting to situate the second source of pleasure: it goes along with the third at the beginning of the sentence, with the first at the end. Furthermore, we know nothing about this "pure and simple" pleasure of sensation: can any perceived object at all become its source? But one thing is certain: imitation is not the only basic principle of art, its "truth" is matched by the "charms of harmony."

Unfortunately, this promise of the *Lettre sur les sourds et muets* (along with several others) is not kept. Diderot devotes episodic remarks to harmony in painting and in the theater; but he connects them solely with the artist's working technique (as in the article "Composition" in the *Encyclopedia*), without setting them up as a principle rivaling that of imitation. If he turns his attention to the relationship between the two principles, it is always in order to affirm the superiority of imitation. Concerning the theater: "The acts [of a play] are required to be of roughly equal length: it would be much more reasonable to ask that their length be proportional to that of the action they encompass" (OE, p. 243). We ask that the colors of a painting be in harmony with each other? We ought instead to seek to have them harmonize with the colors of nature (see OE, pp. 678–679). Harmony indeed remains the slave of imitation.

We come to the same impasse with Lessing. He is perfectly capable, on occasion, of formulating a clear-cut opposition between imitation and harmony. Here, for example, is an opinion very close to the one Diderot expressed in the "Lettre à Mlle de la Chaux." "What would happen next?" Lessing asks in the seventieth section of his Hamburg Dramaturgy, discussing the justification of imitation:

> The example of nature which is to justify the combination of solemn gravity with farcical merriment can justify as well every dramatic monster that has neither plan, nor connexion, nor common-sense.[13] Imitation of nature would consequently either be no principle of art, or if it still remain so, it would by means of art cease to be art. At least it would be no higher art than that art which imitates the colored veins of marble in plaster of Paris; their direction and course may go as they like, the strangest cannot be so strange but that it might seem natural; only that does not seem natural in which too much symmetry, proportion and equality is shown, in which too much is seen of that which in every other art, constitutes art. In this sense the most labored is the worst, the most arbitrary the best.[14]

Symmetry, or proportion, is certainly in complementary distribution here with imitation—they are treated as two independent principles, both of which govern artistic activity. Nowhere in his own work, however, does Lessing depend upon this dichotomy, nor does he inquire into the exact relationship between the two. And the Laocoön depends entirely upon a theory of imitation.

13. Diderot finds a similar argument in Jacques the Fatalist and His Master: "Nature is so diverse, especially in the question of instincts and characters, that there is nothing so strange in the mind of a poet that experience and observation cannot offer you a model of it" (OR, p. 553; in J. R. Loy, trans. [New York, 1959], p. 59).

14. Hamburg Dramaturgy, trans. H. Zimmern (New York, 1962), pp. 169–170.

For a time, other notions appear capable of counterbalancing the all-powerful one of imitation; but their inadequacies are quickly discovered. A first, timid attempt to identify a principle of art that would be irreducible to imitation surfaces in Diderot's use of the term *manière*: such a timid use that the term scarcely appears before it is condemned. The idea seems to come from the antagonism between two complements of the verb "imitate": imitate nature, imitate the ancients. Diderot sometimes demands, within a single sentence, that we imitate nature and imitate Homer (cf. *OC*, 7, 20); but he recognizes most of the time that to imitate other works does not mean simply to "imitate nature": it also involves a style, a type of imitation. This fact might have led him to nuance the notion of imitation, but, once he has made such an observation, he uses it only to pronounce the condemnation of what he calls a "manner." We are to imitate the ancients only to the extent that they imitate nature; the rest is contrary to art. Nothing makes actors so heavy-handed as the imitation of other actors (see *OE*, p. 268). "There would be no manner either in the design or in the color if one were scrupulously imitating nature. Manner comes from the master, from the school, and even from antiquity" (*OE*, p. 673). Diderot nurtures no sympathy for manner: "Manner is in the fine arts what hypocrisy is in morals" (*OE*, p. 825). Diderot's blindness goes so far as to make him argue that there exists just one manner worth keeping, because it is the mannerless: "He who copies La Grenée will be brilliant and solid, he who copies Le Prince will be grey and purple in tone; he who studies Chardin's style will be accurate" (*OE*, p. 677; in Tollemache, p. 47). Chardin, a mannerless painter? Diderot himself renders impassable the path he is attempting to break.

A second prospect for displacing imitation, as little exploited as that of manner, is the one that the notion of *convention* seems to open up.[15] Diderot seems to subordinate convention—when he recognizes its existence—to imitation. He defines it yet again in the negative: it arises from the impossibility of imitating to perfec-

15. Rousseau writes, on the other hand: "We still have no idea whether our system of music is not based on pure conventions; we have no idea whether its principles are not entirely arbitrary, and whether any other system substituted for ours would not end up, through familiarity, by pleasing us just as much. . . . Through a rather natural analogy, these thoughts could provoke others on the subject of painting, on the harmony of colors, on certain parts of the design, in which there is perhaps more arbitrariness than we think, and in which imitation itself may have conventional rules."

tion. Diderot's impotence in the face of a question that has none-theless been well put is particularly apparent in a passage of the *Paradoxe* where he notes that a posture that would be most upset-ting in life would be ridiculous on stage. Why?

> Because people do not come to see tears, but to hear speeches that make them cry, because this truth of nature clashes with the truth of convention. Let me explain: I mean that neither the dramatic system, nor the action, nor the poet's text could be reconciled with my stifled, broken, tearful delivery. You see that it is not even permissible to imitate nature, even beautiful nature, too closely, and that there are limits within which we must remain. —And who set these limits? —Common sense, which would not have one talent be used to the detriment of another. [*OE*, p. 377]

Starting from a sharp opposition between natural and conven-tional truth, the response dissipates, evaporates little by little, only to refer us in the end to a "common sense" that is even vaguer than convention.

Thus Diderot can no more define "convention" than he can define "ideal model" or "manner." And yet no sooner does he attempt a precise description of the rules of an art than he is drawn toward formulations that cannot be based on imitation alone. Here is what he says, in the form of precepts, about com-position in painting:

> Keep out of your *composition* all idle figures that would chill it instead of bringing warmth; those figures that you use should not be scattered and isolated; bring them together in groups; your groups should be interrelated; the figures in them should offer clear contrasts, but not that contrast of academic positions in which we see the pupil always attentive to the model and never to nature; the figures should overlap in such a way that the hidden parts do not prevent the imagination's eye from seeing them completely; lighting effects should be carefully re-alized; no little scattered areas of light that do not form a whole, or whose forms are only oval, round, square, parallel; these forms would be as unbearable to the eye, in the imitation of objects that should not be rendered symmetrical, as they would be pleasing to it in a symmetrical arrangement. Pay strict atten-tion to the laws of perspective, and so on. [*OC*, 14, 202]

Bring figures together in groups, contrast them, order the ef-fects of light, avoid the round and the square: can all these requirements be justified in the name of imitation? Diderot would like to think so.

To sum up: the principles of imitation and of the beautiful are present together in the thinking of the period, but in this particular area that thinking remains syncretic. It amalgamates the two notions without articulating them; their harmony is recognized, but no inquiry is made into the possible conflict that may obtain between them; or, if the conflict is noted, it is resolved unhesitatingly in favor of imitation. The latter, moreover, bears up rather badly under this favoritism: too much coddling makes it sickly. Aesthetic theory is at an impasse, and the nature of art eludes its grasp. One can only repeat, with respect to Diderot (and even more justly with respect to his predecessors) the words with which he characterized himself: "As for myself, . . . I prefer to spend my time creating clouds rather than dispersing them, questioning opinions rather than forming them" (*Lettre sur les sourds et muets*, p. 65; in Crocker, p. 34).

5

Imitation and Motivation

═══════════

In presenting the various attempts that have been made to
reckon with the principle of imitation, I have deliberately left one
aside, because it appeared to me to warrant special attention. This
approach interprets imitation as a motivation established between
the two faces of the sign, signifier and signified. The aesthetic
problematics is thus explicitly inscribed within the framework of a
semiotics.[1]

This reinterpretation is not usually situated within a general
reflection on imitation; rather it arises when the various arts are
compared in terms of their imitative capacity. The comparison in
question bears upon poetry and painting in particular, sometimes
also upon music.

The first volume of Abbé Dubos's *Critical Reflections on Poetry,
Painting and Music* (1719) provides a convenient point of departure.[2] This is not to say that no one had ever before undertaken to

1. For this and the following chapter I found especially useful the work by B.
A. Sørensen entitled *Symbol und Symbolismus in der äesthetischen Theorien des 18.
Jahrhunderts und der deutschen Romantik* (Copenhagen, 1963).
2. *Réflexions critiques sur la poésie et la peinture*, trans. Thomas Nugent (repr.
New York, 1978), 3 vols.

compare the arts from the viewpoint of their representative capacity. Simonides' formula, according to which poetry is a painting that speaks, and painting is mute poetry, had never been entirely forgotten. Even Leonardo da Vinci, in his *Treatise on Painting*, devoted some lengthy passages to comparing the arts. But the notion of "artistic" sign had not yet crystallized, and Leonardo, who was seeking first and foremost to prove the superiority of painting, considered poetry alternatively as an art of hearing or an art of the imagination (that is, foreign to the senses). He affirmed the preeminence of painting because in painting objects retain a higher degree of presence (I am leaving the spatiotemporal opposition aside here). In the case of such imaginative representations, he wrote,

> we may say that there is the same relationship between the sciences of painting and poetry that there is between a body and its derivative shadow. There is an even closer relationship, for at least the shadow of such a body achieves sensory perception through the eye, but in the absence of the function of the eye the image of that body [in poetry] does not become known to the senses, but remains where it originates.[3]

A man's image is closer to him than his name; in brief, that is what Leonardo is saying. He does not, however, turn his attention to the nature of the signs themselves. Similarly, Roger De Piles writes in his *Cours de peinture par le principe* (1708) that "words will never be taken for the things themselves . . . ; the word is only the sign of the thing" (II, 358), without proposing a genuine typology of artistic signs. We must note that these thinkers never asked themselves to what extent art (painting or literature or, better yet, music) is really a sign; or, in a more nominalist perspective, to what extent the term "sign" retains its initial meaning when it is applied to music, painting, poetry. But let us accept for the moment the premises of a theory that alone provides a meaningful context for the specific propositions of these thinkers.

Dubos is the first to project a semiotic typology of the arts. He offers a clear formulation of the category that allows us to oppose painting and poetry: painting "does not employ artificial signs, as poetry, but natural ones" (I, 321). Where does this subdivision originate? Probably in an anonymous tradition that assimilates

3. *Treatise on Painting*, trans. A. P. McMahon (Princeton, 1956), p. 14.

three things: (a) the two possible origins of language according to Plato, the natural and the conventional; (b) the two varieties of signs according to Augustine, the natural and the intentional; and (c) the transcription of these two sources in the Port-Royal *Logic*, in which signs are called, among other things, natural or institutional. None of these dichotomies stresses the existence or nonexistence of motivation, moreover; although that category is present for Arnauld and Nicole, in their writings it appears among the institutional signs ("a conventional sign is a sign established by convention which may, but need not, have any connection with the thing signified"[4]).

Once painting and poetry have been assimilated to the two classes of signs, painting turns out to be superior, for Dubos, on three counts. In the first place, as Leonardo had already remarked, the things represented possess a higher degree of presence; this observation allows Dubos, again like Leonardo, to speak in praise of sight as opposed to hearing (poetry, for Dubos, is an auditory art): "We may say here, metaphorically speaking, that the eye is nearer to the soul than the ear" (I, 322). Furthermore, the very existence of signs in painting can be questioned (the sign being intrinsically linked to absence): "Perhaps I do not express myself properly, in saying, that the painter makes use of signs; 'tis nature herself which he exhibits to our sight" (ibid.). Second—and this is merely a consequence of the previous affirmation—painting acts more directly, more strongly on men than poetry does. Third, the one is comprehensible to all, with regard to nationality or education, whereas the other is not: the curse of Babel works against poetry. These two consequences are decisive for Dubos, whose entire aesthetic is oriented toward the process of perception and consumption of art.

But Dubos is more attentive than his precursors to the nature of poetry. He does not distinguish between poetic and nonpoetic language: all his criticisms of language in general are likewise imputed to poetry. He does, however, take one step forward in the description of poetic signs when he separates two stages in the process of signification in literature, stages that would correspond, in glossematic terminology, to denotation and connotation: "Words must first excite those ideas, whereof they are only

4. A. Arnauld, *La Logique de Port-Royal* (Paris, 1660), trans. as *Logic; or, The Art of Thinking*, 1865 (repr. London, 1965), I, iv, p. 47.

arbitrary signs. These ideas must be ranged afterwards in the imagination, and form such pictures as move and engage us" (I, 323). Literature would thus be distinguished from the other arts by its oblique, indirect mode of representation. Sounds evoke meaning; but the latter in turn becomes a signifier, whose signified is the world represented. In this sense, poetry is a *secondary* semiotic system.

Furthermore, Dubos recognizes three types of beauty in poetry: one arising from the sounds alone, one that depends upon meaning alone, and one, finally, that results from the harmonious relationship between the two. We need not linger here over the beautiful sounds and beautiful ideas, but we may well ask whether Dubos, by affirming the possibility of equivalence between signifiers and signifieds, is not contradicting his first thesis according to which the signs of language are arbitrary, thus lacking in any possibility of equivalence. He writes: "The second beauty is the particular relation that words bear to the idea they signify. This is the imitating in some measure the inarticulate sound, which we should make to signify it" (I, 251).

Words will never be able to imitate things; but perhaps they are capable of imitating a noise (onomatopoeia? interjection?) that would in turn be a natural expression of the thing; this is a kind of imitation by relay. Still, even those words or sentences that are imitative, as it were, in the second degree, are too few in number, and they grow fewer every day: language was imitative in its origin, but its evolution is characterized by demotivation. Dubos asserts that Latin poetry is superior to French poetry by virtue of the fact that Latin includes more onomatopoeias (the only form of motivation that he dwells upon). Nevertheless, poets have to cultivate this "second beauty":

> It follows, therefore, that words which imitate the sound they signify, or the sound which we should naturally make, in order to express the thing whereof they are the established sign, or that they have any other relation to the thing signified, have a much stronger energy than those which bear no other affinity to the thing signified, than that which has been authorized by custom. [I, 253].

A motivated language would be more convenient for poets; but the meaning of words is nonetheless the most important element—and furthermore, motivated language has almost ceased to exist!

These ideas find an immediate echo. Witness a text by the English grammarian and philosopher James Harris: *A Discourse on Music, Painting, and Poetry.*[5] Harris reverses the traditional hierarchy of the arts, raising poetry to the top by virtue of its aptitude for representing and transmitting the whole of experience; but as far as the nature of signs in the various arts is concerned, Harris and Dubos are not far apart. The arts all imitate nature, but they imitate by different means. Harris says: "A Figure painted, or a Composition of Musical Sounds have always a natural Relation to that, of which they are intended to be the Resemblance. But a Description in Words has rarely any such natural Relation to the several Ideas, of which those Words are the Symbols" (p. 58, note c). Poetry is an auditory art, but it functions through language, which is characterized, according to Harris, by "a sort of Compact assigning to each Idea some Sound to be its Mark or Symbol" (p. 55, note a). Harris is aware of the existence of "natural" verbal signs (onomatopoeia), but he does not consider them very important.

Farther as Words, besides their being Symbols by Compact, are also Sounds variously distinguished by their Aptness to be rapidly or slowly pronounced, and by the respective Prevalence of Mutes, Liquids or Vowels in their Composition; it will follow that, beside their Compact-Relation, they will have likewise a Natural Relation to all such Things, between which and themselves there is any Natural Resemblance. . . . And thus in part even Poetic Imitation has its Foundation in Nature. But then this Imitation goes not far; and taken without the Meaning derived to the Sounds from Compact, is but little intelligible, however perfect and elaborate. [Pp. 70–72]

Harris has no problem using a single name, *imitation*, to designate two series whose profound difference he nonetheless describes; and he does not seek, either, to determine whether poetic signs are set apart from the other signs of a language by some peculiar feature (even though his evocation of onomatopoeia attests to a confused awareness of these two problems).

This latter point is taken up by Diderot, who in other respects only repeats Harris's ideas on the hierarchy of the arts, and Dubos's (or Leonardo's) ideas on the poetry/painting opposition: "The painter shows the thing itself; the musician's expressions,

5. In *Three Treatises* (London, 1744).

and the poet's, are only hieroglyphics" (*Lettre sur les sourds et muets*, p. 81).[6] On the frontier between poetry and nonpoetry within language, we find in the same *Lettre*, on the other hand, a passage that has become famous:

> In all speech, considered generally, we must distinguish between thought and expression; if the thought is rendered with clarity, purity, and precision, that is sufficient for everyday conversation; add to these qualities a nice choice of words, together with rhythmic and harmonious phrasing, and you have a style suitable for use in the pulpit, though you will still be a long way from poetry, especially from that kind of poetry employed in the descriptive passages of epic poems and odes. At such times there is a spirit flowing through the poet's words that gives life and emotion to every syllable. What is this spirit? I myself have sometimes felt its presence; but I know no more of it than that it is the cause whereby things can be spoken and represented simultaneously, so that the mind apprehends them, the soul is moved by them, the imagination sees them, and the ear hears them all at one and the same time; so that the language used is no longer merely a succession of linked and energetic terms expressing the poet's thought with power and nobility, but also a tissue of hieroglyphics, all woven inextricably together, that make it visible. I might say that all poetry is, in this sense, emblematic. [P. 70; in Crocker, p. 36]

Thus Diderot opposes two types of discourse here: the poetic and the everyday, with oratorical prose as an intermediate degree. The specificity of poetic discourse resides in its signifier (although Diderot is more concerned with the difference between the effects of the two types of discourse): the signifier is transparent (nondistinctive) in the case of everyday language, whereas, in the case of poetic language, linguistic signs are transformed into hieroglyphics (or emblems)—they express and represent at the same time.

But what are hieroglyphics? The subsequent pages of the same text give a clear answer.[7] Diderot calls hieroglyphics those sequences of discourse that directly imitate the thing designated, those in which the signifier is in the image of the signified; today they would be called "motivated signs" or "symbols." Thus the word *sigh* (Fr. *soupire*) is a hieroglyphic, that is, it depicts (imitates) the action that it designates, for "the first syllable is muffled, the

6. For editions of Diderot's works, see the Bibliographical Note for Chapter 4.
7. See also J. Doolittle, "Hieroglyph and emblem in Diderot's *Lettre sur les sourds et muets,"* *Diderot Studies,* 2 (1952), 148–167.

second tenuous, and the last one mute" (p. 70; in Crocker, p. 37). In a line from Virgil, "*demisere* is as soft as the stalk of a flower; *gravantur* weighs as much as the flower-cup full of rain; *collapsa* marks an effort and a fall." The hieroglyphic's insufficiency is the insufficiency of imitation (of motivation): "Shall I say it? I find *gravantur* a bit too heavy for the light head of a poppy, and the *aratro* that follows the *succisus* does not seem to me to complete its hieroglyphic representation" (*Lettre*, pp. 72–73).

The fact that language also includes "natural signs" (an observation brought about by the need to unify everything under the aegis of imitation) was only a minor point for Dubos and Harris; it becomes for Diderot an almost militant definition of poetic language. Poetry must use natural (that is, motivated) signs. The problem is that Diderot neglects to discuss not only the details of the motivating processes (which we are in a position to establish today thanks to his examples), but also a more essential question that a skeptic cannot avoid formulating: To what extent is poetry in fact what it "must" be? Is it really onomatopoeia alone that distinguishes it from prose?

Diderot never returns to the themes that he dealt with in this early text, and these questions, for him at least, remain unanswered. The only aspect he goes on to develop later is the comparative study of the arts, and more specifically that of poetry and painting. He starts from the perspective indicated earlier: "Painting shows the thing itself, poetry describes it. . . ." In the *Encyclopedia* article entitled "Encyclopédie" he presents the same opposition:

> Painting does not reveal the operations of the mind . . . ; in a word, there are innumerable things of this nature that painting cannot represent; but at least it shows all that it represents: and although discourse, on the contrary, designates all things, it shows none at all. Paintings of living beings are always very incomplete, but they are not at all ambiguous because they are portraits of objects that we have before our eyes. The characters of written language apply to everything, but they are conventional; they signify nothing in themselves. [*OC*, 14, 433–434]

Twenty years later, Diderot is still insisting on this same opposition:

> The painter is precise; the discourse that paints is always vague. I can add nothing to the artist's imitation; my eye can see no more than what is there; but in the writer's tableau, however

polished it may be, everything remains to be done by the artist who would transpose it from discourse to canvas. [*OE*, pp. 838–839]

As is often the case with Diderot, this affirmation finds its best expression not within a logical argument but in the form of a parable:

A Spaniard or an Italian, spurred by the desire to possess a portrait of his mistress, whom he could not show to any painter, took the only course open to him and decided to describe her in writing, as completely and as exactly as possible. He began by establishing the proportions of her head as a whole; next he passed to the dimensions of her forehead, eyes, nose, mouth, chin, neck; then he went back over each of these features and spared no pains so that his mind would engrave upon the painter's mind the true image he had before his eyes; he overlooked neither colors, nor shapes, nor anything that grew out of his mistress's character: the more he compared his text with the face of his mistress, the better resemblance he found; above all, he believed that the more small details he included in his description, the less licence he would be giving the painter; he omitted nothing that he thought the painter's brush ought to capture. When his description appeared to be complete, he made one hundred copies and sent them to one hundred painters, instructing each one to execute faithfully on canvas what they should read on his paper. The painters set to work; and after a time our lover received one hundred portraits, all of which were scrupulously faithful to his description, and none of which resembled another, nor his mistress. [*OC*, 14, 444]

Producer and receiver do not divide the work in precisely the same manner in painting and in poetry. In a painting, we receive the painter's project simultaneously with its realization: the painter has not only conceived the idea of his painting (he might have been able to manage that much, if necessary, by means of words), but he has also made it perceptible. In poetry, by contrast, an analogous task falls to the reader's imagination: the poet produces only the canvas that the reader potentially materializes. The poet's finished work is still only a (potential) project for the painter; conversely, the spectator perceives but does not construct, whereas the reader must do both. Another text says the same thing: "The [poetic] image in my imagination is only a passing shadow. Canvas fixes the object before my eyes and instills in me its de-

formities. Between these two stimuli there is the difference between *it may be* and *it is*" (*OE*, p. 762). Diderot's attention is thus
drawn more to the process of reception than to the object itself.
At the same time, the parallel cannot be pursued for long: reading
is not necessarily accompanied by the construction of an image,
and verbal representation is not of the same nature as pictorial
representation.

But let us return to the question of the sign's motivation in art.
We now possess all the elements that were at the disposal of the
principal hero of this chapter: Lessing. If I have reported all
the foregoing assertions and reflections at length, it has been
precisely in order to make Lessing's contributions—widely dis-
paraged by historians—stand out the more clearly; for his originality is, we might venture to say, of a new type: it is the originality
of a system. More precisely, Lessing is the first to juxtapose two
commonplace observations of the period: that art is imitation, and
that the signs of poetry are arbitrary. He is the first, too, to decide
that this juxtaposition poses a problem. His rigorous thinking
explodes the framework of classical aesthetics, even if he does not
find a solution to its antinomies; this could never have been accomplished by the approximate and vague reasoning of a Leonardo or a Diderot.

The major thesis of the *Laocoön* (1766) is formulated at the
beginning of chapter 16, but the entire book in fact rests on it.
Here is the key sentence:

> If it is true that painting and poetry, in their imitations, make
> use of entirely different media of expression, or signs—the first,
> namely, of form and color in space, the second of articulated
> sounds in time;—if these signs indisputably require a suitable
> relation to the thing betokened, then it is clear, that signs ar-
> ranged near to one another, can only express objects, of which
> the wholes or parts exist near one another; while consecutive
> signs can only express objects, of which the wholes or parts are
> themselves consecutive.[8]

This sentence condenses a syllogism that can be spelled out as
follows:

(1) The signs of art must be motivated (otherwise we no longer
have imitation).

8. In *Laocoön*, trans. Edward Calvert Beasley (London, 1853), p. 101.

(2) The signs of painting are extended in space, and those of poetry in time.

(3) Thus, in painting, one can only represent what is extended in space, and in poetry, what unfolds in time.

Among the criticisms addressed to Lessing in his lifetime, erudite quibbles aside, the most numerous deal with the second half of the minor premise. His friend Moses Mendelssohn had presented, some ten years earlier, a system of the arts similar to Harris's; upon reading Lessing's early drafts, Mendelssohn made some pertinent comments that Lessing tried to take into account. Mendelssohn affirmed that poetic signs, being arbitrary (like Dubos and with no more ado, Mendelssohn made no distinction between linguistic signs and poetic signs), can depict what is in time just as well as what is in space, succession as well as simultaneity. He noted, for example, in a commentary on Lessing's manuscript: "Poetic signs have an arbitrary signification; that is why they sometimes also express things that coexist side by side, without encroaching, however, on the territory of painting, for they express them rather as a multitude in succession. . . . Signs in succession also express things existing side by side from the moment their signification is arbitrary."[9]

Temporal succession—linearity, as Saussure will call it—is not a constituent element of linguistic signs, according to Mendelssohn; and he suggests that Lessing put music in the place of poetry, as he himself has already done, since music is indeed composed of signs in succession.

The most serious criticism published during Lessing's lifetime, that of Herder, tends in the same direction. Herder devotes the first of his *Kritische Wäldchen* to the problem of the *Laocoön*. Like Mendelssohn, Herder attributes very little importance to what we would call the signifier in poetry today; the only thing that counts for him is meaning. Now meaning is not linear. "What is natural in the sign, that is, letters, sonority, melody, counts for nothing, or nearly nothing, in the effect of poetry: the meaning that resides in the words by virtue of an arbitrary convention, the spirit that inhabits the articulated sounds is everything."[10]

Poetry does not act principally on the senses (as do painting or music) but on the imagination: it acts on "the inferior capacities of

9. *Laocoön*, ed. Blumner (Berlin, 1880), p. 359.
10. *Sämmtliche Werke* (Berlin, 1877–1913), III, 136.

the soul, basically fantasy, through the meaning of words" (ibid., p. 158). This argument subsequently becomes commonplace not only in criticism of Lessing but also in German aesthetics in general: the sensible (and partial) arts are opposed to the absolute and essentially immaterial art of poetry. So we find ourselves back at Leonardo's position, but with his values reversed: absence is celebrated in the place of presence.

I shall not attempt to evaluate Herder's position in itself; it is widely known that a different opinion prevails today on the role of the poetic signifier. It is nonetheless certain that, when he criticizes Lessing (and, through him, a secular tradition), Herder is right in one sense: poetry is not an "auditory" art like music (furthermore, it is perceived through the eyes—by reading— much more often than through the ears); and its mimesis is not achieved by means of isolated sounds. But the important point lies elsewhere: Herder's critique, like Mendelssohn's, bears solely upon one part of the second proposition of the syllogism. In adopting this limited focus, neither one observes that he is dodging the strongest element of Lessing's reasoning, which lies not in the minor premise but in the major, and which is the following: the signs of art must be motivated. Neither one notices, any more than subsequent commentators do, that Lessing overturns the distribution of signs that he inherited from Dubos and Harris according to which the signs of painting were motivated and those of poetry unmotivated.[11] For Lessing (who is closer to Diderot on this point but much clearer than Diderot), both groups must be motivated, otherwise there is no art. His predecessors skim lightly over the fact that they are demanding from poetry on the one hand what they are refusing to grant it on the other. In painting, "imitation" and "natural sign" are synonyms. But how can poetry be imitative while the signs it uses are arbitrary? Confronted with these contradictory requirements, Lessing prefers logic to common sense, even if logic leads, at first glance, toward the absurd. And the position he adopts is consistent: the signs of

11. In the preface to the 1964 Hermann edition of The *Laocoön*, J. Bialostocka repeats this insubstantial cliche: "Lessing . . . was not alone in trying to define the difference between poetry and painting. . . . We can also find in Dubos, Harris, and Diderot a distinction between the natural signs of painting and the conventional symbols of poetry" (pp. 23–24). Lessing's originality is well marked, on the other hand, in the work of M. Marache, *Le Symbole dans la pensée et l'oeuvre de Goethe* (Paris, 1960); see especially p. 30. The first chapter of this book is in several respects parallel to my own work.

poetry, too, are motivated. That is the theorem that remains to be proved.

This affirmation is all the more significant in that it is absent from the early drafts of the *Laocoön*, in which we read, for example: "Where does the difference between poetic and material images come from? From the difference in the signs that painting and poetry use. The former in space, and natural; the latter in time, and arbitrary" (Blümner ed., p. 393). On this specific point, Lessing's thinking does not differ at all from that of his predecessors. Now it is indeed of poetry that Lessing will require, in the definitive version, the use of motivated signs. To be more precise, this idea will never achieve its "definitive" expression, for more than any other it is taken up gain, modulated and transformed in the fragments written by Lessing after the *Laocoön* and published only after his death.

In the place of the simplistic equation proposed by Dubos, Harris, and Mendelssohn, according to which painting is natural and poetry is arbitrary, a four-term structure is elaborated little by little in Lessing's thought. In the first place, language may be arbitrary *or* natural. In the former case, we are dealing with prose (that is, in contemporary terms, with nonliterary discourse), and in the latter with poetry (with literary discourse). Lessing says this quite explicitly in chapter 17 of the *Laocoön*, in response to Mendelssohn's hand-written objection:

> It is true, as the signs of speech are arbitrary, so it is perfectly possible that by it we can make the parts of a body follow each other just as truly as in actuality they are found existing side by side. Only this is a property of speech and its signs in general, but not in so far as it best suits the purposes of poetry. The poet is not concerned merely to be intelligible, his representations should not merely be clear and plain, though this may satisfy the prose-writer. He desires rather to make the ideas awakened by him within us living things, so that for the moment we realize the true sensuous impressions of the objects he describes. . . . Once more, then; I do not deny to speech in general the power of portraying a bodily whole by its parts: speech can do so, because its signs or characters, although they follow one another consecutively, are nevertheless arbitrary signs; but I do deny it to speech as the medium of poetry, because such verbal delineations of bodies fail of the illusion on which poetry particularly depends, and this illusion, I contend, must fail them for the reason that the co-existence of the phys-

ical object comes into collision with the consecutiveness of speech. . . . Wherever, then, illusion does not come into the question, where one has only to do with the understanding of one's readers and appeals only to plain and as far as possible complete conceptions, those delineations of bodies (which we have excluded from poetry) may quite well find their place.[12]

Lessing opposes "illusion" and "comprehension" (or "intelligence") where we would have spoken of motivated and unmotivated signs; he accepts the views of Baumgarten and Mendelssohn, according to whom art is nothing if not perceptible; nevertheless, he brings clearly to light a definition that subtends all of his reasoning and that will be repeated ceaselessly in the centuries to come: poetry is a language whose signs are motivated.

How does this motivation come about? In the *Laocoön* itself, Lessing puts his whole emphasis on the imitation of temporality: the signs of language follow one another in time, they can designate, in a motivated way, all that is successive in time. Now "subjects which or the various parts of which succeed each other may in general be called *actions*. Consequently, actions form the proper subjects of poetry" (Steel trans., p. 55).

But in the posthumous fragments, Lessing envisages several other ways of motivating signs. In the first place he believes, in common with many in the eighteenth century, that language was born from onomatopoeia, that in the beginning words resembled the things they designated. Now, onomatopoeia is at the service of poetry: "From the judicious use of these words in poetry arises what is called musical expression in poetry" (Blümner ed., p. 430). The same is true of interjections, which are universal—and thus natural—expressions of feelings that poets know how to use.

Another motivating device suggested by Lessing brings us very close to the "diagrammatic" phenomena dear to Jakobson. "Poetry also uses not only isolated words but also these words taken in a certain order. Even if the words in themselves are not natural signs, their succession may have the power of a natural sign" (ibid., p. 431). Lessing regrets the fact that this device, such a common one in poetry, should so rarely have attracted the attention of critics. (J. E. Schlegel conceived of imitation in poetry in the form of proportional relationships, but more in the

12. *Laocoön, Nathan the Wise, Minna von Barnhelm*, ed. W. A. Steel (London and New York, 1930), pp. 61, 63.

sense of the analogical transposition so highly appreciated by Aristotle.)

Next comes a device that warrants more attention: the use of metaphor (the word is used here, as often elsewhere, to designate tropes in general). And in this regard we can see once again where the originality that scholars have denied to Lessing lies. To be sure, we find the various ingredients of Lessing's argument in the writings of several of his contemporaries. J. E. Schlegel, as we saw in the preceding chapter, interpreted imitation in poetry as resemblance not between words and things, but between the comparative term and the thing compared, between the two meanings of the metaphorical term (*Abhandlung von der Nachahmung*, 1742). In the same period, the Swiss Breitinger was writing in his *Kritische Dichtkunst* (1740) that the arbitrariness of words is a handicap for poetry, and that, to remedy it, poetry has at its disposal the "pictorial figure" (*mahlerische Figur*), the metaphor, which, unlike ordinary words, is a "necessary, natural, and efficacious sign" (II, 312). Thus he concluded that

> the figured and flowery manner of writing enjoys a great advantage over the common, proper manner; this advantage stems principally from the fact that this manner not only communicates things by arbitrary signs that lack the slightest relationship with their meaning, but it also depicts these things quite distinctly before our eyes by means of similar images. . . .
> Figured and flowery expressions not only allow us to guess at thoughts on the basis of arbitrary signs, but render them visible at the same time. [Ibid., pp. 315ff.]

Described in this way, metaphors belong to the realm of the "marvelous," as opposed to that of the "probable," according to Breitinger.

In the years immediately preceding the appearance of the *Laocoön*, the Augustinian dichotomy (or the one understood as such) between artificial (arbitrary) and natural signs—metaphor being included among the latter—is brought back to life by the Leibnitzians. Georg Friedrich Meier, after evoking it in its generality, applies it to the realm of aesthetics: the beautiful being considered, since Baumgarten, to be a perceptible quality, natural signs—which are not afflicted with the abstractness of arbitrary signs—are conducive to it. "Thus all the arbitrary signs must *imitate* the natural ones to the greatest possible degree, if they aspire to be beautiful. . . . The more natural the arbitrary and artificial signs are, the more beautiful they are."[13] Or, again, Johann Heinrich Lambert writes in his *Neues Organon* (1764):

> If we limit ourselves to proper meaning, we can only consider words, and particularly the root-words of languages, as *arbitrary* signs of things and of concepts. On the other hand, they already contain more resemblances insofar as they serve as metaphors, in which the proper meaning will be presupposed. However, these resemblances lie not in a comparison between the impressions made by the word and by the thing, but in the comparison between the objects that are named by means of the metaphor. [Ch. III, 1, 20; vol. II, p. 14]

That description of the metaphoric mechanism reappears, virtually unchanged, with Lessing.

Once again, then, we might say that all the elements of Lessing's doctrine existed before he wrote. But let us observe more closely the way he proceeds. First, he enumerates all the means at the disposal of poetry for rendering motivated language, and he distinguishes two principal types: natural signs (onomatopoeia, and the like) and signs that are equivalent to natural ones but are not themselves natural. "Poetry disposes not only of authentic natural signs but also of devices for elevating its arbitrary signs to the dignity and power of natural ones" (Blümner ed., p. 430).

Thus metaphor takes its place within a homogeneous series. It is described as follows: "As the capacity of natural signs resides in their resemblance to things, metaphor, lacking that resemblance, introduces another in its place, a resemblance between the thing designated and another thing, so that the concept is renewed in an easier and livelier way" (ibid., p. 432).

Where Breitinger was content to write that metaphor is a sign that resembles, and is appropriate to poetry for that reason, where Lambert accounted for the linguistic nature of metaphor, but without envisaging a theory of poetic language, Lessing formulates a unified theory, at once concrete and general. As a constituent feature, resemblance is *not* the same in metaphor as in motivated signs (such as images, or onomatopoeia); the two are equivalent only from a functional point of view. Furthermore, Lessing exposes the mechanism in question: metaphor is a motivated sign created by means of unmotivated signs. None of these considerations arise in Breitinger's work. Moreover, we have seen

---

13. *Anfangsgründe aller schönen Wissenschaften*, 2d ed. (1755), part 2, pp. 626, 634.

how the Swiss writer insisted on asserting that all metaphor serves to "paint" (a widespread illusion in the eighteenth century).[14] Perhaps Lessing does not yet have a satisfactory response to this argument, but he does not insist on the necessarily visual character of metaphor, and contents himself with saying that metaphors make understanding easier and livelier.

In a letter to his friend Friedrich Nicolai dated May 26, 1769, Lessing sums up his position on the motivation of verbal signs (note that he conceives of no motivation except resemblance): "Poetry must necessarily attempt to raise its arbitrary signs to the level of natural ones; that is the only way it can distinguish itself from prose and become poetry. The means it can use to accomplish this are sonorities, word order, meter, figures and tropes, comparisons, and so forth." All these devices bring poetry close to being an art whose signs are motivated, but the identification is never complete: there still remain unmotivated linguistic signs. Always, except in one case, which thereby takes on exemplary value in Lessing's eyes: "The higher poetic genre is the one that makes arbitrary signs entirely natural. That is the dramatic genre; for here words cease to be arbitrary signs and become natural signs of arbitrary things."[15]

Words then designate words (Leonardo said scornfully that words can designate only words): motivation is total, even if these designated words are, for their part, "arbitrary," that is, incomprehensible outside of a given language and culture. Thus, as Abbé Dubos had done before him, Lessing raises dramatic poetry (tragedy) to the highest rank among poetic genres.

Language has motivated signs (in poetry) and unmotivated ones (in prose); but painting includes both types of signs, and thus has two distinct varieties: here again Lessing separates himself from the orthodoxy represented by Dubos, Harris, and Mendelssohn. "Not every use of successive arbitrary auditory signs is poetry. Why would every use of coexisting natural visual signs be painting, since painting is said to be the sister of poetry?", he wondered in the *Fragments* (Blumner ed., p. 452); and in the same letter to Nicolai: "Poetry and painting may be natural as well as

---

14. Breitinger further insists on this point in the work that he devotes exclusively to the problem of figures of resemblance: *Kritische Abhandlung von der Natur, den Absichten und dem Gebrauche der Gleichnisse*, 1740, for example, pp. 7 and 113.

15. *Lessings Briefwechsel mit Mendelssohn und Nicolai über das Trauerspiel*, ed. R. Petsch, 2d ed. (Darmstadt, 1967).

arbitrary; consequently, poetry and painting must each have a double, or at least both must have a higher and a lower form."

Lessing does not seem to have developed this idea at any length: in his writings we do not come across any list that would be parallel to the preceding one—but its inverse—on arbitrary signs in painting. On the other hand, we do find a suggestion as to the manner in which even natural signs cease to be entirely natural. For, if the features of a portrait retain the same relations as are found in the original, they almost never have the same *dimensions*: "Thus the painter who would use only entirely natural signs must paint in lifelike proportions, or at least in dimensions that do not deviate markedly from nature."

Every miniaturist has his share of "arbitrariness": "A human face with the dimensions of an outstretched palm, of a thumb, is indeed the picture of a man; but it is already, to a certain extent, a symbolic picture: I am more conscious of the sign than of the thing designated" (Blümner ed., p. 428; that consciousness is, for Lessing, the indication of arbitrariness).

Lessing's argument is seductive in its rigor. Even so, does it account for the nature of art in general, of artistic "imitation" in particular? One may well doubt it. The word "imitation" lends itself to misunderstandings, that much is clear: there is hesitation between imitation as representation or staging, and imitation as production of an object that resembles its model. For the art of language, only the first interpretation of the term is meaningful. But, profiting in a manner of speaking from the confusion between the two uses of the word, Lessing pretends to believe, or believes in fact, that, even for poetry, "imitation" is to be understood in the sense of "resemblance." Hence the appearance of a paradox that Dubos and Harris did not need to reckon with: it is said of poetry both that it "resembles" (since it obeys the principle of imitation) and that it does not (since it uses arbitrary signs). But the paradox clearly arises from the fact that Lessing used the words in different meanings from one line to the next.

It is difficult to situate Lessing's ideas with respect to the passage from classicism to romanticism. To the extent that he seeks to consolidate the principle of imitation, he participates, along with Batteux, Diderot, and the others, in the last manifestations of the classical spirit. However, in spite of the fact that he displaces the problematics of imitation, by making it no longer a relationship between signs (or images) and the universe but a relationship between signifier and signified, thus one that is internal to the sign—in other words, in spite of the fact that he brings *imitation* back to *motivation*—Lessing clearly announces the romantic doctrine of poetic language; indeed, he appears to be its founder. The filiation of these two doctrines, classic and romantic, lies very precisely in this passage from the first concept to the second. But how are we to reconcile, in Lessing's thought or in that of his successors, from A. W. Schlegel to Jakobson, the observation that linguistic signs are arbitrary and the affirmation that poetry uses motivated signs? Even repeated two hundred times, an idea does not necessarily become true. . . .

It remains true that Lessing was the first to integrate the theory of art convincingly into a general reflection on the sign; the first, too, to affirm in an explicit way the grounding of each art in its raw material, thus that of literature in language. And perhaps the soundness of his thinking struck a more serious blow to imitation than any other, at the very moment when he was trying to protect it: he proved *a contrario* that the reign of imitation over aesthetic thought was approaching its end. Romanticism was ready to be born.

6

The Romantic Crisis

THE BIRTH OF ROMANTIC AESTHETICS

In order to tell the story of the birth of Western semiotics, I began by choosing a destination: Augustine, whose doctrine I interpreted as the outcome of a whole series of heterogeneous influences; my theme, in short, was Augustine and his predecessors. In order to explore the birth of the romantic aesthetic (but why establish a parallelism between two corpuses of thought that differ so?), I am obliged to adopt a strictly parallel but inverse procedure: I shall start with the writings of a single author, who seems to me to possess the seed of the entire aesthetic doctrine of romanticism, and then I shall trace the influences, direct and indirect, that he exercised on his contemporaries and his juniors. I shall present the romantic aesthetic—or rather, that part of it that interests me in the present context—as an expansion of these initial writings, an expansion of which we ourselves represent perhaps the last avatar. Thus my theme this time will be an author and his successors. The earlier theme closed and synthesized classical antiquity; this one announces and inaugurates our modernity.

A Transitional Figure

And who is the lucky one? One can hesitate among several names. I have chosen Karl Philipp Moritz rather than Herder, Rousseau, Vico, or Shaftesbury (to mention only the most serious candidates); but I remain conscious of a certain arbitrariness in this decision, which is based on a value judgment that is, after all, highly subjective. It seems to me that Moritz is the first to have *combined* in his work all the ideas (he did not, of course, invent them) that are to determine the profile of the romantic aesthetic. This particular role—which is, moreover, a rather limited one (here any parallel with Augustine breaks down)—makes Moritz a convenient point of departure for my study.

There is, to be sure, a second reason for this choice: the fact that the most typical representatives of romanticism, in their systematic presentations of the new doctrine, subject all of the preceding tradition either to criticism or to massive repression, rescuing only one name from oblivion, one single author from scorn—and that is Moritz. This exceptional praise is not without its ambivalence, moreover: as soon as Moritz's special role is recognized, it is undercut in some way, as if there were some danger that unreserved admiration might cast a shadow over the admirer's own worthiness.

Thus it was, first, with August Wilhelm Schlegel, in the first volume of his *Vorlesungen über schöne Literatur und Kunst*, dealing with art theory (*Die Kunstlehre*: notes for a course given in 1801): after reviewing all the theories of the past, after criticizing them all, after presenting his own views, or rather those of the *Athenaeum*, he adds: "Only one writer, to my knowledge, has deliberately used the principle of imitation in art in the highest sense: that is Moritz, in his little text on imitation formative of beauty. The problem with this text is that, in spite of his truly speculative mind, Moritz, finding no support in the philosophy of the day, strayed alone along dangerous mystical paths (*Irrgängen*)" (p. 91).[1]

In the following pages Schlegel quotes or summarizes a number of Moritz's ideas, admiring them all without reservation; and yet that introductory remark, even while placing Moritz in an exceptional position, urges us not to follow him on the wrong path,

1. The references and abbreviations used in this chapter are given in the Bibliographical Note.

one that is summarily labeled mystical. But the strangeness of this attitude becomes really glaring only when we read another passage, this time in Schelling's *Philosophie der Kunst* (Philosophy of Art) (notes for a course given in 1802) which deals with mythology (a central concept for Schelling):

> It is very much to Moritz's credit that he was the first among the Germans, and in general, to represent mythology with that characteristic of poetic absoluteness that is peculiar to it. Even though he did not carry this idea to its final fulfillment, even though he can only show that such is the case but cannot show the necessity and the basis (*Grund*) for this state of affairs, the poetic sense dominates his entire presentation nevertheless, and perhaps (*vielleicht*) we can detect here the traces of Goethe, who expressed these ideas throughout his own work and who no doubt (*ohne Zweifel*) awakened them also in Moritz. [v, 412]

This statement is more complex than Schlegel's. Schelling begins with a superlative evaluation: Moritz is the first, not only among the Germans but in general (let us further note, on Moritz's behalf, that Schlegel and Schelling grant him first place in different areas). A first limitation follows: far from being too mystical, this time Moritz is, in a way, not mystical enough: he does not know how to get to the bottom of things, he lacks *Grund*. But even before the sentence ends, a second, much lower blow is struck: what is good in Moritz is perhaps a trace of Goethe—a "perhaps" that quickly becomes "no doubt" in the following (and final) clause.

So many coincidences deserve an explanation. I shall seek it in the man to whom Moritz—like so many others—owed so much, the man whose immense shadow kept those whom it hid in prolonged oblivion: Goethe. Goethe met Moritz in Rome in 1786; he seduced him, he became his inspiration, he made him his mouthpiece (so we are told, in any case); he took care of him on the occasion of an illness. After returning to Germany, he invited him to Weimar, where Moritz was introduced into a distinguished society, after which Goethe found him a post in Berlin, where Moritz remained until the end of his life, four years later.

Moritz is widely regarded as Goethe's reflection, his spokesman. As proof that this opinion is false, I need cite only one piece of evidence: Moritz's *Essay* (*Versuch einer Vereinigung und Wissenschaften unter dem Begriff des in sich selbst Vollendeten*), which contains all of his major ideas, dates from 1785; thus it was written a year before his meeting with Goethe. So where does this wide-spread opinion come from? From Goethe himself. In the sum-mary-review he devotes to Moritz's book on imitation, he an-nounces that he was present at the creation of the work. In his *Travels in Italy,* still speaking of the same book he is more brutal: "It grew out of our conversations, which Moritz has used and elaborated after his own fashion" (JA 27, 254). Thirty years later, in a note entitled *Einwirkung der neueren Philosophie* (1820), he still needs to reassert his position: "I had long discussions with Mor-itz, in Rome, about art and its theoretical requirements; a small printed volume bears witness even today to our fruitful obscurity of yesteryear" (JA 39, 29).

If such was the written version, what are we to think of the oral appreciations that Schlegel and Schelling could not have failed to hear, having been Goethe's intimates during precisely these early years of the century? We can get some idea of this by referring to two other places where Moritz is mentioned in the *Travels In Italy,* always in an amiable and condescending fashion: "He is a remarkably good man; he would have gone much farther if he had occasionally come across people who were both capable and affectionate enough to enlighten him on his own state" (JA 26, 202–203). "He has a most felicitous and accurate way of seeing things; I hope he will also find the time to become profound (*gründlich*)" (JA 27, 94).

In the sentence where Schlegel is regretting Moritz's isolation, do we not seem to hear an echo of this earlier description? And in Schelling's text, where he deplores the absence of *Grund,* a para-phrase of the second? If for no reason other than this remarkable fate, consisting of praises that mainly contributed to covering up his ideas and his true role, Moritz deserves to be awarded a privileged place here in his turn.

The End of Imitation

But let us pick up the thread of our story where we left off before this anecdotal intermission: namely, with the uneasiness that aesthetics experiences when confronted with the concept of imitation. The concept is unsatisfying, yet there is no way to be rid of it; as a result, we find the series of more or less awkward adjustments that we have surveyed in the two preceding chap-ters.

Such was the state of affairs in, say, 1750. Let us now leap forward fifty-five years and open A. W. Schlegel's *Die Kunstlehre* to the pages dealing with imitation. From this text we get a wholly different impression: in this half-century the crisis that gave birth to romanticism has occurred. One difference is immediately apparent: it is now permissible to criticize the principle of imitation openly; indeed, the very objections or questions that I raised about this notion above are already clearly and brilliantly formulated in Schlegel's presentation.

In the first place, the strict application of the principle of imitation (the one I have called its "zero degree") leads to absurdity. If art succeeded in plying itself to this principle, thus in producing perfect copies, it is difficult to see where its value would lie, since the prototype already exists. Schlegel imagines amusingly that art's advantage would lie in the absence of any physical inconvenience that might accompany the perception of the model itself.

> Thus, for example, the superiority of a painted tree over a real tree would consist in the fact that no caterpillars or insects would land on its leaves. Thus it is that villagers in the north of Holland, concerned with cleanliness, indeed do not plant real trees in the little courtyards that surround their houses. They are satisfied with painting trees, hedges, cradles of greenery all around, on the walls; furthermore, the greenery lasts all winter. Landscape painting would then serve simply as a means of having around oneself, in one's room, an abridged version of nature, as it were, where one would prefer to contemplate mountains without being exposed to their chill temperatures and without being obliged to climb them. [P. 85]

But such an idea about the nature of art is not simply ridiculous, it is false: for it is clear to everyone that the work of art obeys conventions that have no counterpart in nature, the supposed object of imitation (Hermogenes takes revenge on Cratylus here). So it is with the *line of verse* in poetry, with *rhythm* in music; so it is even with the plastic arts: if the conventions are forgotten, "we should not make fun of the man who did not consider a bust a good likeness, because the person it represented, according to him, certainly had hands and feet". Or we will be like that Chinese who, "seeing English paintings, asked whether the people represented were really as dirty as they appeared owing to the effects of light and shadow" (pp. 86–87).

The principle of imitation cannot be improved by amending the object, as Batteux (and in a different way Diderot) wanted to do: to say that we are imitating "beautiful nature" is to introduce a second principle, beauty, without providing a way to comprehend it. "It must be one or the other: either we imitate nature as it is offered to us, and then often it may not appear beautiful; or we represent it always as beautiful, and then we are no longer imitating. Why not say rather that art must represent beauty, and leave nature entirely aside?" (p. 85).

Schelling brings out this paradox even more clearly a few years later, in his *Oration on the Relation between the Plastic Arts and Nature*:

> Should, then, the disciple of nature imitate, without distinction, all things in her, and in each thing, all things? Only beautiful objects should be reproduced, and only the beautiful and perfect in them. Thus the principle would be more narrowly determined; but at the same time it would be maintained that in nature the perfect is mixed with the imperfect, the beautiful with the unlovely. How, then, could he who looks upon nature with an eye of slavish imitation distinguish the one from the other? [vii, 294; Eng. trans., p. 4]

Schelling himself had drawn the conclusions from this contradiction in an earlier text, the last chapter of his *System of Transcendental Idealism* (1800). If the rule of art is beauty, art is an incarnation of beauty superior to nature, which is (also) governed by principles other than beauty. Consequently, far from having to imitate nature, art provides us with a yardstick for the judgment that we bring to bear on natural beauty: the hierarchy of art and nature is reversed: "Whence it is self-evident what we are to think of the imitation of nature as a principle of art; for so far from the merely contingent beauty of nature providing the rule to art, the fact is, rather, that what art creates in its perfection is the principle and norm for the judgment of natural beauty" (iii, 622; Eng. trans., p. 227).

The earlier interpretation of the principle of imitation is untenable. How then can we explain the relationship, which undeniably exists, between works of art and nature? By interpreting the principle of imitation in an entirely new way. The discovery and practice of this new interpretation are, if Schlegel is to be believed, the particular contributions of Moritz.

Doctrine

The innovation Moritz introduces is in fact a radical one. Whereas, formerly, in order to accommodate the principle of imitation to observed facts, it seemed sufficient to couple a modifying adverb with the verb "imitate" or else—a supremely audacious measure—to characterize its object differently ("beautiful nature," "ideal"), Moritz changes the subject of the verb, and by the same token changes its meaning. The work no longer imitates; the artist does.

Imitation in the arts resides, if anywhere, in the activity of the creator. The artist, not the work, copies nature, and he does this by producing works. But the meaning of the word "nature" is not the same in the two instances. The work can only imitate the *products* of nature, whereas the artist imitates nature inasmuch as the latter is a *productive* principle. "The *born artist*," Moritz writes, "is not content to observe nature, he has to imitate it, take it as his model, form (*bilden*) and create as nature does" (*S*, p. 121). It is therefore more accurate to speak of construction rather than of imitation: the artist's characteristic capability is a *Bildungskraft*, a formative (or productive) faculty; Moritz's major aesthetic treatise is called, significantly, *Über die bildende Nachahmung das Schönen* (On the Creative Imitation of the Beautiful: 1788). *Mimesis*, yes, but on condition that the term be understood in the sense of *poiesis*.

Schlegel is going too far, of course, when he attributes this idea to Moritz and Moritz alone. Before him, Shaftesbury in England and Herder in Germany had begun to situate imitation between creator and Creator, not between two creations (these are the immediate sources; one can go back as far as Empedocles for a first formulation of the parallelism). They had exploited the evident analogy between God, creator of the world, and the artist, author of his work. Herder even wrote that "the artist has become a creator God." Shaftesbury had appealed to the image of Prometheus, a particularly appropriate one in this context: the creator god comes to symbolize the artist. Moritz belongs to that same tradition; he writes in *Götterlehre*:

Prometheus moistened with water the earth which was still impregnated with celestial particles, and he created man in the image of the gods, in such a way that man alone raises his eyes toward heaven whereas all the other creatures incline their heads toward earth. . . . That is why Prometheus is represented, in ancient works of art . . . , with a vase at his feet and a human torso before him; he is forming them with clay; all the power of his thought seems concentrated on their perfection. [Pp. 24, 25][2]

Consequently, the moment of formation takes precedence over the already formed result: every important term is drawn to the side of the process of production. Moritz writes: "The nature of the beautiful consists in this, that its inner being lies beyond the limits of the power of thought, in its emergence, in its own becoming" (S, pp. 77–78). The first part of this sentence affirms a certain irrational aspect of beauty; the last two phrases situate this aspect in the act of becoming. This preferential attention explains why, in the romantic aesthetic, the accent no longer falls upon the relationship of representation (linking the work and the world), but upon the relationship of expression, the one that links the work and the artist.

In this new framework, the work of art has in common with nature the fact that each is a closed totality, a complete universe— since the creation of works in no way differs from the creation of the world, and since the same can be said of the products created. The resemblance no longer resides in the appearance of similar forms, but in the possession of an identical internal structure: the relationship of the constituent parts is the same, only the coefficient of size varies. The work is not the image but the diagram of the world. "The beautiful totality emerging from the hands of the artist who forms it is thus an impression of the higher beauty that resides in the great totality of nature" (S, p. 73). "The capacity to act . . . seizes upon the dependency in things, and with what it has taken, similar in this respect to nature itself, it forms an *arbitrary* whole existing in itself" (p. 74). The same organization obtains in both cases—but in nature it appears life-size, whereas in art the scale is reduced (p. 76). We have come back to the neo-Platonic doctrine of microcosm and macrocosm.

This new perspective not only changes the content of the notion of imitation, but also its position. I began my presentation of Moritz's doctrine with his new interpretation of imitation, be-

2. On the history of this comparison, see O. Walzel, *Das Prometheussymbol von Shaftesbury zu Goethe*, 2d ed. (Munich, 1932). Another of Walzel's books, *Grenzen von Poesie und Unpoesie* (Frankfort, 1937), deals with all the basic concepts of the aesthetics of the period.

cause my point of departure here was the previous aesthetic theory, of which imitation was the central concept. But imitation is no longer central for Moritz. Like the world, the work of art is a self-sufficient totality; precisely to the extent that the work resembles the world, the former no longer needs to assert its relationship with the latter. The central concept of Moritz's aesthetics is, in fact, totality, and this is what he prefers to call the beautiful.

Moritz's ideas taken one by one are not new, but his synthesis is. This is particularly striking in the case of his notion of the beautiful, which combines—for the first time, it would seem—two ideas expressed frequently in his day. On the one hand, like his master Mendelssohn, Moritz wants to separate aesthetics and ethics, beauty and usefulness. More specifically, he gives up defining the beautiful by the pleasure it procures (a definition found in J. E. Schlegel), for on that basis one would be unable to distinguish between beauty and usefulness; for Moritz, such a definition is far too psychological and subjective. The necessity of a separation from the useful leads him to define the beautiful first in a negative way: "Thus a thing cannot be beautiful because it gives us pleasure, for then everything useful would also be beautiful; but what gives us pleasure without being in itself useful is what we call beautiful" (S, p. 6).

Paradoxically, beauty is closer to uselessness than to usefulness: "The concept of uselessness, to the extent that it has no purpose, no reason for being, is all the more easily and all the more closely linked with the concept of beauty, to the extent that this latter also needs no purpose, no reason for being outside itself, but possesses its entire value and the goal of its existence in itself" (S, p. 69).

This proximity is not a definition. The beautiful is useless for a specific reason: whereas the useful, as the word itself indicates, finds its purpose outside itself, the beautiful is that which needs no external justification. A thing is beautiful to the extent that it is intransitive.

> The purely useful object is thus not a whole in itself, not a finished product (*Vollendetes*), and it becomes a completed whole only when it attains its goal in me. —In the consideration of the beautiful, however, I remove the goal from myself and I replace it in the object: I consider it as something *accomplished in itself*, and not in me: it thus constitutes a whole in

itself, and gives me pleasure *for itself.* . . . I love the beautiful
object rather for itself, whereas I only love the useful object for
myself. [*S*, p. 3]

And again: "The beautiful object does not require an end outside
itself, for it is so perfected in itself that the entire purpose of its
existence is found in itself" (p. 69). "The essence of the beautiful
object consists in its *accomplishment* in itself" (p. 79). The concepts
of beauty and wholeness thus become virtually synonymous:
"The concept of a whole existing in itself is inalterably attached to
that of beauty" (p. 71).

The affirmation according to which each totality, each work,
finds its end in itself has important implications. Let us recall the
way Augustine opposed use and enjoyment: we use an object for
some other end, we enjoy it for itself. But in the Augustinian
optic, and in that of Christianity in general, there is only one
object that can both be considered an ultimate end and also be
enjoyed in itself, and that is God. Let us not underestimate the
importance of the reversal, and of its implications, which I take to
be political: hierarchy is replaced by democracy, submission by
equality; all creation may and should be the object of enjoyment. To the same question—can man become the object of
enjoyment?—Augustine responds in the negative, and Moritz by
praising man. "Man must learn to realize anew that he is here for
himself—he must feel that, in every thinking being, the whole is
present in view of each individual, exactly as each individual is
present in view of the whole" (*S*, p. 15). "The individual man
must never be considered as a purely *useful* being, but also as a
noble being, who has his own value in himself. . . . The spirit of
man is a fully realized whole in itself" (p. 16).

To be, intransitively, becomes a supreme value for Moritz, and
he ends his treatise on "the formative imitation of beauty" with
these exclamations: "That we ourselves *are*, this is our highest and
noblest thought. —No more sublime word on beauty can escape
from mortal lips than this: he is!" (*S*, p. 93).

On the other hand, however, Moritz maintains a second definition of beauty that he could have found in Diderot, or in one of
his innumerable predecessors, according to which beauty results
from the harmonious relation of the parts that make up an object.
He writes, for example: "The more the parts of a beautiful object
are in relation to their whole, that is, to the object itself, the more
beautiful it is" (*S*, p. 72). "The more *necessary* the separate parts of

a work of art and their respective positions, the more beautiful the work" (p. 120).

Moritz's genius lies in the fact that, far from setting up an opposition between these two ideas, or simply keeping them separate, he combines them and uses the one to complete the other harmoniously. It is precisely because the beautiful object is in no way necessary that its parts have to be necessary, both with respect to the other parts and with respect to the whole that they constitute. Moritz establishes this interdependence in his very first text on aesthetics, dating from 1785:

> Where an object lacks external utility or purpose, these must be sought in the object itself, if this object is to arouse pleasure in me; or else I must *find so much finality in the separate parts of this object that I forget to ask: but what good is the whole?* To put it in differents terms: seeing a beautiful object, I must feel pleasure uniquely for its own sake; to this end the absence of external finality has to be compensated for by an internal finality; the object must be something fully realized in itself. [S, p. 6]

Moritz's terminology is not entirely stable: sometimes he opposes the absence of ends to the presence of finality, sometimes he opposes internal and external finalities. His idea, however, is clear, and from this starting point the internal *coherence* of the beautiful object turns out to be indissolubly linked with its external *intransitivity*: "finding its purpose in itself" goes hand in hand with "being endowed with a systematic character." On this specific point, the Kantian aesthetic (that aspect of it summed up in the formula "finality without end") is in no way more advanced than Moritz's.

Winckelmann was already saying that "the goal of the true art is not imitation of nature but creation of beauty"; but he was unable to work out the consequences of this assertion. Not until Moritz does art become essentially an incarnation of beauty. Here is a statement synthesizing this new attitude: "Every beautiful work of art is more or less an impression of the great whole of nature that surrounds us; it must also be considered as *a whole existing for itself* which, like nature at large, *has its end in itself*, and is there for itself"(S, p. 122). Thus it is not by chance that the title of Moritz's first text on aesthetics, which recalls and inverts Batteux's, already announces the dominion of beauty over art: it is the *Versuch einer Vereinigung aller schönen Künste und Wissenschaften unter dem Begriff des in sich selbst Vollendeten* (Essay on the

Union of All the Arts and Sciences in the Concept of the Perfect in Itself: 1785).

If art and nature are similarly subject to analysis in the name of the beautiful, still, they are not equivalent: nature's works can also be *used,* whereas works of art cannot. From the standpoint of beauty, then—here Moritz anticipates the passage from Schelling quoted above—art is superior to nature.

> The progressive movement of thoughts toward each other, or the progressive transformation of external finality into internal finality, or, more briefly, *realization in itself,* appears to be the *leading* purpose, properly speaking, of the artist in his work of art. The artist must seek to replace the end, which in nature is always exterior to the object, within this object itself, and thus render it fully realized in itself. Then we see a whole where before we only saw parts with divergent purposes. [*S,* p. 153]

This passage establishes both art's privilege over nature and its law: the conversion of external to internal finality.

A striking example of the application of this principle to the theory of the various arts is provided in the *Versuch einer deutschen Prosodie* (Essay on German Prosody 1786), in which Moritz defines the opposition between verse and prose in terms of the opposition between the heterotelic and the autotelic; or rather, by a comparison (originating with Malherbe; we also find it in Condillac's *Art d'écrire*) the terms of which are opposed in the same fashion: dancing to walking.

> The situation of discourse is almost like that of walking. Ordinary walking has its goal *outside itself,* it is purely a *means* to reach an end, and it tends constantly toward this end, without taking into account the regularity or irregularity of each separate step. But passion, for example as when one jumps for joy, *turns walking back upon itself,* and the separate steps are no longer distinguished among themselves by the fact that each draws the walker closer to the goal; they are all equal, for walking is no longer directed toward a goal, but takes place rather *for itself.* As in this way the separate steps have acquired equal importance, the desire to *measure and subdivide what has become identical in its nature* is irresistible: in this way dance is born. [*S,* pp. 185–186]

From the moment that walking no longer serves to move us closer to a goal, its internal organization appears: the measure. Likewise, when words are produced "for themselves," when dis-

course is "turned back upon itself," the line of verse, that is, the
internal organization of discourse in the name of an autonomous
law, makes its appearance (p. 187). The line of verse is a dancing
discourse, for dance is at once an intransitive and a structured
activity.[3]

Internal coherence is the characteristic feature of the work of
art at every level, and thus applies also to art's spiritual and
material aspects, to its content and its form. But form and content, matter and spirit are contraries; one can thus characterize
the work of art differently by saying that it achieves the fusion of
contraries, the synthesis of opposites. Moritz makes this point,
for art—he writes that "the higher tragic beauty is formed by the
juxtaposition of opposites" (S, p. 203)—as well as for mythology,
which plays for him, as it later will for Schelling, a role analogous
to that of art. The images of Greek mythology, high point of
mythological evolution, are characterized by this syntheticism,
this capacity to absorb and resolve the incompatibility of contraries: "The fact that in Minerva's lofty divine creation, just as in
Apollo's, we find total opposites brought together, renders that
poetry beautiful and it becomes here, as it were, a higher language which combines in a single expression a good number of
concepts that resound harmoniously together, whereas elsewhere
they are dispersed and separate" (Götterlehre, pp. 101–102).

The autonomy of a totality is a necessary condition of its beauty. This proposition has a paradoxical consequence having to do
with the description that can be given of a work of art. A perfect
work of art leaves no room for explanation: were it to do so, it
would not be perfect, for it would depend upon something beyond itself, something external to itself, whereas the beautiful
object is defined precisely by its absolute autonomy.

> The nature of the beautiful object consists in the fact that the
> parts and the whole become expressive and significant, one part
> always through another and the whole through itself; in the
> fact that the beautiful object explains itself—describes itself
> through itself—and thus needs no explanation or description
> besides the finger that merely points to the content. No sooner
> would a beautiful work of art require, beyond that index finger,

3. On this idea of Moritz's, see H. J. Schrimpf, "Vers ist tanzhafte Rede. Ein
Beitrag zur deutschen Prosodie aus dem achtzehnten Jahrhundert," in W. Foerste
and H. K. Borck, eds., Festschrift für Jost Trier zum 70. Geburtstag (Cologne-Gratz,
1964), pp. 386–410.

a special explanation, than it would become by that very token imperfect: since the first requirement of the beautiful is that clarity by means of which it unfolds itself before our eyes. [S, p. 95]

The work of art signifies itself, through the interplay of its parts; thus it constitutes its own description, the only one that can be adequate. "Works of figurative art are themselves their most perfect descriptions, and these descriptions cannot be repeated" (p. 102).

This fact in turn leads to a still more paradoxical implication, according to which, if it is true that within a single medium (poetry, painting) the work of art in question is its own sole possible description, a new possibility arises in the comparison of the various arts to each other: since the beautiful object is always achieved through the operation of the same principle, all beautiful works are secretly identical; the most beautiful poem is thus, *ipso facto*, the equivalent, and at the same time the description, of the most beautiful painting—and vice versa.

In a description of the beautiful formed by words, these words, taken together with the trace they leave in the imagination, must themselves be the beautiful object. And in a description of the beautiful achieved by lines, these same lines, taken together, must be the beautiful object which can never be designated except by itself; for it begins where the thing becomes one with its description. Authentic works of poetic art are thus the only true descriptions of the beautiful in words among works of figurative art. . . . In this sense, we could say that the most perfect poem would be at the same time, unbeknownst to its author, the most perfect description of the highest masterpiece of figurative art, just as the latter is in turn the incarnation, or the accomplished presentation, of the masterpiece of fantasy. [S, pp. 99–100]

Or, more briefly: "Poetry *describes* the beautiful object of the figurative arts, in that it grasps in words the same relations that the figurative arts designate through drawing" (p. 120).

The beautiful may be equaled; it cannot be translated. Poetry, painting, and music are "higher languages," as Moritz puts it elsewhere, that express what lies beyond the "limits of the faculty of thinking," the faculty that words express. The artistic message is *expressible* through poetry, painting, and so on; and at the same time, it is *inexpressible* by means of ordinary language. The impossibility of describing a beautiful object results as much from a kind of incapacity on the part of the language of art to be converted into the language of words, as from the inherent autonomy of the object. Art alone can express what art expresses.

We might say, then, that all the characteristics of a work of art are concentrated in a single notion, which the romantics will later call *symbol*. But Moritz still uses this word in its old meaning (that of arbitrary sign), and in fact he has no term to designate this characteristic signifying capacity of art; he settles for beauty, art, mythology. On the other hand, he does have a term designating the opposite of symbol (and in this he will be followed by the other romantics): *allegory*. The presence of the morpheme *allos* in this word may suffice to account for the animosity that Moritz bears toward it: allegory requires something beyond itself, unlike the beautiful object, which is a fully realized whole in itself.

> No sooner does a beautiful image have to indicate and signify something outside itself than it approaches the status of pure symbol [= arbitrary sign], which does not really depend upon beauty in the proper sense, any more than do the letters with which we write. —The work of art then no longer has its end only in itself, but rather outside itself. —True beauty consists in the fact that a thing signifies nothing but itself, designates only itself, contains only itself, that it is a whole realized in itself [S, p. 113]
>
> To the extent that allegory thus contradicts this notion of beauty in the figurative arts, it deserves no place in the series of beautiful objects, whatever expense of zeal and effort it may offer; it has no value, no more than do the letters with which I write. —Guido's Fortuna, with her flowing hair, touching the moving ball with the tip of her toes, is a beautiful image not because she designates happiness accurately, but because the image as a whole possesses a harmony in itself. [P. 114]

As before, the beautiful (and therefore art) is defined here as a "completed whole in itself"; allegory is foreign to it, as is anything finding its justification outside itself. But a further problem arises: Moritz recognizes that the work of art signifies; now is it not a generic characteristic of every sign, and not just of allegory, to refer to something other than itself? Moritz thus needs to conceive of a new class of signs, characterized by their intransitivity (and consequently, since the sign is by definition transitive, by a new fusion of contraries). The work of art is "a thing which signifies itself" (but is this still signification?); this is what is achieved by the harmonization of the parts among themselves and with the whole, by the object's internal coherence.

In another text, Moritz writes:

An authentic work of art, a beautiful poem, is something finished and completed in itself, something that exists for itself, and whose value lies in itself, and in the ordered relationship of its parts; on the other hand, pure hieroglyphics or letters may be, in themselves, as formless as one likes, provided that they designate that of which one is to think in perceiving them. —He who can ask, after reading them, "What does the *Iliad* signify? What does the *Odyssey* signify?", must be little moved by Homer's lofty poetic beauty. —All that a poem signifies is found in itself. [S, pp. 196–197]

Hieroglyphics and letters are arbitrary signs that designate by convention; what will later be called symbols are motivated signs—but that simply means that an "ordered relationship" exists among the symbol's various levels, just as it does among its parts; and this inner harmony in turn becomes a new form of signification, intransitive signification—which art brings to life but which no words can render. Whence the inanity of the question, "What does the *Iliad* signify?" As another formula asserts: "To the extent that a body is beautiful, it has nothing to signify, nothing external to itself of which to speak; it has only to speak, with the help of its external surfaces, of itself, of its inner being, it has to become a signifier through this" (p. 112). Signification in art is an interpenetration of the signifier and the signified; all distance between the two is abolished.

If, then, allegory is admitted sometimes to the ranks of the arts, it can be only on a marginal basis, in an auxiliary role: "If a work of art were to exist *only* to indicate something outside itself, it would become by that very token an *accessory thing*—whereas the work of art must always, where beauty is concerned, itself be the principal thing. —If allegory appears, it must therefore always remain subordinate, and come as if by chance; it never constitutes the essential or the proper value of a work of art" (p. 113).

Art is not the only place where intransitive signification (the future symbol) is to reign; the same is true in mythology, to which Moritz devotes a separate work, the *Götterlehre*, which might well be considered the point of departure for all contemporary studies of myth.[4] Instead of reducing the Greek myths to pure historical accounts, or else—the inverse and symmetrical error— reducing them, by means of a catalogue of allegories, to the illustration of some abstract teaching, Moritz merely brings to light the constituent parts of each myth, of each mythic image, showing their mutual relations and those of myths among themselves. Here is how he accounts for this in a programmatic preface (quoted here from the *Schriften*, where the subject is taken up again):

> Seeking to transform the story of the classical gods into pure allegory, with the help of all sorts of interpretations, is as foolish an enterprise as seeking to transform these poems into good true stories, with the help of all sorts of forced explanations. . . . In order to avoid changing these beautiful poems in any way, it is necessary to take them first *as they are*, without regard for what they are supposed to signify and, to the extent that it is possible, to examine the whole in a comprehensive way, in order to discover progressively the traces of relationships and relations, even the most distant ones, among the individual fragments that have not yet been integrated. . . . —In the area of fantasy, the concept *Jupiter* signifies itself first of all, just as the concept *Caesar* signifies Caesar himself in the series of real things. [P. 196]

It is because Moritz conceives of mythology in this way that Schelling addresses to him the ambiguous praise cited above; praise that will disappear entirely at the point when, nearly fifty years later, Schelling is drafting his *Philosophie der Mythologie*, usually taken as the point of departure of modern mythology. Not that Schelling's view have moved very far from Moritz's in this time, since he formulates the core of his own conception of myth as follows:

> Mythology . . . has no meaning other than the one it expresses. . . . Given the necessity with which its *form* likewise is born, mythology is entirely proper, that is, it must be understood just as it expresses itself, and not as if it thought one thing and said

4. On the aims and method of this work, see H. J. Schrimpf, "Die Sprache der Phantasie. K. Ph. Moritz' *Götterlehre*," in H. Singer and B. v. Wiese, eds., *Festschrift für Richard Alewyn* (Cologne-Gratz, 1967), pp. 165–192. Karl Kerényi had already recognized Moritz as the founder of modern mythology; cf. his study "Gedanken über die Zeitmässigkeit einer Darstellung der griechischen Mythologie," *Studium Generale*, 8 (1955), 272.

another. Mythology is not *allegorical*; it is *tautegorical* [Schelling borrows this term from Coleridge]. For mythology, the gods are beings that really exist; instead of *being* one thing and *signifying* another, they signify only what they are. [Part II, 1, 195–196]

ROMANTICISM

Symphilosophy

In Friedrich Schlegel's notes and fragments, we find a singular proposition formulated in various fashions. "Wieland and Bürger together would make one good poet" (*LN*, 1103). "We do not yet have a suitable moral author (in the way that Goethe is a poet, Fichte a philosopher). (Jacobi, Forster, and Müller ought to be synthesized for this purpose.)" (*LN*, 1100). This latter note is amplified and explained in fragment 499 of the *Athenaeum*:

> As yet we have no moral author who could be compared to the great poets and philosophers. Such an author should combine Müller's sublime old politics with Forster's great economy of the universe and with Jacobi's moral gymnastics and music; similarly, in his style of writing, he should combine the heavy, dignified, and enthusiastic style of the first with the fresh colors and agreeable finesse of the second and with the sensitive character of the third, who echoes everywhere like a faraway harmonica from the spirit world.

To synthesize individuals for the purpose of producing complete beings is in fact one of the young Friedrich Schlegel's cherished ideas. This dream applies not only to the authors he is reading, but also to himself and his friends (Novalis in turn dreams of a collective production). When the result of such activity is a philosophical work, the activity is called "symphilosophizing"; when it is a poem, the activity is called "sympoetry." Schlegel explains the undertaking in more general terms with regard to another example:

> Perhaps a whole new epoch of science and art will begin when symphilosophy and sympoetry become general and internal, when it will no longer be a rare thing to see several mutually complementary natures form collective works. Often one cannot help thinking that two spirits ought indeed to be combined, like separated halves, and that only together are they all that

they could be. If there were an art of amalgamating individuals, or if desiring criticism could do something other than desire— an activity for which it finds so much material everywhere—, I would like to see Jean Paul and Peter Leberecht [i.e., Ludwig Tieck] combined. Everything that is lacking in the one is found in the other. Jean Paul's grotesque talent and Peter Leberecht's fantastic education combined would produce an excellent romantic poet. [A, 125].

These examples make it obvious that symphilosophy is undertaken not in the name of resemblance but in the name of complementarity. Another fragment puts it more bluntly still: "Sympathy alone ordinarily links philosophers who are not against one another, not symphilosophy" (A, 112). On the one hand, those who are going to symphilosophize must be "up to it," as still another fragment puts it (A, 264); they must function at the same level, and, on the other hand, they must think "against each other." These are the optimal conditions for creation, be it philosophical or poetic.

If the idea is seductive in itself, how much more impressive is the discovery that the German romantics succeeded in practicing this symphilosophy (knowingly or not)? Romantic symphilosophy had a material basis first of all: the communal life, during the last five years of the eighteenth century, of the core group that crystallized around the review *Athenaeum*. The literal brotherhood of August Wilhelm and Friedrich Schlegel became the nucleus of a more extensive fraternity, which included—with interruptions and nuances—Novalis, Schleiermacher, Schelling, Tieck, and others. During a five-year period, these men frequented the same houses, the same women, the same museums; they had countless conversations and exchanged innumerable letters. The works written or inspired by Friedrich Schlegel (the *Dialogue on Poetry*, the *Fragments* of the *Athenaeum*) in particular bear traces of symphilosophical activity.

These facts impose a particular attitude upon any student of the romantic doctrine. It is not possible here, nor would it be interesting, to present in succession, as I have just done for Moritz, the theses upheld by each member of the group. There is one doctrine and one author, even if their names are several: not that each repeats the others (that would be no more than sympathy); but each one formulates, better than any other, some part of the same single doctrine.

By thus taking as a reality what was perhaps after all nothing but a dream of the romantics, and, what is more, by making this reality a methodological principle for reading their texts, I am exposing myself to two criticisms.

The first, an objection on principle, would consist in demonstrating (and this would not be hard to do) the irreducible difference between one author and another. The argument is legitimate in itself, but irrelevant here. The debate that sets partisans of unity in the romantic movement against supporters of each particular author's specificity is a false one. Both sides are right, and there is no contradiction; for the two affirmations are on different levels. In attempting to characterize a movement of ideas, one is sensitive to resemblances and contiguities among the participating authors, and to their global opposition to representatives of other movements. Conversely, in examining the place of one author within the movement, one accentuates whatever separates this author from kindred spirits. At a certain level of approximation, Schelling, Schlegel, and even K. W. F. Solger produced one and the same symphilosophy; at another level, they differ in significant ways. Each of these affirmations is true, and each is approximate. In order to avoid fruitless argument, it suffices to specify carefully the level of generality at which one has decided to operate.

The second objection is historical in nature, and it obliges us to revise the description of symphilosophy that we obtained from Friedrich Schlegel's writings. What counts for me here is not a biographical and anecdotal belonging-together, a community perceived by the very people who participated in it, but a complementarity of ideas. The latter does not always coincide with a community of feelings and intentions. One historical fact, in particular, seems to me to have played a misleading role insofar as the knowledge of ideas is concerned: that is the opposition between romantics and classics (in the German sense of the word), between Jena and Weimar. Personal relations certainly figure in this context too (A. W. Schlegel and Schelling, in particular, were frequent visitors at Weimar and were highly regarded there; Friedrich Schlegel took Schiller as his inspiration, and Humboldt maintained a correspondence with A. W. Schlegel); however, age differences and personal rivalries were such that Goethe never identified himself as a romantic (the romantics, for their part, saw him for some time as the embodiment of their ideal). These biographical quibbles have some interest, no doubt, but they cannot play a decisive role for us here: in our perspective, and to put matters bluntly, Goethe is sometimes a romantic, and Friedrich Schlegel is not always one. What I am attempting to do is to present a doctrine that was developed in Germany between 1785 (the year Moritz's *Essay* was published) and 1815 (the year Solger's *Erwin* appeared), and it matters little to me whether the authors got along well with one another or not. The very label "romantic" is, after all, one of sheer convenience (and our authors used the word in a different sense).

All this may appear trivial. However, the implications of an apparently innocent gesture are important. Instead of "finding" the past, I am constructing it. In order to make the past intelligible, I must keep my distance from it—as if faithfulness required betrayal. I can defend myself only by saying that I add nothing to these texts that is not there already: I choose, and that is enough. My counterargument is a different one: the romantic ideology, born in Moritz's era, is not yet dead; we share in it, and by this token our own intuitions and our judgment (mine, in the present case) remain relevant. I am perhaps part of the picture I am drawing of the romantics; but that is because they are part of me. The romantic doctrine I am presenting is thus not exactly the one which was developed and practiced in the time of Friedrich Schlegel; it is the one that belongs to us, today, when we look back at that period. Certain features then deemed essential have fallen by the wayside; others have become sharper, as if crystallized, through the action of time. It is the birth and the development of these latter features that I should like to discuss.

Production

We have already seen, thanks to A. W. Schlegel's account, what the romantic critique of imitation comprised. The romantics had the means to reject what Novalis called the "tyranny of the principle of imitation" (VII. 288). The same Novalis was prepared to place music at the pinnacle of the arts, precisely because it is not imitative; and if he refrained from doing so it was because the other arts, particularly painting, appeared to him in fact to be no more imitative than music. A well-known fragment (which could be compared with a similar page in the second chapter of *Ofterdingen*) thus contrasts music and painting:

The musician takes and draws out of himself the essence of his art; he cannot be charged with the slightest suspicion of imitation. As for the painter, one would say that visible nature prepares everywhere for him a model that he will absolutely not, that he will never, succeed in attaining; and yet the painter's art is, to tell the truth, as perfectly independent, as totally a priori as the musician's. Only the *language of signs* that the painter uses is infinitely more difficult than that of the musician. The painter, to be sure, paints with his eye; his is the art of seeing harmoniously, and of seeing beauty. His sight is entirely active, a wholly productive (*bildende*) activity. His image (*Bild*) is only his cipher, his expression, his instrument of reproduction. [III. 210]

Painting and music are thus both nonimitative arts, in the classical sense of the word; for the work comes from the artist. If there is a difference between the two arts, it is that the painter's creation is situated, as it were, at a point anterior to that of musical creation: within perception. It is true that the painter perceives images; but this perception is itself creative, because it is selective and organizing. The painter's language of signs (*Zeichensprache*, as opposed to that of words), owing to the preexistence of its forms, is more difficult to practice—precisely to the extent that it aims to accommodate already existing images to subjective and expressive ends, an effort that the musician does not have to make. Abstract painting is evoked here by omission: it would make the painter's language as "easy" as that of the musician.

Art does not imitate nature, it is nature; it does not resemble nature, it is part of nature. "It is idle chatter to seek to distinguish between nature and art," writes Novalis again (VII. 162); and "art is part of nature" (VII. 178). Which means: nature's works are totalities like those of art, obeying the same organizational rules. Or, in Schelling's words: "He is far beyond the times who does not see art as a closed, organic and necessary whole in all its parts, like nature" (V, 357).

If one must still distinguish between art and nature on this level, it is only in order to say that art brings to fulfillment in a purer or denser fashion the principles that are seen to be at work in nature. Thus Schelling is ready to grant primacy to art, and for this reason alone—which he develops through an organic metaphor: "If we are interested in pursuing as far as possible the construction, the internal disposition, the relations and entanglements of a plant or, generally speaking, of any organic being, how much more strongly ought we to be attracted by the recognition of these same entanglements and relations in that plant, so much more highly organized and bound up in itself, that is called a work of art" (v, 358). Novalis observes that nature can sometimes be asymmetrical, disordered, whereas the work of art is necessarily harmonious; out of this difference arises the function of art (vii. 258).

There are henceforth two possible imitations (according to A. W. Schlegel, it can be said to Moritz's credit that he observed this): the wrong one and the right one, that of perceptible appearances and that of the productive principle. Or, in Novalis's words: "There is a symptomatic imitation and a genetic imitation. The only living one is the second" (iii. 39). Schelling describes this opposition in more detail (but his ideas on imitation go in yet another direction: the new imitation has as its goal the revelation of the spiritual in the material); thus he writes in his *Oration on the Relation between the Plastic Arts and Nature*:

> It is with this spirit of nature, which acts within beings, which expresses itself through their forms and figures, as if through so many signifying images (*Sinnbilder*), that the artist, no doubt, must compete; and it is only insofar as he grasps it by imitating it in an authentic manner that he has himself produced something true. For the works born of a juxtaposition of forms (*Formen*), beautiful ones, moreover, would still remain entirely without beauty, since what must give the work of art as a whole its beauty can no longer be form, but must be something above form, namely: the essence, the general element, the look, the expression of the spirit of nature that must dwell there. [vii, 302]

Rather than being content to juxtapose forms, the artist has to rival the spirit of nature that is expressed through these forms. Nature herself is imbued with an artistic impulse; and, conversely, artistic creation extends divine creation. As Novalis says, "nature possesses an artistic instinct" (vii. 162). And Friedrich Ast writes: "Artistic production (*Bilden*) is consequently as much a goal in itself as the divine production of the universe; and the one is as original and based on itself as the other: for the two are one, and God is revealed in the poet as he produces (*gebildet*) corporally in the visible universe" (*System*, p. 8).

The shift of attention from the relationship among forms (im-

itation of symptoms) to the process of production (genetic imitation) implies a valorization of every process in its becoming, as
opposed to the being-already-become. Friedrich Schlegel writes,
in the absolute: "That which does not cancel itself out is worth
nothing" (LN, 226), and, speaking of philosophy: "One can only
become a philosopher, not be one. As soon as someone thinks he
is one, he ceases to become one" (A, 54). In the opposition between ancients and moderns, the valorized term is the one that
becomes, not the one that is: "In the ancients we see the perfected letter of all poetry; in the moderns we see its growing
spirit" (L, 93). Let us recall, as well, that the romantics' favorite
genres are specifically the dialogue and the fragment, the one for
its unfinished character, the other for the way it stages the search
for and the elaboration of ideas: both share in the same valorization of production with respect to the product.

Wilhelm von Humboldt is foreign to the romantics in the narrow sense, on several levels. First, he was a friend of Goethe and
Schiller rather than of F. Schlegel and Schelling. Second, texts we
are about to consider were written some thirty years after the
Athenaeum era. Finally, the object, in this later period, is not art
but language. However, Humboldt remains, and remains entirely, within the romantic tendency, in the sense in which I am
using this term. That does not mean that there are no differences:
the most important comes from the change of object that I have
just mentioned. No longer seeking to oppose art to other activities, still less to demand of one form of art (modern art) what
would be lacking in another (that of antiquity), Humboldt passes
from prescription to description, from the optative to the con-
stative. He does not demand that language be production rather
than product: he observes that this is the case and asks rather that
the science of language take this fact into account.

The object of the science of language is not to be the empirically observable linguistic forms, but the activity of which they are
the product. This faculty is language much more than are the
words and sentences uttered. "Language must be regarded not as
a dead product of the past but as a living creation" (vii, 44; LV, p.
26). "Indeed, language may be regarded not as a passive entity,
capable of being surveyed in its entirety, nor as a something
impartable bit by bit, but rather as an eternally productive medium" (vii, 57–58; LV, p. 37).

Observable linguistic forms are only the obvious part of the act of production, and the point of departure for the act of comprehension; and it is always the act that counts, more than the contingent substance that signals its presence for us. "The word, [element of language] which we may retain for the sake of simplicity, does not impart as a substance something already produced, nor does it contain an already closed concept; it merely stimulates construction of these through independent power and in a definite way" (vii, 169; *LV*, p. 130). The forms are dead, whereas the productive principle participates in life (we have not left organic metaphors behind): "A language cannot under any conditions be investigated like a dead plant. Language and life are inseparable concepts, and learning them from these two aspects is always recreation" (vii, 102; *LV*, p. 73).

Somewhat as with Schelling, the utterance here is on the side of the material, enunciation on the side of the spiritual. "In the individual word as well as in connected discourse, language is an action, a truly creative operation of the intellect" (vii, 211; *LV*, p. 161). Or, in a more detailed presentation:

> Since language, as I have already remarked frequently, has only an ideal existence in the minds and hearts of men but never possesses a material existence even though engraved in stone or bronze, and since the power of tongues no longer spoken— to the extent that they may still be perceived by us—largely depends upon the strength of our intellectual power to revive them, there can be in language an instant of true static status that is only as great as that found in the incessantly burning ideas of men themselves. It lies in the nature of language to be a progressive development under the influence of the intellectual power of its speakers in every case. [vii, 160; *LV*, p. 121]

Humboldt thus rediscovers, transposed to another level, the principal affirmations of the romantics on the subject of the work of art. Language is a living being; its production counts more than the product. It is an uninterrupted becoming. One cannot describe linguistic forms accurately without going beyond them: to give an exact description one would have to reconstitute the mechanism of which they are the product. The concrete utterance is at once an instance and an image of the act of production in general, the one that has as its product not the particular sentence but the entire language. This is expressed in the most famous passage of *Linguistic Variability and Intellectual Development* (the terminological opposition between *ergon* and *energeia* comes from Aristotle via Herder and Harris):

> In itself language is not work (*ergon*) but an activity (*energeia*). Its true definition may therefore only be genetic. It is after all the continual intellectual effort to make the articulated sound capable of expressing thought. In a rigorous sense, this is the definition of speech in each given case. Essentially, however, only the totality of this speaking can be regarded as the language. . . . The real language lies in the act of its physical production. [vii, 46; *LV*, p. 27]

One of the most important consequences of this change of perspective is the focus on the process of expression, at the expense of imitation, or, more broadly, of representation and designation—as well as the focus on the process of acting on others, or, to use a comparable term, of impression. Words are not the image of things but of the speaker; the expressive function takes precedence over the representative function. Language "must be abstracted from all that it effects as a designation of comprehended ideas. Furthermore, we must revert to a more meticulous examination of its origins and its interaction with intellectual activity" (vii, 44; *LV*, p. 26). "Language never represents the objects, but always the concepts independently constructed by the intellect in the course of speech production" (vii, 90; *LV*, p. 63).

Sometimes Humboldt is more moderate: a relationship between objects and words does exist, but this relationship cannot be direct: it passes necessarily through the intermediary of the speaker's mind. The word "is an offprint not of the object per se, but of the image of the latter produced in the soul" (vii, 60; *LV*, p. 39).

Clearly, the expression in question is not that of a purely individual and capricious subjectivity, as one of the later variants of romanticism would have it; but the relationship of expression is affirmed as forcefully as one could wish: "Language is forged by speaking, and speech is the expression of an idea or of a sensation" (vii, 166; *LV*, p. 127). Thus, "language . . . is the organ of the internal being" (vii, 14; *LV*, p. xix). Thus language "permits us to gaze into the inner recesses of the speaker" (vii, 178; *LV*, p. 136).

The valorization of production, and consequently of all that is in a state of becoming—such is the central idea of this chapter of the romantic aesthetic. The critique of classical imitation and the replacement of classical by genetic imitation lead to this point.

The accent on the relationship between producer and product, between creator and work, is one of the chief consequences.

Intransitivity

Novalis relies constantly in his writings upon an opposition that he could have found in Kant between the pure and the applied arts, the former being intransitive and the latter utilitarian.

> Art . . . is divided . . . into [two] main portions, the one being art either defined by its objects or else directed toward other central functions of the senses by determined, finite, limited, mediate concepts; the other being art that is undefined, free, immediate, originary, unguided, cyclical, beautiful, autonomous, and independent, art that realizes pure ideas, art that is enlivened by pure ideas. The first portion is only a means to an end; the second is the end in itself, the liberating activity of the mind, the enjoyment of the mind by the mind. [III. 239]

Novalis is in no doubt as to the way these two terms will be evaluated. Utilitarian art is at once primitive, in the sense that the artist has not yet freed himself from the constraints imposed by need, and artificial, because it moves away from the authentic nature of art, subjecting art to external demands.

> The primitive artist attaches no value to the intrinsic beauty of form, to its coherence and its equilibrium. His aim and sole desire is the sure expression of his intent: his goal is the intelligibility of his message. What he wants to transmit, what he has to communicate has to be comprehensible. . . . The distinguishing feature of artificial poetry is its adaptation to a goal, to an intent foreign to itself. Language, in the most proper meaning of the term, belongs to the realm of artificial poetry. Its goal is determined communication, the transmission of a definite message. [III. 201]

All external functions must be prohibited, not only usefulness in the strict sense but also, for example, the effects that a certain poem might produce in its readers (this was the effect rhetoric called "touching" or "moving"). "That poetry must avoid effects goes without saying, for me: affective responses are quite like illnesses; they are fatal" (VII. 33). The expressive, impressive, and referential functions of language, subsumed by the communicative function, are thus opposed as a group to another, unnamed function, in which language is appreciated for itself. The example of the Sanskrit man illustrates this function: "The true Sanskrit would speak in order to speak, because speech is its delight and essence" (*The Novices of Saïs*, p. 5). Here we see how the various aspects of romantic doctrine, although interdependent, may end up in contradiction. The expressive function challenges the function later called poetic in a struggle for primacy.

Thus, for Novalis, language has two uses. Language as we ordinarily think of it is utilitarian: "Language in the proper sense is the *function of an instrument as such. Every instrument expresses, impresses* the idea of the person using it." But there is a second, intransitive language, and it is this one that is suited to poetry:

> Language to the second power, for example the fable, is the expression of an entire thought—and it belongs to the hieroglyphics of the second power—to the *language of sounds and of pictograms* of the second power. It has poetic qualities and it is not *rhetorical*—subordinated—when it is the perfect expression—when it is *euphonic* to the second power—correct and precise—when it is, so to speak, an *expression* for expression—when at least it does not appear as a means—but as being in itself a perfect production of the *higher linguistic power*. [III. 250]

Language may be rhetorical (for Novalis as for Kant, that term means "instrumental") or poetic—that is, an "expression for expression."

The beautiful cannot be useful: "A beautiful utensil is a contradiction in terms" (VI. 43). In the name of the same principle Novalis condemns all music that has any relation whatsoever to something outside itself: "Music for singing and music for dancing are not really true music, but only a bastard form. Sonatas, symphonies, fugues, variations: there is real music" (VII. 302). Pure and true art, *legitimate* art is art produced for itself. It is embodied in the image: "An image is neither the allegory nor the symbol of something else, but the symbol of itself" (III. 174). Or in poetry: "The pure poetic anecdote refers directly to itself, has interest only through itself" (III. 195). Or in the novel: "The novel aims at no goal; it depends upon nothing but itself, absolutely" (VIII. 280).

A short text called "Monologue" (III. 194) absorbs these various ideas and goes even further, bringing out the paradox inherent in intransitive language. Here, it is language in the proper sense that Novalis describes as intransitive; what is called utilitarian language (referential, communicative, expressive) is only an erroneous idea that people have about language.

Speaking and writing are at bottom peculiar things; real conversation is a pure word game. One cannot help but be astonished
at the ridiculous error of people who think they are speaking
for the sake of the things said. But as for the defining characteristic of language, namely that it is concerned only with itself, no
one knows it. . . . If it were only possible to make people
understand that language is like mathematical formulas—these
constitute a world in themselves—they interact only with each
other, express nothing but their own marvelous nature. . . .

The paradox of intransitive language is that the expressions
that express only themselves may be—or better still, are—at the
same time invested with the most profound meaning. It is even
precisely at the moment when one seems to be speaking about
nothing at all that one says the most. "When someone speaks just
for the sake of speaking, he utters the most magnificent and the
most original truths." How is this possible? Here we come back to
the conflict between the two forms of imitation: the wrong one,
which attempts to reproduce visible forms, and the right one, in
which imitation occurs simply because entities as coherent and
self-contained as natural beings have been created. Linguistic entities, like mathematical formulas, are part of nature, and do not
need to designate nature in order to express it. "They are part of
nature only by their liberty, and it is only through their free
movements that the soul of the world is made to appear, making
them a delicate measure and the basic design of things."

Novalis's "Monologue" is particularly interesting in that it
does not stop here. No sooner is the doctrine formulated than it is
applied to the very utterance that contains it. If one can speak of
things only by not speaking about them, how is it possible that
he, Novalis, has just spoken of language and of its essence which
is poetry? "I may well believe that I have given the clearest possible idea of the essence and function of poetry, I know too that
no man can understand it, and that I have said something completely idiotic, for I have sought to say it, and no poetry has come
forth."

The paradoxical logic of language is in play here too: if Novalis
has succeeded in expressing ("saying") poetry, it is not owing to
the referential capacities of language, but because no utterance is
made under the governance of a referent. Language is speaking
through Novalis, and it says to itself: "What if this drive toward
speech, toward speaking, were the distinctive sign of the inter-
vention of language, of the effectiveness of language in me? What

if my will had wanted only what I was intended to want, so that in the final analysis, without my knowing it or believing it, all this were poetry, and were to make comprehensible a mystery of language?"

The speaking subject is only a mask borrowed by the unique and constant subject of any utterance, language itself. The writer is not someone who uses language, but someone whom language uses: "A writer is a person animated by language" (*Sprachbegeisterter*).

As we know, the poetic practice of the romantics—excluding Hölderlin, who in fact does not belong to the *Athenaeum* group—lags behind their theory (one might say that they produced theory for the poetry that was to come a century later). Novalis writes in the series of fragments called "Great General Repertory. Future Literature": "What a fine day it will be when we shall read nothing but beautiful compositions, literary works of art. The other books are all only means which are forgotten as soon as they cease to be useful means, which happens to books very quickly" (VI. 155). And in another famous fragment, he describes with precision these future compositions, which are to be beautiful and pure:

> Disconnected, incoherent narratives that have associations nevererthless, like *dreams*. Simply poems that are perfectly harmonious, beautiful with perfect words, but also without coherence or any meaning, with at most two or three intelligible stanzas—which must be like pure fragments of the most disparate things. Poetry, true poetry, may at the very most have, broadly speaking, an allegorical meaning and may produce, like music and so forth, an indirect effect. [VII. 188]

For Augustine, only God could be an end in himself. For the romantics, everything must be: man, art, right down to the smallest word. A hierarchical state dominated by absolute values has been followed by a bourgeois republic all of whose members have the right to consider themselves equal to the others, a republic in which no person is a means with respect to others. Friedrich Schlegel captures the parallel evolution of poetry and politics in the following formula: "Poetry is republican speech: a speech which is its own law and end unto itself, and in which all the parts are free citizens and have the right to vote" (L, 65).

Coherence

Novalis rejects one form of coherence, that of reason, in order to affirm another, that of dreams, and its system of associations. In a general way, the affirmation of coherence goes hand in hand with that of intransitivity: an abundance of internal finality, as Moritz was wont to say, has to compensate for the absence of external finality. And Schelling expresses this solidarity, which is at the same time a definition of poetic language, in the following way:

> The poetic work . . . is possible only through a separation of the discourse by means of which the work of art expresses itself from the totality of language. But this separation on the one hand and this absolute character on the other are not possible if the discourse does not have in itself its own independent movement and thus its time, like the bodies of the world; thus it separates itself from all the rest, obeying an internal regularity. From the external point of view, the discourse moves freely and autonomously; it is only in itself that it is ordered and subject to regularity. [v, 635–636]

In the abstract, we can imagine two forms of coherence for a given work. Coherence among its strata, first of all: a certain number of levels, running the full length of the text, can be identified in the work, and their harmony is affirmed in a *vertical* sense, so to speak. Then, coherence among its segments: here continuity is disrupted and each part is judged necessary, each one has solidarity with the others; this would be, as it were, a *horizontal* correspondence.

In reality, the romantics were unconcerned with the distinction between these two forms of coherence. If there are variations among these authors, they stem from the diversity of metaphors used, or of contexts imposed; it falls to us to sort out what was muddled together, or to combine what was translated by diverse terminologies.

The most traditional form of vertical coherence is probably the one which takes the signs of poetry to be motivated, as opposed to those of language, which remain arbitrary. This is Lessing's theory, as we have seen: here imitation, once an omnipotent principal, is reduced, in the form of motivation between sound and meaning, to being only one among the numerous features of the work of art.

It is A. W. Schlegel (who knows and quotes Augustine's *On Christian Doctrine*) who, among the romantics, demands this form of poetic coherence. In the outlines of his lectures on art theory, we find the following notation: "Requirement that linguistic signs bear a resemblance to what is designated. Satisfaction by poetic treatment in general" (*Die Kunstlehre*, p. 281). And here is an expansion of this idea:

> As we have just seen, language passes from pure expression to arbitrary usage for the purpose of representation; but when arbitrariness becomes its dominant feature, representation, that is, the connection of the sign with what it designates, disappears; and language is no longer anything but a collection of logical ciphers, suited to handling the accounts of reason. In order to make it poetic once again, it is necessary to reestablish its imaged character (*Bildlichkeit*), that is why the improper, the transposed, the tropic are considered essential to poetic expression. [Ibid., p. 83]

We can see that this idea is modeled, in A. W. Schlegel's case, on a characteristic historical schema: in its origins, language is pure expression (we saw this theme developed by Humboldt), thus motivated; then it becomes arbitrary; but poetry can intervene to make up for this deficiency of languages. Poetry rejoins primitive language, and Schlegel rediscovers Johann Georg Hamann's phrase: poetry is the mother tongue of humanity (Herder's opposition between natural and artificial poetry fits in here as well).

> Through all that precedes, we have established that onomatopoeias, metaphors, all the varieties of trope and personification, figures of speech that the poetry of art seeks intentionally, are found in the proto-language on their own, are at home there of ineluctable necessity, are even dominant there in the highest degree; therein lies the elementary poetry announced in the origin of language. In this sense, what is often said is true: poetry came before prose—an affirmation that could not be made if we think of poetry as an established artistic form. [Ibid., p. 242]

Even though Schlegel evokes the imaged character of tropic expressions, it is clear that the possible visualization is not what matters to him, but rather the motivation: this is what onomatopoeia and metaphor have in common. The signifier has to be as close as possible to the signified. The same requirement is expressed in another vocabulary of which we have already encountered some samples: the work of art is described as an organic being, in which the motivated relationship is no longer situated between sound and meaning but between form and content. Form is organic (with respect to content): this means that it is not arbitrary but necessary; the form does not necessarily resemble the content, but it is in every case determined by the content.

It is A. W. Schlegel once again who formulates most eloquently the idea of organic form, and the opposition between organic and mechanical. This subject is too well known for me to linger over it;[5] I shall limit myself to recalling just two passages, particularly explicit ones, from his writing. The first is located in *Die Kunstlehre* and deals, to be sure, not with works but with critics' conceptions of them (this shift from a typology of objects to a typology of discourse is comparable to the shift we observed in Novalis regarding the intransitivity of language). Schlegel writes: "One could call the latter atomistic criticism (by analogy with atomistic physics), in that it considers the work of art as a mosaic, as the laborious assembly of dead particles; whereas the work of art that deserves that name is organic in nature, in that the particular exists only through the intermediary of the whole" (p. 27). Every work of art, or at least every authentic one, is organic: here the adjective seems to refer as much to horizontal as to vertical coherence. The organic is opposed to the mineral as the living is to the dead: if one can always take away from or add to the latter, it is because its closure, and thus its composition, are arbitrary.

The second passage, perhaps the most famous of any that Schlegel ever wrote, expresses the opposition between organic form and mechanical form with respect to the history of drama. I quote it in full:

> Form is mechanical when, through external force, it is imparted to any material merely as an accidental addition without reference to its quality; as, for example, when we give a particular shape (*Gestalt*) to a soft mass that it may retain the same after its induration. Organical form, again, is innate; it unfolds (*bildet*)

5. A detailed study of organic metaphor in romantic literary theories is found in M. H. Abrams, *The Mirror and the Lamp* (New York, 1953); Abrams's object is chiefly English romanticism.

itself from within, and acquires its determination contemporaneously with the perfect development of the germ. We everywhere discover such forms in nature throughout the whole range of living powers, from the crystallization of salts and minerals to plants and flowers, and from these again to the human body. In the fine arts, as well as in the domain of nature—the supreme artist, all genuine forms are organical, that is, determined by the quality (*Gehalt*) of the work. In a word, the form is nothing but a significant exterior, the speaking physiognomy of each thing, which, as long as it is not disfigured by any destructive accident, gives a true evidence of its hidden essence (*Wesen*). [*Vorlesungen*, II, 109–110; *Lectures*, p. 340]

Let us focus on several points in this text. Even minerals have organic form, at least in the dynamic process of crystallization. The work of art is cast in the same mold as the works of nature. Art is like nature, it does not need to imitate it. Mechanical form is arbitrary (accidental, haphazard); organic form is natural (thus in both senses of the word). Form is the consequence (rather than the image) of substance; this leaves no doubt as to the anteriority and the superiority of the latter over the former.

The concept of "internal form" is related to that of organic form.[6] Internal form is directly related to content, which by the same token it necessarily reveals. In certain cases, internal form becomes a convenient intermediary between form and content, the link in the chain that makes it possible to reestablish the relationship of motivation throughout: it is more abstract than form, more structured than content.

In all that precedes, what is in question—even if it is not clearly expressed—is what we have called vertical coherence. The other type of coherence has attracted less attention, but it is this second type that Novalis seems to have in mind when he speaks of the necessary cohesion of works of art. A work is a pure network of relations among its constituent elements: hence Novalis's frequent assimilations between poetry, music, and mathematics (each of these activities makes still more explicit this character of pure internal coherence). "Language is a musical instrument for ideas. . . . A fugue is entirely logical, entirely scientific. It can also be treated poetically" (VI. 492). "Algebra is poetry" (VI. 244). "We

6. For the history of this concept, see R. Schwinger, *Innere Form. Ein Beitrag zur Definition des Begriffes auf Grund seiner Geschichte von Shaftesbury bis W. v. Humboldt* (Munich, 1935), the first ninety pages of a collective work.

ought to write as we compose music" (vii. 51). Or, in a unifying formula: "Logic in the general sense includes the same sciences, or will be divided in the same way, as the science of language and tonal art. Applied linguistics and applied logic meet and form a superior science of connections (*Verbindungswissenschaft*)."

The work of art is nothing but connections; this is also something like the definition of poetry. "It would be impossible to define what the essence of poetry consists in, properly speaking. It is an infinite and simple coherence, nevertheless" (vii. 284). Poetry transforms discourse by making each of its elements necessary: "Poetry raises up each separate element by a particular connection with the rest of the ensemble, of the whole" (iii. 29). Here coherence plays the role attributed to motivation by Diderot, Lessing, and A. W. Schlegel; motivation becomes "horizontal" in its turn. From there it is but one step further to the formal analysis of texts—and Novalis indeed sketches out such an analysis of *Wilhelm Meister*—thus of the novel—by establishing a veritable inventory of "narrative possibles." He thereby lays the groundwork for a passage from the paradigmatic to the syntagmatic, from resemblance to participation—although the ideal relation, for Novalis as for the others, is the one in which an element is both part and image of the whole, in which it "participates" without ceasing for all that to "resemble."

A somewhat marginal development with respect to the main current of romantic aesthetics, and yet closely linked to romantic ideas on the coherence of the work, is the one that deals with the hermeneutic circle. The "circle" itself is actually a consequence of the integral coherence of the work; it is therefore not just by chance that the theory is formulated by a disciple of Friedrich Schlegel and Schelling—Ast—and by their friend Schleiermacher. But, somewhat as in A. W. Schlegel's passage on organic criticism, these theoreticians of interpretation, Ast and Schleiermacher, refrain from opposing two types of works (organic and mechanical, motivated and unmotivated). They recognize, implicitly or explicitly, that all works are coherent; it is simply a shortcoming of interpretation if it fails to notice this, or is unable to bring this unity to light.

Ast writes, for example:

The true being of things can only be known if we relate their exterior life to the inner life, to the spirit, if we establish a harmonious unity between outside and inside. The interior can scarcely subsist without the exterior, and vice versa (for the existence of the interior can only be proved by its exteriorization, and exteriority in turn is nothing but the way out of the interior, and therefore supposes an interior as its principle); no more can they be separated; they are one life, and the truth of all life is their unity. [*Grundriss*, pp. 1–2]

All things are thus an inseparable unity of outside and inside, form and content, and it is the task of knowledge to reestablish this relationship, whatever its direction (vertical or horizontal): "Truth lies only in the idea of the whole, in the correct and harmonious linking of all the particular instances in a living corpus. That is why only he who judges each individual thing in the spirit of the whole has an authentic view of Antiquity" (ibid., p. 25).

But this solidarity of the parts (segments or strata) among themselves, and of the parts with the whole, quickly poses a problem for knowledge, one which results precisely from this reciprocal determination: how can we know the one, when it always already implies knowledge of the other? Schelling had formulated the problem with all due precision (in his *System*): "Since the idea of the whole cannot in fact become clear save through its development in the individual parts, while those parts, on the other hand, are possible only through the idea of the whole, there seems to be a contradiction here" (III, 624; Eng. trans., p. 228).

It is this apparent contradiction that will be called the *hermeneutic circle*. Ast characterizes it as follows:

> But if we can only know the spirit of all Antiquity through its manifestation in the works of writers, and if these works in turn presuppose knowledge of the universal spirit, how is it possible to know the individual, since it presupposes knowledge of the whole (and since we can only grasp the one after the other, never the whole at the same time)? That I can only know a, b, c, and so on, through A, and this A in turn only through a, b, c, and so on, is an insoluble circle if A and a, b, c, are conceived as opposites that condition and mutually presuppose one another, without their unity being recognized. [*Grundlinien*, pp. 179–180]

How can we get out of this vicious circle? Ast's reply is simple—too simple, perhaps. Each part of the whole, he says, is at the same time an image of it; the whole is already given to us in each part, and we need not worry about knowing it in any other way. If we are to believe Ast, in the end the circle does not exist.

> A does not stem from a, b, c, and so on, is not composed of them, but precedes them, penetrates them all equally; a, b, c, are thus nothing but individual representations of the unique A; a, b, c already reside originally in A; these members are the particular manifestations of the unique A, which thus already resides in each in a special way, and I do not need to cover the infinite series of particular instances first in order to establish their unity.
>
> It is only in this way that the particular can be known through the whole and, conversely, the whole through the particular; for the two are given together in each particular instance; when we suppose a, we suppose A, for the former is only the revelation (*Offenbarung*) of the latter, thus with the particular also the whole; and the more I progress in grasping the particular, going down the line a, b, c, and so on, the more the spirit becomes manifest and evident to me, the more the idea of the whole (already born in me through the first member of the series) unfolds. [Ibid., pp. 180–181]

Schleiermacher says essentially the same thing: each individual object implies knowledge of a totality, which is composed, however, only of such individual objects; the solution that he proposes (and that was in fact implicitly present in Ast's statement) is to begin by acquiring a rapid acquaintance with the whole, before studying the parts in depth. Is this not what Friedrich Schlegel had already suggested with the word *cyclic*, in a notebook that both Ast and Schleiermacher had doubtless consulted? "Would the cyclic method be exclusively philological?" "Every critical reading . . . is cyclic." "One is bound to arrive quickly at a presentiment of the whole by applying the cyclic method" ("Philosophie der Philologie," pp. 48, 50, 53). Schleiermacher, for his part, writes: "Every particular thing can be understood only through the intermediary of the whole, and thus every explanation of the particular already presupposes the comprehension of the whole" (*Hermeneutik*, p. 160). "Even within a single text, the particular can be understood only on the basis of the whole; that is why a cursory reading which gives an overview of the whole has to precede a more precise interpretation" (p. 89).

This remains true for the two types of interpretation envisaged by Schleiermacher, grammatical and technical. Comprehension of a given linguistic utterance implies knowledge of the entire language (grammar, vocabulary) as well as knowledge of the entire discourse (the author's entire corpus[7]).

Motivated signs, organic form and internal form, cohesion and connection of poetic elements, hermeneutic circle, these are only a few of the varied and yet unified manifestations of a single idea: necessary internal coherence. And once again, we note that the characteristic features of the romantic aesthetic, though they are all interrelated, may find themselves in conflict, indeed in contradiction with one another: thus the valorization of coherence is not always in close harmony with that of incompleteness. This explains perhaps why these two precepts are exploited later on by different artistic schools; even among the German romantics, the same authors do not always defend both theses—which does not prevent them from being close, or even brothers, as with August Wilhelm and Friedrich Schlegel.

Syntheticism

To demand unity of form and content, or of the material and the spiritual, is to affirm the unity of two contraries. This requirement is fully accepted by the romantics, and it goes a great deal further than the simple postulation of the coherence of the work. Thus Friedrich Schlegel defines both the idea in general and its key concept of irony: "An idea is a concept realized even to the point of irony, an absolute synthesis of absolute antitheses, the ceaseless and self-creating exchange of two thoughts in conflict" (A, 121; we are reminded of the characteristics of symphilosophy). And Novalis dreams of a logic in which the law of the excluded middle would be suppressed: "To annihilate the principle of contradiction is perhaps the highest task of the higher logic" (VII. 180). *Syntheticism*, or the fusion of contraries, is a constituent feature of the romantic aesthetic.

Schelling contributed more than any other romantic author to the establishment of syntheticism. He had precursors in a long philosophical tradition, from Nicholas of Cusa to Kant, but none of them attributed a comparable role to this figure: all *philosophy of identity* is based upon it. What interests us, in the present context,

7. I undertake a detailed examination of these forms of interpretation, along with the other concepts of contemporary hermeneutics, in *Symbolisme et interprétation* (Paris, 1978: English translation forthcoming, Cornell University Press).

is that the honor of absorbing all contraries falls to art in particular. This is why art is found at the pinnacle of the construction
presented in the *System of Transcendental Idealism*; this is no doubt
also the reason why Schelling, a philosopher, is interested in art.
His affirmation of the role of art has the weight of a definition,
and he returns to it on several occasions in his *System of Transcendental Idealism*. "Just as aesthetic production proceeds from the
feeling of a seemingly irresoluble contradiction, so it ends likewise, by the testimony of all artists, and of all who share their
inspiration, in the feeling of an *infinite* harmony" (III, 617; Eng.
trans., pp. 222–223). "An infinite dichotomy of opposed activities . . . is . . . the basis of every aesthetic production, and by
each individual manifestation of art it is wholly resolved" (III,
626; Eng. trans., p. 230). The poetic gift . . . [is the] one whereby
we are able to think and to couple together even what is contradictory" (ibid.).

The artist starts by opposing contraries and ends with their
reconciliation; recognition of these two moments is essential. This
gives us, too, the definition of genius: "Genius is thus marked off
from everything that consists in mere talent or skill by the fact
that through it a contradiction is resolved, which is soluble absolutely and otherwise by nothing else" (III, 624; Eng. trans., p. 228).
Likewise the definition of beauty: "Every aesthetic production . . .
presents . . . an infinite finitely displayed. But the infinite finitely
displayed is beauty" (III, 620; Eng. trans., p. 225).

Art absorbs all oppositions; thus it is superfluous to enumerate
them one by one. Some of them, however, are more important
than others. In the *System of Transcendental Idealism*, Schelling
places particular stress on the opposition between the conscious
and the unconscious. "Conscious and unconscious activities are
to be absolutely one in the product [of art]" (III, 614; Eng. trans.,
p. 220). "The work of art reflects to us the identity of the conscious and unconscious activities" (III, 619; Eng. trans., p. 225).

In the *Philosophie der Kunst*, this pair of categories is coupled
with another, freedom and necessity. The global affirmation remains the same: "Art is an absolute synthesis or a mutual interpenetration of freedom and necessity" (v, 383). "Necessity is related to freedom as the unconscious is to the conscious. Art rests
then upon the identity of the conscious and unconscious activities" (v, 384).

For Friedrich Schlegel, the terms are "intentional" and "instinctive": "Every good poem must be wholly intentional and wholly instinctive. That is how it becomes ideal" (*L*, 23). Or even art and nature: That work "is accomplished which is at once natural and artificial" (*A*, 49); he also speaks of "this wonderfully perennial alternation of enthusiasm and irony" (*GP*, pp. 318–319; Eng. trans., p. 83).

That first opposition and its resolution have to do with the process of creation; moreover, we are already familiar with the fusion of form and content (or matter and mind, or real and ideal, and so forth), as characteristic of the work of art itself. The following are just a sampling of the various formulations. According to Schelling, form and matter emerge inseparable from art (v, 360): art is the indifferentiation of the ideal and the real (v, 380). Friedrich Schlegel describes art as the interpenetration of allegory and personification, which he defines in turn as follows: "At the root of personification, we find this imperative: *Make spiritual all that is perceptible.* At the root of allegory: *Make perceptible all that is spiritual.* The two together determine art" (*LN*, 221). Novalis is more laconic and more general: "For man, the equation is: body = soul; for the human race: man = woman" (vi. 624).

The interpenetration of the masculine and the feminine appears again in Schelling, who would be ready to affirm that the sole reason for castration in antiquity was to create objects for art that would allow it to achieve its greatest perfection.

> Beyond the general moderation, the Greek artists sought to imitate in art those natures in whom the masculine and the feminine were blended, which the Asian softness produced by the castration of young boys; in this way they sought to represent after a fashion a state of nonseparation and of identity of the genders. That state, achieved by a sort of equilibrium which is not a sheer annulment but a true amalgam of the two opposing characteristics, belongs to the highest achievements of art. [v, 615–616]

More than anything else, Schelling insists on the resolution, in art, of the opposition between the general and the particular. "The *in-itself* of poetry is that of all art: it is the representation of the absolute or of the universal in an individual" (v, 634). Each part of the work is at the same time a whole. "It is a reunion of the individual and the general that we find in every organic being as in every poetic work in which for example the various figures are each members serving the whole, and yet, in the perfect formation of the work, each is an absolute in itself" (v, 367). The mode of artistic signification is this interpenetration of the general and the particular (equivalent, here, to the signified and the signifier): "The requirement of absolute artistic representation is representation with *complete indifference*, and specifically in such a way that the general be entirely the particular, and that simultaneously the particular be all the general, but without signifying it" (v, 411). The opposition between the general and the particular is in turn in harmony with several others, such as those between spirit and matter, ideal and real, truth and action: "One can say that beauty is present everywhere that light and matter, ideal and real are in contact. Beauty is neither only the general or the ideal (that is truth), nor the pure real (that is in action), it is thus only the perfect interpenetration, or mutual incorporation, of the two" (v, 382).

It is thus in the nature of the romantic spirit to aspire to the fusion of contraries, whatever they may be, as A. W. Schlegel's somewhat chaotic enumerations testify: "The romantic delights in indissoluble mixtures; all contrarieties: nature and art, poetry and prose, seriousness and mirth, recollection and anticipation, spirituality and sensuality, terrestrial and celestial, life and death, are by it blended together in the most intimate combination" (*Vorlesungen*, ii, 112; Eng. trans., p. 342). Or Novalis's: "These are alloys full of wit, for example, Jew and cosmopolitan, or childhood and wisdom, or brigandage and nobility of heart, concubinage and virtue, excess and lack of judgment in naïveté, and so on to infinity" (i, 365). Friedrich Schlegel was able to apply the ironic consequences of this principle to himself: "It is as deadly for the spirit to have a system as to have none. Thus it may as well decide to join the two" (*A*, 53).

This valorization of the amalgam over the separate essences has implications for the romantic system of genres. Friedrich Schlegel, who was more concerned with this than the others, has an ambiguous position on the issue: on the one hand, true to Lessing's teaching, he recognizes the constraints imposed by literary form on individual works; on the other hand, however, he appreciates the irreducible difference of each work, thereby anticipating the extreme attitude of a Croce: "The modern poetic types are either only one or infinite in number. Each poem a genre in itself" (*LN*, 1090). It is precisely his admiration for syntheticism that tips the scale in the direction of transcending genres: he does place a genre at the top of the poetic pyramid, but it is one that is itself an amalgam of all the other genres, whether pure or already mixed: this is the novel, in the romantic sense of the word. "The novel is a mixture of all poetic types, natural poetry devoid of artifice and mixed genres of artistic poetry" (LN, 55). And this mixture transcends the limits of literature itself; it encompasses all discourse: "The whole history of modern poetry is a running commentary on the following brief philosophical text: all art should become science and all science art; poetry and philosophy should be made one" (L, 115).

The very word "romanticism" is defined with reference to this synthesis of contraries. "Romantic" (the term refers, at the time, to Christian and Renaissance art as opposed to Greek art) is defined, to be sure, in relation to "classic"; and the two terms are related to the fusion of contraries. But the amalgam of nature is, in a sense, anterior to the separation of contraries; that is *syncretism*, whereas the amalgam of art is posterior to the separation of contraries, and this is what I am calling *syntheticism*. Schelling writes, in his *System*: "The art-product differs from the organic product of nature . . . in . . . that the organic being still exhibits unseparated what the aesthetic production displays after separation, though united" (III, 621; Eng. trans., p. 226). And in the *Philosophie der Kunst*: "The organic product of nature exhibits the same still unseparated indifference, whereas the work of art exhibits it *after* separation, but still as indifferentiation" (V, 384).

The most popular formulation of the classic/romantic distinction belongs to A. W. Schlegel; it is modeled on the distinction between nature and art as found in Schelling. The classics practice syncretism; the romantics practice syntheticism.

> The Grecian ideal of human nature was perfect unison and proportion between all the powers,—a natural harmony. The moderns, on the contrary, have arrived at the consciousness of an internal discord which renders such an ideal impossible; and hence the endeavor of their poetry is to reconcile these two worlds between which we find ourselves divided, and to blend them indissolubly together. . . . In Grecian art and poetry we find an original and unconscious unity of form and matter; in the modern, so far as it has remained true to its own spirit, we observe a keen struggle to unite the two, as being naturally in opposition to each other. [*Vorlesungen*, I, 26; Eng. trans., p. 342]

This definition of the moderns, or romantics, poses a problem that could have been foreseen in logical terms, and that indeed arises in practice. If romanticism is defined by the resolution of all contraries, sooner or later it is bound to encounter the classic-romantic pair: if it absorbs the opposition, it achieves one of those paradoxes that Bertrand Russell knew how to explain, in which a whole comes to figure as an element within itself. Such absorptive capacity clearly has troubling consequences here: it rules out any separation between classic and romantic, and in effect it robs the term "romantic" itself of all meaning. This transformation of the concept is particularly striking in Friedrich Schlegel. In the *Dialogue on Poetry*, using one of his characters, Marcus, as spokesman, he defines "the ultimate goal of all literature" as "the harmony of the classical with the romantic" (p. 112), and through another character, Antonio, he declares, in what is both the affirmation of the supremacy of romanticism and of its dissolution, that "all poetry should be Romantic" (p. 101).

The Inexpressible

Art expresses something that can be said in no other way. This romantic affirmation comes up more often as the statement of a typological difference than as a mystic credo (although the latter occurs as well). Friedrich Schlegel took care to distinguish himself from those who, on the pretext that art alone is capable of expressing what it expresses, reject all analysis of the poetic phenomenon: "If some mystical art lovers who think of every criticism as a dissection and every dissection as a destruction of pleasure were to think logically, then 'wow' would be the best criticism of the greatest work of art. To be sure, there are critiques which say nothing more, but only take much longer to say it" (*L*, 57).

Novalis himself is just as categorical: "I am convinced that we attain *true revelations* more rapidly through cool technical understanding and through a calm moral sense than through fantasy, which seems to lead only to the realm of ghosts, and antipodes of the true heaven." And in *Henry von Ofterdingen*, he has Klingsohr say: "The calm animating warmth of a poetic mind is the direct opposite to the wild heat of a morbid heart. This wild heat is poor, bewildering and short-lived; but poetic warmth discriminates all forms cleanly, fosters the development of the most diverse relations, and eternally exists in itself" (p. 109).

When we reach this point—it is difficult not to start from that paragraph of the *Critique of Judgement* in which Kant deals with aesthetic ideas, a concept essential to his system: "BEAUTY (whether it be of nature or of art) may in general be termed the *expression* of aesthetic ideas" (p. 532). "Aesthetic ideas" are thus the content of works of art. But what is an aesthetic idea?

> By an aesthetic idea I mean that representation of the imagination which induces much thought, yet without the possibility of any definite thought whatever, i.e., *concept*, being adequate to it, and which language, consequently, can never get quite on level terms with or render completely intelligible. [P. 528]

> In a word, the aesthetic idea is a representation of the imagination, annexed to a given concept, with which, in the free employment of imagination, such a multiplicity of partial representations are bound up, that no expression indicating a definite concept can be found for it—one which on that account allows a concept to be supplemented in thought by much that is indefinable in words, and the feeling of which quickens the cognitive faculties, and with language, as a mere thing of the letter, binds up the spirit (soul) also. [P. 530]

I shall not deal with the status of this category in Kant's overall conceptual system; we shall limit ourselves here to considering the following characteristics of the aesthetic idea: it is what art expresses; no linguistic formula can say the same thing; art expresses what language does not say; this initial impossibility provokes a compensatory activity which, in the place of what is inexpressible at the core, expresses an infinite number of marginal associations. Eluding language, the aesthetic idea in fact offers language an enviable, because interminable, role: where there appeared to be less there is more.

The forms that transmit aesthetic ideas are the aesthetic attributes. "Those forms which do not constitute the presentation of a given concept itself, but which, as secondary representations of the imagination, express the derivatives connected with it, and its kinship with other concepts, are called (aesthetic) *attributes* of an object, the concept of which, as an idea of reason, cannot be adequately presented" (p. 529).

The vocabulary with which Kant designates the relationship between the inexpressible concept and the forms that evoke it is revealing: "consequences," "kinship"; as he says, the relation always follows "laws that are based on analogy" (p. 529). We are not far from the tropic matrix established by rhetoric and based on the categories of participation, causality, and resemblance.

Even though language may be its raw material, poetry is endowed with aesthetic attributes and can thus express aesthetic ideas to which language as such has no access; poetry is what allows language to transmit the inexpressible.

> It is not alone in the arts of painting or sculpture, where the name of *attribute* is customarily employed, that fine art acts in this way; poetry and rhetoric also drive the soul that animates their work wholly from the aesthetic attributes of the objects— attributes which go hand in hand with the logical, and give the imagination an impetus to bring more thought into play in the matter, though in an undeveloped manner, than allows of being brought within the embrace of a concept, or, therefore, of being definitely formulated in language. [P. 529]

Poetic language (art in language) is opposed to nonpoetic language by that superabundance of meaning—even if it lacks the clarity, the explicitness, of logical attributes and of concepts. Or, again as Kant says, it arouses in us "a whole host of kindred representations that provoke more thought than admits of expression in a concept determined by words" (p. 529). The multiplicity of secondary representations compensates for the lack of a principal representation; logical language is adequate, poetic language is not, but owing to its multiplicity it expresses the inexpressible. This is also a definition of genius (different from Schelling's).

Among the German romantics, Wilhelm Wackenroder is the one who comes closest to our traditional image of the romantic persona: he is sentimental, irrational, and loves art above all else. Not entirely by accident do we find in this student of Moritz's the most extensive treatment of art as expression of the inexpressible. Moreover, art does not stand alone at the pinnacle of human activities: it shares that place with religion. The comparison is sustained throughout Wackenroder's writing, in the name of a common irrationality.

Art's irrational character is manifested throughout the entire process leading from creator to consumer: the former can never explain how he produced a given form, the latter can never succeed in fully grasping it. But the insistence on the irrational is at its strongest when it comes to characterizing the work of art itself. And if nature is sometimes assimilated to art, this is because art and nature are both "marvelous languages" in contrast to the impoverished language of words.

Verbal language can express only the rational, the terrestrial, the visible. "We rule over the entire globe by means of words;

with easy effort we acquire for ourselves through trade all the treasures of the earth by means of words. Only the invisible force which hovers over us is not drawn down into our hearts by words" (p. 118). "Language can only inadequately count and name the changes, not visibly portray for us the interdependent transformations of the drops [of water in a rushing river]" (*Confessions and Fantasies*, p. 191). The language of words grasps neither the invisible nor the continuous; it is "the grave of the inner frenzy of the heart" (p. 191). Because of this, it is quite particularly ill suited to the description of works of art: "A beautiful picture or painting, in my opinion, is actually not to be described" (p. 104).

Art (and nature), on the contrary, allow men "to perceive and to comprehend heavenly things in their full force" (p. 118). Art expresses "mysterious things . . . which I cannot set down in words" (pp. 118–119). These mysterious or celestial things, equivalent to Kant's "aesthetic ideas," set the tenor of works of art; as a result, seen from the viewpoint of reason, the latter will always appear obscure, mysterious, indescribable. Music gives the impression of something dark and indescribable (p. 188); its language is obscure and mysterious (p. 150). The language of art cannot be translated into the language of words (p. 184); and Wackenroder exclaims: "What do they want, the faint-hearted and doubting reasoners, who require each of the hundreds and hundreds of musical pieces explained in words, and who cannot understand that not every piece has an expressible meaning like a painting? Are they trying to measure the richer language by the poorer and to resolve into words that which disdains words?" (p. 191).

Just as with Kant, the fact that art's content cannot be named in words, the untranslatability of the artistic work is in a sense counterbalanced for Wackenroder by the multiple, infinite interpretation to which the work gives rise.

A precious painting is not a paragraph of a textbook which, when with a brief effort I have extracted the meaning of the words, I then set aside as a useless shell: rather, in superior works of art the enjoyment continues on and on without ceasing. We believe that we are penetrating deeper and deeper into them and, nevertheless, they continuously arouse our sense anew and we foresee no boundary at which our soul would have exhausted them. [P. 127]

The inexpressible here again provokes a superabundance of words; the signified overflows the signifier.

Need I add that Wackenroder does not hesitate in choosing the language he prefers? He is happy only when he has withdrawn "into the land of music . . . where all our doubts and our sufferings are lost in a resounding sea,—where we forget all the croaking of human beings, where no chattering of words and languages, no confusion of letters and monstrous hieroglyphics makes us dizzy but, instead, all the anxiety of our hearts is suddenly healed by the gentle touch" (p. 179).

This set of assertions—what art expresses cannot be rendered by the words of everyday language; such an impossibility gives rise to an infinite number of interpretations—can be found again intact among the members of the *Athenaeum* group. This should not surprise us: the affirmation of poetry's untranslatability goes hand in hand with that of its intransitivity; to assert that its meaning is inexhaustible is entirely compatible with asserting that its nature is a perpetual becoming and that its character is organic. Friedrich Schlegel is bent on describing the two terms of that relation, art and its content; in so doing, he rediscovers an idea that was familiar to Origen and to Clement of Alexandria, namely, that one can only speak indirectly of the divine (Origen wrote, for example, that "there are certain things, the meaning of which it is impossible to explain by any human language": *On First Principles*, iv, iii, 15. And Clement: "All then, in a word, who have spoken of divine things, both Barbarians and Greeks, have veiled the first principles of things, and delivered the truth in enigmas, and symbols, and allegories, and metaphors, and such like tropes. Such also are the oracles among the Greeks. And the Pythian Apollo is called Loxias (oblique)" (*Miscellanies*, v, iv, pp. 233–234). In the *Dialogue on Poetry*, Ludovico declares that "the sublime, because it is unutterable, can be expressed only allegorically" (pp. 89–90); and Antonio comments that "the divine can communicate and express itself only indirectly in the sphere of nature" (p. 100; the second version of this text substitutes "the purely spiritual" for "the divine"). An unpublished note goes so far as to establish mutual solidarity between the indirect or allegorical mode of expression and the divine tenor of such a message: the meaning of the allegory necessarily participates in the divine (here we must remember that for Friedrich Schlegel the term "allegory" has a generic meaning and is not opposed to

"symbol," as it is for the other romantics). "Every allegory signifies God, and one cannot speak of God save allegorically" (xviii, v.
315). Thus, on the one hand, "every work of art is an allusion to
infinity" (xviii, v. 1140); on the other, "symbols are signs, representatives of elements that are never representable in themselves"
(xviii, v. 1197). Conversely, indirect expression is not only present
in poetry, it is the constructive principle of poetry. "Allegory is
the heart of poetic play and poetic appearance" (xviii, iv. 666).
"Allegory, symbolism, personification as well as symmetry and
rhetorical figures are *principles*, not elements, of poetry: the *elements* are a dead mass" (xviii, iv. 148).

Ordinary language is incapable of reaching these heights; poetry cannot be rendered in prose; *art criticism* is a contradiction in
terms. "Criticism of poetry is nonsense," writes Novalis (vii. 304).
Or rather, such criticism is indeed possible, but only, as Moritz
has suggested, on condition that it become poetry, music, painting, itself. "One cannot really speak of poetry except in the language of poetry," "a theory of the novel would have to be itself a
novel," the characters of Schlegel's *Dialogue* affirm; and a fragment of the *Lyceum* asserts: "Poetry can only be criticized by way
of poetry. A critical judgment of an artistic production has no civil
rights in the realm of art if it isn't itself a work of art, either in its
substance, as a representation of a necessary impression in the
state of becoming, or in the beauty of its form and open tone, like
that of the old Roman satires" (*L*, 117).

Since art expresses the inexpressible, its interpretation is end-
less. According to Schelling, "every true work of art . . . lends
itself to an infinite number of interpretations without our being
able to say whether this infinity is the work of the artist himself or
resides solely in the work" (iii, 620). For A. W. Schlegel, "the
nonpoetic view of things is the one that sees them as governed by
the perceptions of the senses and the determinations of reason;
the poetic view is the one that interprets them ceaselessly and
sees in them an inexhaustible figurative character" (*Die Kunstlehre*,
p. 81). Poetry is defined by plurality of meanings.

Athenaeum 116

[1] Romantic poetry is a universally progressive poetry. [2] Its
vocation is not only to unify once again all the separate genres
of poetry, and to establish contact between poetry and the phi-

losophy of rhetoric. [3] It desires, and is obliged as well, sometimes to blend and sometimes to amalgamate poetry and prose,
genius and criticism, artistic poetry and natural poetry, to make
poetry a living, social thing, and make life and society poetic, to
poeticize *Witz* [wit, joking] and fill and saturate art forms with
all sorts of solid formative matter, and animate them by im-
pulses of humor. [4] It embraces all that is only poetic, from the
broadest system of art that contains several others itself, right
down to the sigh and the kiss whispered by the child-poet in an
artless song. [5] It can lose itself to such an extent in what it
represents that one would like to believe that its unique and
ultimate goal is to characterize poetic individualities of all sorts;
and yet there exists no form capable of expressing the author's
spirit fully: so that a given artist who wanted only to write a
novel has by accident represented himself. [6] It alone can, like
the epic, become a mirror of the entire surrounding world, a
tableau of the century. [7] And yet, it can float still better in the
middle, between what is represented and what represents, on
the wings of poetic reflection, free from all real and ideal interest, and give this reflection an ever-increasing power and mul-
tiply it like an infinite series of mirrors. [8] It is capable of the
highest and most complete formation, not only from the inside
toward the outside but also from the outside toward the inside;
so that it organizes similarly all the parts of what must be a
whole in its products, and in this way there opens to it the
perspective of a classicism whose growth is unbounded. [9]
Romantic poetry is among the arts what *Witz* is to philosophy,
and what society, relationships, friendship and love are in life.
[10] The other forms of poetry are completed, and can now be
dissected in their entirety. [11] Romantic poetry is still in a state
of becoming; that is even its specific nature, not to be able to do
anything but become, eternally, and never to be accomplished.
[12] It cannot be exhausted by any theory, and only a divinatory criticism should dare attempt to characterize its ideal. [13]
It alone is infinite, as it alone is free, and its first law is that the
poet's arbitrariness is subject to no law. [14] The romantic genre
is the only one that is more than a genre, that is in a certain
way poetry itself: for in a certain sense all poetry is or has to be
romantic.

This fragment of the *Athenaeum* is the work of Friedrich
Schlegel, and it is generally considered the manifesto of the romantic school. I quote it here because it presents in condensed

form all the characteristic features of the romantic aesthetic as I have enumerated them up to now.[8]

How is this fragment composed? Sentence 1 is a definition of romantic poetry that includes two terms pregnant with meaning, "universal" and "progressive"; sentences 2–8 discuss the term "universal"; sentences 8–13 have to do with the word "progressive." The last sentence, 14, once again characterizes the object in its generality; it is in a sense on the same level as sentence 1.

"Universal," the term explained in sentences 2–8, here takes on a meaning close to the one I attributed to "syntheticism" (and, incidentally, to "intransitivity"): romantic poetry is universal in the sense that it transcends the usual oppositions. We are provided with several graded examples. First, within poetry itself, it synthesizes all the genres, including artificial poetry and natural (popular) poetry; then, just one step up, the synthesis bears upon the different types of discourse (of which poetry is just one example): poetry, eloquence, philosophy, or again poetry and prose. Then we go beyond the realm of language: the synthesis concerns poetry and life, form and matter, mind and intuition, and, in the realm of creation, genius and critical sense. Along the way, Schlegel has abolished an earlier distinction between poetry and what is not poetry, thus transforming the very definition of poetry: there exists an uninterrupted movement from the sigh of the child, who participates in poetry by this very token (*das Dichtende Kind*), to the most complex poetic constructions: poetry is grasped in its genesis, starting with the most elementary discursive forms.

Sentence 5 explores two other oppositions brought out by romantic poetry: the difficulty of interpreting it arises from the fact that Schlegel's expression itself participates in the exchange of contraries that constitutes its object. After the first proposition ("it can lose itself to such an extent in what it represents") and the beginning of the second ("that one would like to believe that its unique and ultimate goal is . . ."), we expect to find something like "to represent the word and not the individual"; acting as if this beginning said exactly the opposite of what it has in fact set forth, Schlegel continues: "to characterize poetic individualities of all sorts." The same reversal is reproduced in the second half of the sentence: after "and yet there exists no form capable of ex-

8. A line-by-line commentary on fragment 116 by Hans Eichner is found in the introduction to vol. II of the Kritische Ausgabe, pp. lix–lxiv.

pressing the author's spirit fully," we expect to find "so that a given artist, who sought only to represent himself, has by accident written a novel"; but the result clause is once again reversed: "who wanted only to write a novel has by accident represented himself." These connections are no doubt contrary to logic, but so is romantic poetry, and Schlegel has found a way here to represent what he is in the process of saying. Thus the oppositions between expression and imitation, between (subjective) transparency and opacity are resolved.

What follows returns to more conventional forms of expression. The distance between outside and inside is traversed in both directions (in the same way, poetry was presented as a synthesis of personification and allegory), just as the "realism" and the "formalism" of the work of art—which floats between what is represented and what it represents—are maintained simultaneously. The apparently banal metaphor of art as mirror of the world, which appears in sentence 6, changes meaning in sentence 7: can the "infinite series of mirrors" stem from anything other than one mirror placed opposite another? But then the world would always already itself be a reflection? The intransitivity of art receives a rapid mention here: art is "free from all interest."

Sentence 8 represents the transition from "universal" to "progressive." But before reaching this point, Schlegel evokes in passing another canonical property of romantic poetry: its internal coherence, due both to the resemblance among the parts and to their integration into a whole. It is here that we pass on to the "unbounded growth" that characterizes a "classicism" that—as the reader will have noticed—is decidedly not in opposition to romantic poetry.

In sentences 8–13, Schlegel evokes characteristics that I have designated with the words "production" or "expression of the inexpressible"; the two seem to go together in his text. *Witz*, love, and poetry are, each in its own area, agents of change, propelling forces rather than tangible substances; up to and including sentence 11, Schlegel stresses romantic poetry's aspect of "becoming"; and, on this level, romantic poetry is opposed to "other forms of poetry."

Sentences 12 and 13 transfer our attention to the ineffable aspect of that art; a consequence, as it were, of its limitless character. Theory, stemming from reason and discourse, cannot fully account for it, and the only effective critique of poetry is more poetry: this is what the expression "divinatory criticism" means. Schlegel goes even further, formulating a maxim that is contradicted, as he knows full well, by other fragments of the *Athenaeum*: namely, that the poet's arbitrariness is subject to no law.

Finally, sentence 14 relates directly to sentence 1, even as it takes up again a question that had been illuminated, in contradictory fashion, by sentences 2 and 10: is romantic poetry a genre among genres? The answer is neither yes nor no: insofar as romantic poetry is a generative principle, it is at the root of all poetry, and cannot therefore be enclosed within a genre; but at the same time, there exist works that embody this principle more successfully than others; and these make up what we commonly call the "romantic genre" (*die romantische Dichtart*). Whence the paradoxical but perfectly explicable phrase according to which this genre is not a genre.

Athenaeum 116 achieves something like the inverse of symphilosophy: rather than being the unique thought of several people, it is the plural affirmation of a single individual.

SYMBOL AND ALLEGORY

In 1801, when A. W. Schlegel presented the romantic doctrine in a systematic way, he made reference to the work published the previous year by his friend Schelling. That work in fact already contained the principles of romantic doctrine; Schlegel approved of it in its entirety and suggested only a terminological modification.

> According to Schelling, *the infinite represented in finite fashion* (III, 620) is beauty, a definition in which the sublime is already included, as it should be. I am in full agreement on this point, I should simply prefer to formulate this expression as follows: the beautiful is a symbolic representation of the infinite; for in this way we also see clearly how the infinite can appear in the finite. . . . How can the infinite be drawn to the surface, made to appear? Only symbolically, in images and signs. . . . Making poetry (in the broadest sense of the poetic that is at the root of all the arts) is nothing other than an eternal symbolizing. [*Die Kunstlehre*, pp. 81–82]

Without exaggerating, we could say that if we had to condense the romantic aesthetic into a single word, it would certainly be the word "symbol" as A. W. Schlegel introduces it here. The entire romantic aesthetic would then be, in the last analysis, a semiotic theory. Conversely, in order to understand the modern meaning of the word "symbol," it is necessary and sufficient to reread the romantic texts. Nowhere does the meaning of "symbol" appear so clearly as in the opposition between symbol and allegory—an opposition invented by the romantics and one that allows them to oppose themselves to all other viewpoints. I shall briefly examine the principal statements of this opposition.

Goethe

> The objects will be determined by a deep feeling which, when it is pure and natural, will coincide with the best and loftiest objects and will ultimately render them symbolic. The objects represented in this way appear to exist for themselves alone and are nevertheless significant at the deepest level, because of the ideal that always draws a certain generality along with it. If the symbolic points to something else beyond representation, it will always do so indirectly. . . . Today there are also works of art that sparkle by virtue of reason, wit, gallantry, and we include in this category all allegorical works as well; of these latter we expect the least, because they likewise destroy our interest in representation itself, and shove the spirit back upon itself, so to speak, and remove from its field of vision all that is truly represented. The allegorical differs from the symbolic in that what the latter designates indirectly, the former designates directly. [JA 33, 94]

This quotation comes from a brief article entitled *Über die Gegenstände der bildenden Kunst* (On the Objects of the Plastic Arts), written in 1797 but published a long time after Goethe's death. The passage marks the first time that Goethe has formulated the symbol/allegory opposition in a text intended for publication (even though this intention was not realized during the author's lifetime).

The prehistory of this opposition in Goethe's work is well known. Until 1790, the word "symbol" had a very different meaning from the one it was to acquire in the romantic era. Either it was simply synonymous with a series of other, more commonly used terms such as allegory, hieroglyph, figure (in the sense of number), emblem, and so on, or else it designated primarily the purely arbitrary and abstract sign (mathematical symbols). This second meaning was especially widespread among Leibnitzians, as for example with Christian Wolff. Kant is the one who reversed the usage, in the *Critique of Judgement*, and brought the word "symbol" very close to its modern meaning. Far from characterizing abstract reason, the symbol belongs to the intuitive and sense-based manner of apprehending things. "Notwithstanding the adoption of the word *symbolic* by modern logicians in a sense opposed to an *intuitive* mode of representation, it is a wrong use of the word and subversive of its true meaning; for the symbolic is only a *mode* of intuitive representation" (§59, p. 547).

Schiller, an immediate and attentive reader of Kant, adopted the new use of the word "symbol"; moreover, it was in Goethe's correspondence with Schiller, during the period that preceded the drafting of the brief article that interests us here, that Goethe began to use the word in its new meaning. (This is not to suggest that Kant, Schiller, and Goethe had the same view of the symbol, but only that their use of the term was uniformly opposed to that of earlier writers.) On the heels of this correspondence, Goethe decided to write a short text in collaboration with his friend Heinrich Meyer, the art historian; later, each wrote a separate piece under the same title, and only Meyer's was published.[9]

Whatever the role of Goethe's predecessors may have been in determining either the signifier or the signified of the word "symbol," the fact remains that, apart from Meyer's essay (to which we shall return), Goethe was the one who introduced the opposition between symbol and allegory.

In *Über die Gegenstände der bildenden Kunst*, this opposition appears at the end of the exposition. Goethe has already compared the respective merits of various objects from the point of view of the painter. He then moves on to consider the way these objects are treated (*die Behandlung*); it is here that the terms symbol and allegory appear. How do they differ?

Let us first identify their common feature: symbol and allegory

---

9. The genesis and structure of the symbol in Goethe's work are studied attentively by: J. I. Rouge, "Goethe et la notion du symbole," in *Goethe. Etudes publiées pour le centenaire de sa mort par l'Université de Strasbourg*, 1932, pp. 285–310; C. Müller, *Die geschichtliche Voraussetzungen des Symbolbegriffs in Goethes Kunstanschauung*, 1937, and "Der Symbolbegriff in Goethes Kunstanschauung," in *Goethe. Viermonatsschrift der Goethe-Gesellschaft*, 8 (1943); M. Marache, *Le Symbole dans la pensée et l'oeuvre de Goethe* (Paris, 1960), especially chapters vi and x: B. A. Sørensen, *Symbol und Symbolismus in der ästhetischen Theorien des 18. Jahrhunderts und der deutschen Romantik* (Copenhagen, 1963), chapter vii. Rouge's study provides a good overview; Sørensen's goes into more detail.

both allow us either to represent or to designate. By introducing a term that is not found, in fact, in Goethe's text, we might say that symbol and allegory are two types of signs.

The first difference between them arises, then, from the fact that in allegory there is an instantaneous passage through the signifying face of the sign toward knowledge of what is signified, whereas in the symbol this face retains its proper value, its opacity. Allegory is transitive, symbols are intransitive—but in such a way that they do not cease to signify for all that; the symbol's intransitivity, in other words, goes hand in hand with its syntheticism. Thus the symbol speaks to perception (along with intellection); the allegory in effect speaks to intellection alone. We should observe that Goethe identifies as the "represented" term what is for us the representing term (the perceptible object).

This particular mode of signification allows us to state a second difference. Allegory signifies directly; that is, its perceptible face has no reason for being save to transmit a meaning. Symbols signify only indirectly, in a secondary fashion: a symbol is present first of all for itself, and only in a secondary phase do we discover what it signifies. In the allegory, designation is primary; in the symbol, it is secondary. We might perhaps say, too, forcing Goethe's vocabulary somewhat, that the symbol represents and (potentially) designates; the allegory designates but does not represent.

A third difference can be deduced from something Goethe attributes to the symbol: it concerns the nature of the signifying relation. In the case of the symbol, this relation has a very specific character: it is a passage from the particular (the object) to the general (and to the ideal); in other words, for Goethe, symbolic signification necessarily belongs to the class of *examples,* that is, particular cases through which (but not in the place of which) we see, by transparency as it were, the general law of which each is the emanation. The symbolic is the exemplary, the typical, that which allows itself to be considered as the manifestation of a general law. In this way the value of the relation of participation is confirmed, for the romantic aesthetic, to the detriment of the relation of resemblance, which had reigned uncontested over the classical doctrines (most notably through the expedient of imitation). The signifying relation on which allegory is based is not specified for the time being.

A fourth and final difference lies in the mode of perception. In the case of the symbol, we encounter something of a surprise resulting from an illusion. One supposes at first that the symbol exists simply for itself; then one discovers that it also has a (secondary) meaning. As for allegory, Goethe insists upon its kinship with the other manifestations of reason (wit, gallantry). The opposition is not really articulated, and yet its presence is felt: reason is mistress in the one case but not in the other.

*

916. Such an application, coinciding entirely with nature, might be called symbolical, since the colour would be employed in conformity with its effect, and would at once express its meaning. If, for example, pure red were assumed to designate majesty, there can be no doubt that this would be admitted to be a just and expressive symbol. All this has been already sufficiently entered into.

917. Another application is nearly allied to this; it might be called the allegorical application. In this there is more of accident and caprice, inasmuch as the meaning of the sign must be first communicated to us before we know what it is to signify; what idea, for instance, is attached to the green colour, which has been appropriated to hope? [1808; JA 40, 116–117; Eng. trans., pp. 350–352]

These two short paragraphs appear in Goethe's *Theory of Colours* at the end of the didactic exposition, under the heading "Allegorical, Symbolical, Mystical Application of Colour." A third term, "mystical," is indeed present here, but it may be set aside, for "symbolic" and "allegorical" again share the quality of signification, which is not a determining one for the mystical use of color.

The opposition expressed in the passage quoted is a very simple one; the only surprise stems from the fact that it differs from the dichotomies set forth in *Über die Gegenstände der bildenden Kunst*. For this time it is a question of motivated and unmotivated signs, or of natural and arbitrary (conventional) signs. From this first difference a second follows: the signification of the symbol, being natural, is immediately comprehensible to all; that of the allegory, proceeding from an "arbitrary" convention, has to be learned before it can be understood. The categories of innate and acquired are superimposed here on those of universal and particular. The examples given are perhaps somewhat less convincing: is majesty more naturally inherent to red than hope to the color green? The fourth difference noted above reappears here in the background: the symbol produces an effect, and only by means of this effect does it signify; the allegory has a meaning that can be transmitted and learned. The role of reason thus seems once again to differ in the two instances.

*

Natural fire will be presented, subjected only to the most limited extent to an artistic purpose, and we are right to call such presentations symbolic. . . . It is the thing itself, without being the thing, and yet the thing; an image summarized in the mirror of the spirit and nevertheless identical with the object. How far behind allegory remains, in contrast: it may be full of wit, but it is in most instances nonetheless rhetorical and conventional, and its merit always increases to the extent that it comes closer to what we call symbol. [1820; WA 41–1, 142]

This text appears in a commentary on the paintings of Philostratus, and it is explicitly presented as a defense of the concept and the word "symbolic." Goethe takes as his example a painting (Saint Peter near the fire, the night of Jesus' arrest) which he describes as very "laconic"—and because of this quality no one would be so bold as to attribute allegorical character to it; on the other hand, it is symbolic. Let us look once again at the features that characterize the symbol as opposed to the allegory.

The first relates to the difference noted in our first text between direct and indirect designation: the fire that is represented is first of all a fire; if it also signifies something, it only does so at the extreme limit, in a second phase.

The second difference is also a familiar one: although endowed with signification, the symbol is intransitive. This paradoxical status is brought clearly to light by an equally paradoxical sentence: the symbol is the thing itself without being it even while being it (intransitivity again goes hand in hand with syntheticism). The symbolic object at once is and is not identical to itself. Allegory, on the other hand, is transitive, functional, utilitarian, without value in itself; this is doubtless what the adjective "rhetorical" means in this context.

A third already familiar difference: the allegory is conventional, and thus may be arbitrary, unmotivated. The symbol for its part is an image (*Bild*) and derives from the natural.

A fourth difference: allegory is "full of spirit"; the symbol has only an oblique relationship with the "mirror of the spirit." Here we recognize the rational character of allegory as opposed to the intuitive nature of the symbol.

Finally, in two places, Goethe insists on the laconic, condensed character of the symbol. What seems to be in question here is symbolic density, as opposed to discursive expansiveness: only a fire is represented, and it is the symbolic interpretation that adds new values to it. Allegory is less laconic in the sense that in it there is something like an obligation to interpret; expansiveness is almost as present as in explicit discourse.

Let us note that here, as in the preceding texts (the first one in particular), Goethe does not conceal his preference for the symbol.

> There is a great difference according to whether the poet is seeking access to the general through the particular or sees the general in the particular. From the first of these approaches, allegory is born; in this the particular has value solely as an example of the general. The second approach is nevertheless properly the nature of poetry: it states a particular without thinking on the basis of the general and indicating it. But the reader who immediately grasps this particular receives the general at the same time, without realizing it, or realizing it only later. [1822; JA 38, 261]

This is the best-known formulation of the opposition between symbol and allegory. It follows a comparison between Goethe himself and Schiller: the difference between the two concepts is also the difference between the two poets. One of the two opposed terms continues to be valorized here, not only because Goethe identifies with it, but also because poetry, all poetry, is or should be fundamentally symbolic. Let us note that the opposition is applied here for the first time to poetry and no longer to a visible substance.

The insistence on the passage from particular to general is stronger here; at the same time, it is more precise. Obligatory for the symbol, this passage is equally present in allegory: thus the two cannot be distinguished by the logical nature of the relationship between what symbolizes and what is symbolized, but on the basis of the mode of evocation of the general by the particular.

Goethe seems then to pay more attention to the process of production and reception of symbols and allegories. In a finished work, we are always dealing with a particular; and this particular can always evoke a general. But there is a difference in the creative process according to whether one begins with the particular and discovers the general in it after the fact (this is the case for the symbol), or whether one begins with the general and looks to it later for an embodiment of the particular. This difference in approach influences the work itself: one cannot separate the production from the product. Hence the most important opposition: in allegory, signification is obligatory ("direct," as the first text said) and the image present in the work is therefore transitive; with the symbol, the image present does not indicate in itself that it has another meaning; it is only "later" or unconsciously that we are led to the task of reinterpretation. Thus we have passed from the process of production, through the intermediary of the work itself, to that of reception: in the last analysis, the decisive difference seems to lie especially there, in the way we interpret; or, in Goethe's terms, the way we pass from a particular to a general.

Goethe is not affirming radically new ideas here with respect to the earlier texts, and yet he sheds new light by his rapid evocation of the author-work-reader trajectory, and especially by his insistence on the difference in psychic processes (of production and reception), rather than on the logical differences inherent in the work itself.

*

Allegory transforms the phenomenon into a concept, the concept into an image, but in such a way that the concept remains nevertheless still contained in the image so that it can be entirely held and possessed and expressed in it. The use of symbols transforms the phenomenon into an idea, the idea into an image, and in such a way that the idea still remains infinitely active and inaccessible in the image so that, even expressed in all languages, it remains inexpressible. [Nachlass; JA 35, 325–326]

This is Goethe's final maxim devoted to the symbol/allegory opposition; it was written in his old age. Here, as in the preceding text, attention is drawn to an ideal genesis. The analogies between the two notions remain strong, even stronger than in the preceding text, since the difference in approach (from particular to general in the symbol, from general to particular in allegory) now disappears; every production follows the particular-general-particular trajectory. There is always a concrete phenomenon at the beginning, then a phase of abstraction, before the image, equally concrete (and alone present in the finished work) is reached at the end. But from this point onward, differences develop. First, the degree of abstraction is not the same in the two instances: in allegory, the *concept*, belonging strictly to reason, is opposed to the *idea* in symbol—we may suppose that this "idea" is drawn by Kantian overtones toward a global and "intuitive" apprehension. This difference is important, and new: for the first time, Goethe affirms that symbol and allegory do not have identical content, are not just two vehicles for expressing "the same thing." To return to the initial distinction made in our first text, the difference no longer lies in the manner of dealing with the object but in the very object dealt with.

A second difference had been anticipated by the other texts, but had never found such a strong formulation: this is the difference between the expressible, in allegory, and the inexpressible (*Unaussprechliche*), in the symbol; it obviously depends upon the difference between concept and idea. It is paired with another, which is no more than its consequence and which leads us to the difference between production and product, between becoming and being: the meaning of the allegory is finite, that of the symbol is infinite, inexhaustible; or again: meaning is completed, ended, and thus in a sense dead in allegory; it is active and living in the symbol. Here again, the difference between symbol and allegory is fixed primarily by the task that the one and the other impose on the mind of the receiver, even if these differences in attitude are determined by properties of the work itself (which Goethe this time leaves unmentioned).

All these evocations of the symbol/allegory pair in Goethe's writing should be considered complementary rather than divergent; only when these statements are collated do we have the complete definition. As far as the symbol is concerned, we find the full panoply of characteristics accredited by the romantics: it is productive, intransitive, motivated; it achieves the fusion of contraries; it is and it signifies at the same time; its content eludes reason: it expresses the inexpressible. In contrast, allegory, obviously, is already made, transitive, arbitrary, pure signification, an expression of reason. To this romantic stereotype are added some more specific remarks. Rather than being distinguished by their logical forms (symbol and allegory alike designate the general through the intermediary of the particular), the two types of signifying reference are distinguished through the process of production and reception of which they are the end result or the point of departure: the symbol is produced unconsciously, and it provokes an unending task of interpretation; the allegory is intentional, and can be understood without "remainder." The interpretation of the symbol as representation of the typical is equally personal. Finally, there is a morphological difference, thus a particularly interesting one, between the direct and indirect character of designation (let us recall the importance of this difference for Clement of Alexandria and for Augustine); although present, it does not seem to play a primordial role for Goethe.

Schelling

Influenced by A. W. Schlegel's suggestion and doubtless by the spiritual proximity of Goethe, Schelling introduces the notion of symbol into his conceptual system as he presents it in his courses of 1802–1803, published after his death as *Philosophie der Kunst*. Still more significantly, his notion of the symbol, defined in opposition to allegory, occupies the highest position in the entire edifice as it is described in this work. To be more precise, the symbol/allegory pair appears in two places in the text, and it is not clear that the meaning of the term remains the same in these two contexts. It is thus preferable to examine them separately.

The word "symbol" first appears not in an opposition to allegory but within a three-term series: schematic, allegorical, symbolic. Here again, it is imperative to recall the Kantian usage of certain terms. We have seen that Kant was responsible for the reversal in meaning of the word "symbol": in the same paragraph of the *Critique of Judgement*, he opposes the symbolic to the schematic (a term that had appeared in the *Critique of Pure Reason*).

> All *hypotyposis* (presentation, *subjectio sub adspectum*) as a rendering in terms of sense, is twofold. Either it is *schematic*, as where the intuition corresponding to a concept comprehended by the understanding is given *a priori*, or else it is *symbolic*, as where the concept is one which only reason can think, and to which no sensible intuition can be adequate. In the latter case the concept is supplied with an intuition such that the procedure of judgement in dealing with it is merely analogous to that which it observes in schematism. [§59, p. 547]

Schemas and symbols have something in common, beyond the fact that they signify: they are hypotyposes, or presentations,

that is, units whose perceptible component is not purely transparent and indifferent, as it is in the case of characters, words, or
algebraic signs; in other words, these are motivated signs, as opposed to the other, unmotivated signs, in which this same perceptible component is "devoid of any intrinsic connection with
the intuition of the object" (ibid.). This first, common property
serves to oppose them better in other respects: the schematic
signified can be adequately expressed, consequently its designation is direct; the symbolic signified, on the other hand, such as
an aesthetic idea, does not have an adequate designation, a "sensible intuition" appropriate to it; it can only be evoked indirectly,
by analogy with some other schematization. The expressible goes
hand in hand with the direct, the ineffable with the indirect, and
thus with the symbol.

Schelling combines the two oppositions, in a way—Kant's
schematic/symbolic opposition, Goethe's allegorical/symbolic one
—and he obtains a three-term series. But the content of the words
has changed. Schelling's definitions depend much more upon
logic than do those of his predecessors: the difference between
the three notions results from the combination of two fundamental categories, the general and the particular.

> That representation (*Darstellung*) in which the general signi-
> fies the particular, or in which the particular is apprehended
> through the general, is the *schematic*. That representation, how-
> ever, in which the particular signifies the general, or in which
> the general is apprehended through the particular, is *allegorical*.
> The synthesis of the two, in which the general does not signify
> the particular nor does the particular signify the general, but in
> which the two are absolutely one, is the *symbolic*. [v, 407]

Schematicism has become the designation of the particular by
means of the general. The most common case of schematicism is
obviously language: words, always general, are nonetheless capable of designating individual realities. Schelling cites another
example: the artisan who fashions an object according to a design
or an idea achieves the same relationship between the general
and the particular.

Conversely, allegory is the designation of the general by means
of the particular. This use of the word is new with respect to the
earlier tradition, in which the relationship between the two terms
of allegory, when it is specified at all, is one of resemblance, and

thus links two particulars. Even in the eighteenth century, in his treatise on fables (*Fabeln*, 1759), Lessing contrasted the *allegory*, the designation of a particular by another particular, to the *example*, the designation of the general by a particular. Schelling's "allegory" is thus closer to what Lessing called example (and, of course, to Goethe's allegory) than to classical allegory. Schelling adds that there is a difference between the allegorical text and the allegorical reading: one can read any book at all allegorically. "The charm of Homeric poetry and of all mythology rests in truth on the fact that it also contains allegorical signification as a *possibility*—it would indeed be possible also to allegorize everything. Upon this rests the infinite meaning in Greek mythology" (v. 409).

As for the symbol, it is characterized by the fusion of two contraries, the general and the particular, or, to use Schelling's favorite formula, by the fact that the symbol does not simply signify, but also *is*: in other words, by the intransitivity of that which symbolizes. In the symbol, "the finite is at the same time the infinite itself, and does not merely signify it" (v, 452–453). "An image is symbolic whose object does not merely signify the idea but is that idea *itself*" (v, 554–555). The examples studied all point in the same direction: "We must not say, for example, that Jupiter or Minerva *signify* or *must* signify that. In so doing we would have canceled out all the poetic independence of these figures. They do not signify, they *are* the thing itself" (v, 400–401). And, elsewhere: "Thus Mary Magdalen does not only *signify* repentance, but is living repentance itself. Thus the image of Saint Cecilia, the patron saint of music, is not an allegorical image but a symbolic one, since it exists independently of signification without losing its signification" (v, 555).

It is evident that, even if he repeats Moritz in this insistence on the heterotelism of allegory and the autotelism of the symbol ("what is not for itself but for another *signifies* that other," he writes later, v, 566), Schelling never loses sight of the fact that the symbol is and *at the same time* signifies (whereas Moritz tended to say that it is *instead of* signifying). In this the symbol differs from the image, the sensible perception of which may leave no residue.

We are not content, it is true, with the purely nonsignifying being, the one rendered, for example, by the pure image, nor is pure signification any better; we want what must be the object of an absolute artistic representation to be so concrete that it is equal to itself like the image, and at the same time as general and charged with meaning as the concept; that is why the German language renders the word "symbol" by *Sinnbild*, meaningful image. [v, 411–412]

Defined in this way, the symbol coincides in its extension with art, or in any case with the essence of art. "Thought is pure schematicism; all action, on the contrary, is allegorical (for it signifies a general as a particular); art is symbolic" (v, 411).

At the same time, the symbolic coincides with the beautiful: "Based on these observations, we can reduce all the requirements of the painting in the symbolic style to one, namely, that everything is subordinated to beauty, for beauty is always symbolic" (v, 558).

The assimilation of symbol and mythology is more forceful still (it is in this context that Schelling recognizes his debt to Moritz). "In allegory, the particular does no more than *signify* the general; in mythology, it *is* at the same time itself the general" (v, 409). "This entire investigation leads to a necessary consequence: mythology in general, and each of its poetic texts in particular, are not to be grasped either schematically or allegorically, but *symbolically*" (p. 411). "The requirement of a mythology is thus rightly *not* that its symbols simply signify ideas, but that they be beings that signify for themselves, that they be independent" (p. 447).

As with the symbol in general, in the case of mythology Schelling insists particularly on the paradoxical side of his definition: mythology is *at once* general and particular, it is *and* it signifies; even more, it signifies only because it is:

Each figure in mythology is to be taken for what it is, for it is precisely in this way that it will be taken for what it signifies. The signifying here is at the same time the being itself, it has passed into the object, being one with it. No sooner do we allow these beings to *signify* something than they are *no longer anything* themselves. . . . Indeed, their greatest attraction lies in the fact that, whereas they only *are*, without any relation, absolute in themselves, they still allow signification to shine through. [v, p. 411]

Such is the first meaning Schelling attributes to the terms "symbol" and "allegory." This meaning appears in paragraph 39 of the *Philosophie der Kunst* and the terms retain this same meaning in other passages. There exists, however, one other lengthy discussion of these two notions; it arises in connection with painting.

First, the schematic-allegorical-symbolic triad is reduced to two terms, owing to the fact that in art one perceives only the particular, and thus can never start from the general. "Either figurative art causes the general to be signified through the particular, or else the latter, even while signifying the former, *is* at the same time the general. The first type of representation is *allegorical*, the second *symbolic*" (v, 549).

The words "symbolic" and "allegorical" have the same meaning here they had earlier, but this soon changes. In fact, in his concrete analysis of symbolic and allegorical painting, Schelling seems to start from an old opposition, one characteristic of Stoic hermeneutics: the opposition between literal or historical meaning and allegorical meaning. "Symbolic painting coincides wholly with what is called historical painting, it simply designates its superior power. . . . According to our explanation, the historical itself is no more than a species of the symbolic" (v, 555). As for allegory, it is subdivided according to categories that are equally familiar to the old hermeneutics: "In paintings, the allegory may be physical, and have to do with natural objects, or moral, or historical" (v, 552).

This last allegory is not the same as the one evoked in the earlier texts; the examples chosen make this clear, for they no longer illustrate a relation between a particular and a general entity, but rather, as in the ancient view of allegory, a relation between two particulars. Here is an example of physical allegory: "The Nile and its flood-stage, sixteen feet high, signifying great fertility according to the ancients, would be reproduced by that number of children, seated at the foot of the colossal figure" (v, 552). And an example of historical allegory (the word "historical" here has acquired a meaning different from the one it has in the expression "historical meaning," or literal meaning): "The rebirth of a city through the favor of a prince will be represented on ancient coins by a feminine body raised above the earth by a masculine body" (v, 554). Now the river and the children, the city and the human body are so many particular entities; they can be related only through resemblance, and no longer through exemplification.

A passage from this second section, which is devoted to allegory (and to the symbol), illustrates the change in meaning particularly well. Schelling seems to distinguish between an allegory in the loose sense, corresponding to his first definition (in which the particular designates the general), and an allegory in the strong sense, one which is limited (in a much looser fashion, in my view) to marking the difference between that which designates and that which is designated. Curiously, it is precisely on this occasion that Schelling calls up (as Kant did) another classical theory, the one opposing motivated and unmotivated signs.

> By and large, allegory can be compared to a *general* language which, unlike specific languages, is based not on arbitrary signs but on natural signs, signs that are objectively valid. Allegory is the signification of ideas through real and concrete images, that is why the language of art, and of figurative art in particular, which according to the expression of an ancient writer is mute poetry, has to present its thoughts personally, as it were, by means of figures. But the strong concept of allegory, which we presuppose here as well, is that what is represented signifies something other than itself, points to something different from itself. [v, 549]

It is striking to observe that, once he has begun to undertake concrete analyses, Schelling returns to an earlier meaning—and thus, in his own context, a banal one—of the opposition between allegory and symbol (even though the latter term had not been employed in this sense previously). It remains true nonetheless that his use of these words to link his own thought to the whole of the romantic tradition is in fact the first such use, and it is the one that he developed in the general part of his work.

Others

The first writer to have publicly contrasted symbol and allegory was not Kant (who did not refer to allegory in the passages in which he redefined the symbol), nor Schiller (who only reflected on it in his letters to Goethe), nor Goethe (who kept the text that he had devoted to the subject locked up in a drawer), nor Schelling (who did not publish the *Philosophie der Kunst* in his lifetime), but Heinrich Meyer, art historian and friend of Goethe. In 1797, the year in which Goethe drafted his first presentation of the dichotomy, Meyer published an essay with the same title, *Über die Gegenstände der bildenden Kunst*, an essay apparently inspired by the discussions he was having with Goethe. Even if we cannot attribute the paternity of this essay to Goethe, we can understand why Meyer did not play an essential role in the history of these two concepts: he used the words quite uncritically, and he made no effort to specify exactly where the difference between them lay. The following passages from his essay contain the texts most closely resembling definitions:

> We call purely allegorical the objects that hide an important and profound truth under the surface of the poetic, historical, or symbolic image, objects that reason discovers only after sense, satisfied, expects nothing more. . . . In the symbolic images of divinities, or their properties, figurative art elaborates its loftiest objects, it forces ideas and concepts themselves to make their appearance in a perceptible way, it requires them to enter into space, to take shape and to present themselves to the eye. [*Kleine Schriften*, pp. 14, 20]

In the symbol, it is the signified itself that has become a signifier; the two faces of the sign have merged. In allegory, on the other hand, the two faces are quite distinct: first, we contemplate what is perceptible; then, once the senses find nothing more, reason intervenes and discovers a meaning independent of these perceptible images. Let us note, however, that the relations Meyer evokes are the opposite of those we found in Goethe (in a text that appeared more than twenty years later, to be sure): here, it is allegory that moves from the particular to the general (from "image" to "truth"), and symbols that move from the general to the particular (from "ideas" and "concepts" to what can be seen). Meyer's lack of attention to the opposition is underlined by the fact that, in the first sentence quoted, which is nevertheless almost a definition of allegory, the word "symbol" appears in a nontechnical sense.

Another of Meyer's formulas attracted more attention from his contemporaries, but it was not written until some ten years later. In order to explain the opposition between symbol and allegory, he had recourse to the opposition between "to be" and "to signify," one that Schelling used in the same way, as we have seen. The connection between these two verbs is even older and better established. In a letter to Meyer himself dated March 13, 1791, Goethe wrote the following ("allegory" designates here what he later calls "symbol"): "As far as invention is concerned, it seems to me that you have drawn the fine line that allegory should not cross. These are figures signifying the whole, but they do not signify any more than they show, and—I shall be so bold as to say—than they are." Meanwhile, in 1800, Herder too had written in *Kalligone* that musical tones "do not merely signify but also are." Here now is Meyer's text on symbol and allegory (which he criticizes Winckelmann for not distinguishing):

> [Symbols] have no other relation but are really what they represent: Jupiter, image of the greatest dignity in unlimited power . . . , Venus, woman created for love, and so forth; thus features of the highest sort, or general concepts incarnated by art; such representations are called symbols, as opposed to what are properly called allegories. . . . Symbolic representation is the general concept itself, rendered perceptible; allegorical representation signifies only a general concept different from itself.
> ["Notes" for the edition of Winckelmann's *Werke*, pp. 684–685]

The symbol is, the allegory signifies; the first fuses signifier and signified, the second separates them.

Between Meyer's two texts, another formulation appears; this one derives not from Goethe but from Schelling. Friedrich Ast's *System der Kunstlehre* (Method of Art Instruction), published in 1805, contains what we might call a schematic and dogmatic presentation of Schelling's (as yet unpublished) aesthetics. The distinction that follows is part of a passage in which Ast opposes nature and art, by way of the category of transitivity: "The particular product of the universe is only an allegory of the absolute, that is, it is connected to the absolute and signifies the whole without representing it, thus without representing an absolute; the work of art, on the contrary, is a symbol of the absolute, that is, it is at once a signification and a representation of the absolute" (p. 6).

Ast has rediscovered, no doubt unwittingly, the terms Diderot had used to oppose poetic and utilitarian uses of language: in the first, we signify and represent at the same time; in the second, we stop at signification. By referring to the ideas that Ast developed elsewhere on the nature of the work of art or even on discourse in general, we can readily interpret this distinction. The relationship between the perceptible and the intelligible is motivated in the case of symbol, unmotivated in the case of allegory; this in turn relates to the greater or lesser coherence among the various levels of a work (a question with which, as we saw earlier, Ast was particularly concerned).

Another author who dealt with the same problem in this peri-

od is Wilhelm von Humboldt. His discussion of the relation between symbol and allegory appears at the end of an essay devoted to the Greek state. Humboldt inquires into the forms of art
proper to the Greeks (I omit his examples):

> The concept of symbol is not always correctly understood, and
> it is often confused with that of allegory. It is true that in both
> cases an invisible idea is expressed by a visible figure, but [this
> comes about] very differently in the two instances. . . . [In] true
> and authentic symbols, . . . whereas they begin with simple
> and natural objects, . . . they end up with ideas that were
> unfamiliar to them at the outset, ideas even that remain per-
> petually inaccessible in themselves, unless they are stripped, if
> only in a tiny measure, of their individuality and their proper
> nature. . . . For it is a property of the symbol that the represen-
> tation and what is represented, in constant mutual exchange,
> incite and constrain the mind to linger longer and to penetrate
> more deeply, whereas allegory, on the contrary, once the idea
> to be transmitted has been found, like an enigma resolved,
> produces only a cold admiration of, or a mild satisfaction with,
> the gracefully executed figure. [III, 216–218]

Like Goethe in this respect, Humboldt does not forget the
characteristics that symbol and allegory have in common: as Kant
would say, they are presentations, or hypotyposes. But Humboldt
stresses the differences. He characterizes allegory in a more succinct fashion: it is, on the one hand, arbitrary, in the sense, probably, of unmotivated; on the other hand, it has a finite sense,
which is stated exhaustively. The symbol is not described as motivated, but one can deduce that it is indeed motivated from the
fact that it is opposed to allegory. Whereas the meaning of allegory is a completed product, the symbol manifests a simultaneity
between the process of production and its end result: meaning
exists only at the moment it comes into being. Likewise, the
closed character of allegorical meaning is opposed to the inexhaustible signifying process characteristic of the symbol; for this
very reason, the symbol is capable of expressing the inexpressible. Moreover, the symbolizing and symbolized faces are in constant interpenetration; in other words, the symbolizer signifies,
but does not, for all that, cease to *be*.

Humboldt's text warrants special attention. At a time when,
even if he were reading the unpublished writings of his contemporaries he would have discovered in them only simple opposi-

tions between symbol and allegory, he produced a description that synthesized all the categories characterizing the romantic doctrine of art: the symbol is at once production, intransitivity, motivation, syntheticism, and expression of the inexpressible; furthermore, the difference between the two notions lies in the attitudes that the objects of interpretation evoke rather than in the objects themselves. Let us keep in mind, too, his affirmation of a ceaseless mutual exchange between symbolizer and symbolized.

It is interesting to note that, some fifteen years later (in 1822), when Humboldt is dedicating himself exclusively to his work on language, he uses the same opposition again, but with different terms: it is no longer a question of symbol and allegory, but of art and language. It is art, this time, that fuses the perceptible and the intelligible, whereas language separates them; art is natural, whereas language is arbitrary. Witness the following:

> From one angle, language . . . is comparable to art, for, just as art does, language tends to represent the invisible in a perceptible fashion. . . . But from another angle, language is to a certain extent opposed to art, for it is considered only to be a means of representation, whereas art, abolishing reality and idea inasmuch as these latter present themselves separately, puts its work in their place. From that more limited property of language as sign arise other differences in nature between the two. A language shows more marks of usage and convention, manifests more arbitrariness; whereas art bears in itself more of nature. [IV, 433]

Creuzer and Solger

The ideas presented in the texts that we have just been surveying are, it is clear, wholly indebted to the aesthetic doctrine of the romantics. Such is not the case with our last two authors, Friedrich Creuzer and K. W. F. Solger. It is true that more than ten years separate them from the *Athenaeum* period. Both men move in the shadow of the romantics and take up some of their ideas unaltered. But each makes an original contribution, if not to the doctrine in general, then at least to the articulation of the opposition and to the meaning of the two terms, symbol and allegory.

Creuzer needs the distinction between the two notions, as he needs many other distinctions, for his own use in a massive construction dedicated to the mythology of ancient peoples; the title of his work begins, significantly, with the words *Symbolik und My-thologie*. Creuzer actively participates in the revalorization of myth and in the establishment of the sign/symbol, or logos/mythos, dichotomy; in another work he even speaks of the Orient as a "symbolic world," and of the Occident as a "syllogistic world." In the introduction to *Symbolik und Mythologie der alten Völker* (1810), he defines the two terms that interest us, as well as several others, in the context of a general tableau of "iconism." He attributes to the symbol many properties that are familiar to us: it is an "expression of the infinite" (pp. 57, 62), of the "limitless" (p. 63), that which signifies and at the same time is, whereas the allegory only signifies (p. 70), and so on. But Creuzer's original contribution is to relate the category of time to the symbol/allegory couple. Here is how he characterizes metaphor, which is for him a subspecies of the symbol: "The essential property of this form of representation is that it produces something that is one and indivisible. What analytic and synthetic reason bring together in a sequential series as individual features, with the objective of developing a concept, this other manner of apprehending gives as a whole and at the same time. It is a single glance; the intuition is achieved all at once" (p. 57).

The general opposition between symbol and allegory is in harmony with the instantaneous character of metaphor. (In another passage Creuzer compares the symbol to "lightning that in one stroke illuminates the somber night" [p. 59], and this formula closely recalls one of Schelling's expressions, which appears in the then-unpublished *Philosophie der Kunst*. "In the lyric poem, just as in tragedy, metaphor often acts only in the manner of a bolt of lightning that suddenly illuminates a dark place, which is swallowed up again by night. In the epic, metaphor lives in itself, and becomes in its turn a little epic" [v, 654]. Creuzer writes:

> The difference between the two forms [symbol and allegory] has to be situated in the instantaneousness that allegory lacks. An idea is exposed in the symbol in an instant, and entirely, and it reaches all the forces of our soul. It is a ray that falls straight from the obscure depth of being and thought into our eyes, and that traverses our whole nature. Allegory leads us to respect and to follow the steps taken by the thought hidden in the image. In the one, there is instantaneous totality; in the other, progression in a series of moments. That is why allegory, but not symbol, includes myth, to which the epic in progres-

sion is most perfectly suited, and which tends to be condensed into symbolism only in the god-myth, as we shall see further on. Thus there is an important truth in the fact that certain rhetoricians used to call allegory the realization or, so to speak, the deployment of one and the same image (trope, metaphor, and so on); for that realization and conduct of the image is in general an innate penchant of allegory. [Pp. 70–71]

Allegory is successive, the symbol simultaneous. The reference to the ancient rhetoricians is misleading. Creuzer evokes Quintilian's opposition between metaphor and allegory, the latter being defined as extended metaphor. But the duration of which Quintilian speaks resides in the linguistic signifier (several words instead of one), whereas the one to which Creuzer refers visibly concerns the psychic activity of comprehension and interpretation. Creuzer's use of the terms "allegory" and "symbol" is different both from that of the classical authors and from the way his contemporaries combine several categories within a single notion: for Schelling, for example, as, I think, for us all, myth goes hand in hand with symbol (not with allegory), in that both tend toward literalism; more generally, it is allegory that suspends time, imposing an atemporal interpretation, whereas the symbol belongs with narrative, thus with temporal development. We can see clearly, however, where Creuzer's conclusions come from: not from the teachings of classical rhetoric, but from the accentuation of other characteristics of symbol and allegory. The symbol's instantaneity is linked with the stress placed in the symbol on the process of production, with the fusion between the symbolizer and the symbolized, with the inability of reason to analyze and express the symbolized in any other way. To the romantic repertory Creuzer added a category that had occurred to no one before, but one that is encountered again in twentieth-century aesthetics (it has been brought back to life by Walter Benjamin in particular).

Let us move on, finally, to Solger. The symbol is the principal notion of his aesthetics; it is coextensive with the beautiful and thus with art, and is opposed only to other signifying relations, such as the sign, the image, or the schema. The symbol, in this sense of the word, is characterized by several familiar features: activity rather than work, an intransitive rather than an instrumental entity, it achieves the fusion of contraries, in this instance the spiritual and the material, the general and the particular, being and signifying. But within this symbolism-in-general it is possible to distinguish several forms, which Solger calls, somewhat disconcertingly, symbol and allegory. It is this opposition between symbol in the narrow sense and allegory that we shall examine here.

The simplest way to explain the meaning Solger gives these terms would be to say that he projects the distinction between classics and romantics, as it is found, for example, in A. W. Schlegel, onto the distinction between symbol and allegory— which becomes its fundamental mode of expression.[10] This projection is assumed by Solger himself, for he writes: "Allegory reigns in Christian art. . . . In ancient art, on the other hand, the symbol reigns [what follows this clause already hints at the content of the opposition] in which the unity that allegory dissolves remains undissolved" (Erwin, p. 301). And in a more complex passage: "Just as, in the spirit of ancient art, essence and manifestation are always already unified symbolically in activity itself, so they are found here [in modern art] in an allegorical opposition that cannot be mediated save through the Witz, which brings together the separate relations of things and in so doing surmounts their isolated character" (ibid., p. 376).

10. Just like Solger, Hegel will seek, in his Ästhetik, to establish solidarities between the typology of forms (symbol, allegory) and historical periods (classical, romantic). But symbol and allegory are not directly contrasted in his work; that is why his doctrine does not really have a place in the present study.

For the historical periods we now have three terms, not just two. The classical period is still defined as it was by A. W. Schlegel, but the opposing category is subdivided into two, according to whether form or idea predominates. Only the latter variety is termed "romantic" by Hegel; when the association of the perceptible and the intelligible is dissolved to the benefit of form, it is called "symbolic"—a misleading term in this context. This triad would thus bring Hegel—passing over Solger and A. W. Schlegel—closer to their common source, Schelling. The two systems could be made to correspond as follows: Schelling, schematism-symbol-allegory; Hegel, symbolic-classical-romantic.

As for the forms (which appear as a subdivision of one of the varieties of symbolic art; but can Hegel be held responsible for this difficult articulation?), he posits another triad, exactly analogous to the first, consisting of enigma, allegory, and image. Thus the following equivalences are established: enigma-symbolic, image-classical, allegory-romantic (this third is also found in Solger).

The most general opposition found in Hegel, the one that plays a role comparable to that of the symbol/allegory pair for the romantics, is that between symbol and sign. The symbol (which seems to be widely separated from the "symbolic" as a period) is defined as being motivated and not necessary (secondary). But we cannot equate Goethe's allegory with Hegel's sign.

Whether we limit ourselves to the words or closely examine the concepts, we have to recognize that, although his Ästhetik is inspired by romantic ideas, Hegel does not take up the symbol/allegory opposition.

Symbol and allegory are characterized by the reunion of contraries. But this reunion may have diverse modalities, as we have known ever since Greek art was contrasted with Christian art (or even, in Schelling's work, nature contrasted with art): the contraries may be harmoniously fused or they may be present together in their essential irreducibility. Unity may be abolished or maintained, just as it may be conscious or not. *Witz* comes to play a role here that I shall not be able to spell out in detail: in the case of allegory, thus precisely in the case of an irreducible and in a sense hopeless copresence of contraries, it comes to offer a means of releasing tension or, as Solger says, of sublation (*Aufhebung*): allegory is a negation of a negation.

From this first characteristic, a second follows, one that no longer involves the syntheticism belonging to allegory and symbol alike, but the fact of being in a perpetual state of becoming. Both are in this state; but as allegory is rather a rending and the symbol a harmony, the former is situated ahead of the latter, in a sense, and thus remains closer to pure becoming, whereas the symbol turns out to be drawn toward the result to which the process leads (thus a temporal dimension is introduced once again).

> The allegory contains the same things as the symbol; however, in allegory we grasp better the idea's functioning, which is already brought to fulfillment in the symbol. . . . When we consider the symbol [in the broad sense] from the point of view of activity, we recognize in it, in particular, (1) all action as exhausted in it, thus as being itself object or matter, in which however it is still perceived as action. This is symbol in the narrow sense. We recognize (2) the beautiful as matter grasped while still in action, as a moment of the activity, which is still related to both sides. This is allegory. [*Vorlesungen*, pp. 131, 129]

The contraries, the becoming, are present in both cases; but the duality is stronger in allegory, more harmoniously absorbed in the symbol. Or, as it is expressed in another formula, activity is tinged with matter in allegory, matter is tinged with activity in the symbol (ibid.)

The opposition *between* symbol and allegory thus comes about, in Solger's case, with the aid of categories familiar to the romantic aesthetic, but ones that ordinarily serve to characterize the romantic symbol alone. For this reason the depreciation of allegory—

obligatory for Goethe, Schelling, Ast, Humboldt et al—disappears, since allegory now shares the qualities of the symbol, in the broad sense—and possesses them sometimes even to a higher degree than does the symbol in the narrow sense. Comparable to Creuzer in this respect, Solger explicitly affirms the equal rights of symbol and allegory: "The two forms have the same rights, and neither is unconditionally preferable to the other" (*Vorlesungen*, p. 134): he is content simply to attribute to each one a sphere of action in which it would be more appropriate than the other. "The symbol has the great advantage of being capable of rendering anything as a perceptible presence, for it pulls together the whole idea into one point of the manifestation. . . . But allegory has infinite advantages for more profound thought. It can grasp the real object as pure thought without losing it as object" (pp. 134–135).

Many other authors dealt with symbol and allegory between 1797 and 1827 (the approximate date of Goethe's last fragment); but I shall stop here. If we agree to recognize the principal features of the romantic aesthetic in the few categories I have enumerated above—production, intransitivity, coherence, syntheticism, expression of the inexpressible—we shall also recognize that the notion of symbol is opposed to that of allegory by virtue of one or the other of these same categories, and thus that in this single notion is concentrated the whole, or at least the major tendencies, of the romantic aesthetic.

7

Language and Its Doubles

The goddess of knowledge does not smile
upon those who neglect the ancients.

Bhartrhari

Augustine recognized the existence of proper and transposed signs; the rhetoricians used to speak of proper and figurative meaning; the romantic aesthetic separated allegory from symbol. As we have seen, these dichotomies do not coincide with one another; however, they all bear witness to an awareness of the difference between several forms that are (sometimes) brought together under the general heading of signs. At the same time, it rarely suffices to note that signs are diverse: as soon as the opposition is formulated, and even before it is formulated, it is accorded much credit. One form of such accreditation, a particularly influential one in the tradition of the social sciences, will be our concern in the present chapter.

In fact, the existence of signs and symbols (for the moment I will adopt these labels for the two major forms of evocation of meaning) provokes two contradictory attitudes with astonishing frequency: on the one hand, in practice, signs are constantly being changed into symbols, and countless symbols are grafted onto each sign; on the other hand, theoretical declarations assert endlessly that everything is sign, that the symbol does not, or should not, exist.

The more intense the symbolizing activity, the more it secretes this antibody, this metasymbolic assertion according to which we have no knowledge of the symbol. All due allowances being made, just as people have been unwilling to admit that the earth is not the center of the universe, or that man is descended from animals, or that reason is not the sole master of human action, they contend that language is the sole mode of representation and that this language is made up solely of signs, in the restricted sense—thus of logic, thus of reason. More precisely, as it is difficult to ignore the symbol altogether, we declare that we—normal adult males of the contemporary West—are exempt from the weaknesses linked to symbolic thought, and that the latter exists only among the *others*: animals, children, women, the insane, poets (those harmless lunatics), savages, our ancestors—who, in turn, know no form of thought but this. As a result, a curious situation exists: men have described their symbols for centuries, but they have done so by claiming to be observing the signs of others. It is as if a vigilant censor had authorized us to speak of the symbolic only if we were to use borrowed words such as "insanity," "childhood," "savages," "prehistory." A taboo that is territorial (savages), temporal (hominoids and children), biological (animals and women), or ideological (the insane and artists) has prevented us from admitting the symbolic into our lives and especially into our language. It is my thesis that descriptions of the "uncivilized" (*sauvage*) sign (that of others) are uncivilized descriptions of the symbol (our own).

Such a situation implies a double reaction.

First, it can be shown that our thinking uses the same mechanisms as that of "primitives" or of people who are "sick." The more closely this task touches our own habits, the more difficult it is to accomplish; nevertheless, it has begun with the exposure of a series of "centrisms": ethnocentrism, anthropocentrism, adultocentrism (the word is Piaget's), logocentrism. As a parallel development, we can become accustomed to identifying the supposedly primitive mechanisms in our own thinking. I should like to give two examples here, chosen in preference to others because they are situated in the very chains of reasoning according to which our thinking knows only signs, and the *other* only symbols!

The first comes from Lucien Lévy-Bruhl. His original characterization of the "primitive mentality," while winning many adherents, had provoked some protests concerning the use of the words "primitive," "prelogical," "participation," "mystical." For nearly thirty years, Lévy-Bruhl was obliged to account at length, in introductions and conclusions, for the way he used these words. "Primitive" did not mean *primitive,* it was only a conventional label; "mystical" did not signify *mystical,* but belief in the real existence of invisible things. . . . Yet he never agreed to replace these *words* (arbitrary ones, according to his own doctrine, which contrasts Western languages and primitive languages on this point) with others. Maurice Leenhardt writes in the preface to the *Notebooks on Primitive Mentality*: "Is it not this same reason, the novelty of his work at the time, which explains the choice of the term 'mystical' in his vocabulary, despite its inadequacy and despite even that it was not acceptable to him? If it should be suggested to him that the term 'mystical' be withdrawn and 'mythical' used instead, he opposed it with his gentle smile."[1]

But Lévy-Bruhl's readers were right. Dozens of explanatory pages did not suffice to convince them that the meaning Lévy-Bruhl had ascribed to the word "mystical" and the ordinary meaning had nothing in common. Concerning names among primitive peoples, Lévy-Bruhl wrote: "In our eyes, naming an object in no way modifies it, and an arbitrarily established homonymy would be unable to produce any real effect. It is totally different with primitive peoples. The name, an essential appurtenance, being the thing itself, homonymy is equivalent to identity."[2] But this is exactly how his readers reacted, readers for whom the homonymy of the two "mysticals" was equivalent to identity or at least to kinship. What is more, this is actually how he reacted himself, for otherwise why would he have insisted on retaining the word even though he was not satisfied with it? In his *Notebooks*, he gives up speaking of prelogic and of the principle of noncontradiction among primitive peoples, but he remains quite as blind as ever to the mechanisms that govern our own thought. Referring to his examples, he writes of the one "which has most struck readers, the Bororo-parrot (Bororo-Araras) duality" (p. 66), but he does not

1. Trans. P. Rivière (New York, 1975), p. xviii.
2. *L'Expérience mystique et les symboles chez les primitifs* (Paris, 1938), p. 236.

notice that this example was so successful not because of its logical singularity but because of the perfectly analogous phonic construction of the two words, Bororo and Araras . . .

The other example is from Jean Piaget. The famous psychologist described the abundance of symbols in the child, of signs in the adult. He showed that, grafted onto the symbol, there occurs a type of reasoning that, following Clara and William Stern, he called "transduction" (as opposed to induction and deduction) and which is defined as "inference that is non-regulated (non-necessary) because it bears on schemas which are still half-way between the individual and the general."[3] Thus, for the child Jacqueline, a hunchbacked boy who has the flu should no longer be hunchbacked when he has recovered from the flu: illnesses are directly assimilated to each other without passing through the general class of illnesses, in which one would distinguish the condition that produced the hump from the others. Now when Piaget looks at the evolution of the semiotic function, he affirms the abundance of "symbols" in the child, their near-absence in the adult, and concludes: "Would it not be legitimate to think of what Saussure called the 'sign' as having evolved from what he called the 'symbol'?"[4]

Let us leave aside the question of whether it is true that "analytic signs" predominate in the adult, or that the sign has its origin in the symbol (something that Piaget explicitly denies elsewhere); let us focus on the form of reasoning alone. A particular property of the symbol (it is less frequent) allows Piaget to infer from it another property (it evolves into a sign). It is as if we were to observe that there was "more" music than painting in the nineteenth century, and vice versa in the twentieth, and were to conclude that music evolved into painting. Here is a fine example of "transduction"—but we find it in the thinking of an adult (Piaget), whereas this thinking ought to have at its disposal only "analytic signs" and therefore correct deductions!

Our first task thus consists in identifying the mechanisms of "symbolic thought" in those who claim to have none. A second, complementary task will focus on reinterpreting the descriptions that have been given, allegedly, of "primitive mentality" or of "original language." Descriptions that are not necessarily false but

3. *Play, Dreams, and Imitation in Childhood*, trans. C. Gattegno and F. M. Hodgson (New York, 1962), p. 248.
4. *Structuralism*, trans. C. Maschler (New York, 1970), p. 97.

that have misidentified their object: in the belief that they were discovering the *other* sign, they have often described *our own* symbol.

We must in fact be suspicious of any excessive reaction against the idea of a "primitive mentality" that would reject not only the obligatory implantation of that "mentality" in others but also the very existence of anything other than the sign and its logic. Returning to look at an affirmation that, at the end of his life, he considered erroneous, Lévy-Bruhl wrote in his *Notebooks*: "The logical structure of the mind is the same in all known human societies, just as they all have a language, customs and institutions; accordingly, to speak no longer of the 'prelogical' character and to say explicitly why I renounce this term and everything which it seems to imply . . ." (p. 49). The structure of the "human mind" is perhaps the *same* everywhere and for all time,[5] but that does not mean that it is *one*—the symbol is irreducible to the sign, and vice versa. Let us consider an assertion by Claude Lévi-Strauss: "It is . . . better, instead of contrasting magic and science, to compare them as two parallel modes of acquiring knowledge. Their theoretical and practical results differ in value. . . . Both science and magic however require the same sort of mental operations and they differ not so much in kind as in the different types of phenomena to which they are applied."[6] We may wonder whether such an affirmation does not stem from an inverse ethnocentrism (or logocentrism) which, after having denied much to magic, now makes too great a concession to it: there is magic in science, and not simply science in magic. Do we not have here two principles, rooted in sign and symbol, which differ indeed in nature and not merely in function, which differ in the mental operations they imply and not simply in the results? Once again, science and magic are perhaps the same thing; but is it a single thing? Rather than casting past research on the primitive mind into oblivion, we ought to look at it to determine whether we might not find there the first, still useful descriptions of the symbol.

The attitudes that I am describing here are not located in any precise historical moment, and the examples that illustrate them may be taken from authors who are far apart in time. Specula-

5. As André Leroi-Gourhan has shown, man does not come from monkeys but from other men.
6. *The Savage Mind* (Chicago, 1966), p. 13.

tions on original language go very far back; those on the language of the insane are still being produced today. We may observe that the romantic crisis did not cause them to disappear; one is tempted to say that the opposite is true. When Wackenroder contrasts verbal language and the language of art according to the categories that separate sign and symbol elsewhere, he partakes of the same paradigm as Vico and Lévy-Bruhl; the difference—although it is not always present—lies in the marks of evaluation—negative or positive—that are attached to the symbol (this judgment obviously does not exhaust the romantic conception of the symbol). Rather than being "classic" or "romantic," the tradition I am speaking of appears to me to be a complement, difficult to avoid, of all such theories: their *double*, of which I choose two versions here, "original language" and "savage language."[7]

ORIGINAL LANGUAGE

My hypothesis is thus the following: thinking that they are describing the origin of language and of the linguistic sign, or their childhood, people have in effect projected onto the past an implicit knowledge of the symbol as it exists in the present.

Speculations on the origin of language are so abundant that an entire book would not suffice to sum them up.[8] Thus I shall not attempt to provide an overview of the history of these specula-

7. This is an arbitrary choice. One might well undertake the same task, for example, on the basis of psychiatric descriptions of the language of the mentally ill. Then we would have statements of the following sort to consider: "Our patients, like M. Jourdain [in Molière's *Bourgeois Gentilhomme*], are unconscious symbolists. . . . Illness is all it takes to discover the laws of symbolism" (J. Pouderoux, *Remarques sur l'incohérence des propos de quelques aliénés* [Bordeaux, 1929], p. 56); "To translate his thought, the schizophrenic prefers this sort of symbolic interjection to the use of words that are banal but ordered in a logical proposition satisfying the laws of syntax" (C. Pottier, *Réflexions sur les troubles du langage dans les psychoses paranoïdes* [Paris, 1930], p. 129). Silvano Arieti, with his equation between schizophrenia and the paleological, would be a fruitful field for research.

8. Such a study already exists, moreover, in the six volumes by A. Borst entitled *Der Turmbau von Babel* (Stuttgart, 1957–1963). For more synthetic views, see B. Rosenkranz, *Der Ursprung der Sprache* (Heidelberg, 1961); A. Sommerfelt, "The Origin of Language. Theories and Hypotheses," *Cahiers d'histoire mondiale*, (1953–54), 885–902; and W. S. Allen, "Ancient Ideas on the Origin and Development of Language," *Transactions of the Philological Society*, 1948, pp. 35–60. *The Origins and Prehistory of Language*, by G. Révész, trans. J. Butler (London and New York, 1956), also provides useful information.

tions, for it would necessarily be superficial, but I shall rather propose a rough sketch, achronic in itself, which retains only a few typical features. I shall limit myself, moreover, to just one of their aspects: the one that has to do with the relation between signifier and signified.

The classical division of these theories opposes *phusei* to *thesei*, natural origin to conventional origin. These terms can include two oppositions: the motivated (natural) versus the unmotivated; and the social (conventional) versus the individual. Now no one, or almost no one (we shall look at the exceptions later on) has affirmed that *natural* language was, by this very token, *individual*; the conventional—in the sense of social and obligatory—character of language is in fact recognized by the adherents of both opposing opinions. One may conclude that the real opposition lies between motivation and its absence. But then the first option alone can be characterized as a hypothesis concerning original language, or more precisely concerning the relation that unites signifier and signified: to see the language of the past in the image of today's language is in fact to renounce the search for a difference other than a temporal one between the latter and the former. In other words, all hypotheses, in the constructive sense, concerning original language are reduced to the search for *motivation* between the two constituent faces of the sign; or, in A. W. Schlegel's formula: "Protolanguage will consist in natural signs, that is, signs found in an essential relation with what is designated" (*Die Kunstlehre*, p. 239).[9] The forms of such motivation, then, are what will concern us particularly here.

Still proceeding in a highly schematic fashion, we can identify three major phases of the search for motivation, listing them in order: (1) from abstract (contemporary) language to figurative language; (2) from figurative language to onomatopoeia; (3) from onomatopoeia to gestural language. This gradation is based upon the degree to which the referent is present in the sign. In fact, if we were to postulate the presence of motivation in advance but were still to limit the field of inquiry to the sign, we could deal with the relation of denotation alone (between sign and referent) or with symbolization alone (no motivation is possible between signifier and signified). With tropes, or verbal symbols, we contrast two homogeneous terms, proper meaning and figurative

9. For citations of Schlegel's work, see the Bibliographic Notes for Chapter 6.

meaning. With onomatopoeia, some part of the referent generally becomes the sign. Finally, in gestural language, the referent remains present almost in its entirety. Let us examine each of these three levels.

When the search for origins remains in the *verbal* arena, and does not refer to some other mode of signification (such as the symbol), it is called *etymology*. Now etymology, on the semantic level, is limited to tropic relations. To illustrate this affirmation I shall refer to Stephen Ullmann's lucid and synthetic presentation of etymological practices.[10] After reviewing numerous classifications of the operations that etymologists perform, Ullmann establishes two irreducible principles leading to a "logical classification" and a "psychological classification." Let us look at the logical classification first. It is "linked to the tradition of classical and medieval rhetoric" (p. 271), for "the pioneers of semantics, Darmesteter, Bréal, Clédat and others could not yet free themselves from the rhetorical point of view" (p. 271). The result is as follows: "The classification is accomplished by means of a purely quantitative comparison of the field of meaning before and after the change. There are thus three possibilities: the field may be wider than before; it may be narrower; or the two notions may find themselves on the same footing" (pp. 271–272).

Hence there are three cases: *extension*—for example, *arripare* in Latin signifies "to reach the river bank," and it produces, in English, *arrive*, with a more general meaning; *restriction*—for example, the Latin *vivenda*, signifying "provisions" (any sort of food), produces in French *viande*, "meat," obviously a narrower meaning; and *displacement*—for example, *canard*, in French, means both "duck" and "tabloid newspaper"—in this case "any comparison of their fields would be absurd" (p. 273).

Here in fact we can see quite clearly the traces of the "rhetorical point of view." Whether we limit ourselves to the classical authors or turn toward modern discussions, we always observe the same tropic relations: on the one hand, synecdoche, which can move from species to genus or genus to species and thus can expand or contract its extension; and on the other hand metaphor and metonymy, which displace extension without changing its

10. The quotations are from Ullmann's work in French, *Précis de sémantique française*, 3d ed. (Bern, 1965).

dimensions. Thus we remain explicitly in the area of rhetorical figures.

The second classification is psychological, that is, it uses the categories of mental association. Here four cases can be identified: (1) resemblance between the two meanings (metaphor); (2) contiguity between the two meanings (metonymy); (3) resemblance between the two names; (4) contiguity between the two names (p. 277).

The *teeth* of a comb would constitute an example of change through metaphor; *style* comes from *stilus*, engraver's point or stylet, through metonymy. The third case is illustrated by the example of the French word *forain*, "itinerant," related to the French *foire*, "fair," whereas it initially meant "foreigner." But even though it is a false one, this etymology functions nevertheless by way of a trope, more precisely through metonymy (itinerants often turn up at fairs); thus it does not constitute a special case. Finally, the fourth possibility is illustrated by the word *capital* used for *capital city*: here we have a generalizing synecdoche, in which the property is substituted for the thing that it characterizes. To speak of contiguity and resemblance amounts to specifying one of the categories of the preceding classification, the very one in fact in which metaphor and metonymy occurred together. Thus the second classification, far from being independent of the first, is only one of its subdivisions. Etymology remains a subdivision of rhetoric.

But perhaps I have chosen the wrong starting point. I can never cite enough examples to prove my hypothesis by that means; I shall thus content myself with looking briefly at the views of one of the most brilliant of contemporary etymologists, Emile Benveniste. In a methodological article entitled "Semantic Problems in Reconstruction,"[11] Benveniste formulates the principal rule of etymology as follows: "In the presence of identical morphemes with different meanings, one must ask oneself whether there is some use in which the two meanings converge" (p. 249). Here are two examples. In English, *story* (narrative) and *story* (of a building) are perfect homonyms. "What keeps us from saying that they are the same is not our feeling that a 'narration' and a

11. In *Problems in General Linguistics*, trans. M. E. Meek (Coral Gables, Fla., 1971), pp. 249–264.

'floor' are irreconcilable, but the impossibility of finding any usage of such a nature that the one meaning might be interchanged with the other" (p. 250). Historical verification confirms the difference between these two words. The inverse case is illustrated by the French verb *voler*, synonym of both the English verbs "to fly" and "to steal." Here a common context exists: "This context is found in the language of falconry; it is the expression 'le faucon *vole* la perdrix' (= reaches and seizes in flight)" (p. 250).

At first glance, the rhetorical criterion of meaning would seem to have been replaced by a formal criterion of distribution. But let us look at the latter criterion more closely. What allows us to affirm that the two meanings of *voler* have a common origin is the possibility of finding a context in which one of the meanings is part of the other: the original meaning is *fly*, and the meaning *steal* is obviously a synecdoche, a specific flight of the falcon. Or, with respect to another example: in Indo-European, "to harvest" and "autumn" are related because in fact "autumn" signifies "time to harvest"; now "harvest" and "time to harvest" are in a metonymic relationship. Thus the old tropic apparatus is once again in play, conjugated, to be sure, with Benveniste's unfailing erudition.

In order to go back to the origins, we rely on the tropic matrix—which, however, characterizes the present state of language, not its past (we saw this assimilation occur for the first time with Augustine). We shall not be surprised, then, to encounter assertions of the metaphoric nature of ancient language, even if they remain outside the etymological framework. Thus Vico writes:

> The second kind of speech, corresponding to the age of heroes, was said by the Egyptians to have been spoken by symbols. To these may be reduced the heroic emblems, which must have been the mute comparisons which Homer calls sēmata (the signs in which the heroes wrote). In consequence, they must have been metaphors, images, similitudes or comparisons, which, having passed into articulate speech, supplied all the resources of poetic expression.[12]

And Ernest Renan: "*Transfer* or metaphor has thus been the principal device in the formation of language."[13] And Otto Jespersen:

12. *The New Science of Giambattista Vico*, trans. from the 3d ed. (1944) by T. G. Bergin and M. H. Fisch (Garden City, N. Y., 1961), p. 102.
13. *De l'origine du langage*, 2d ed. (Paris, 1858), p. 123.

The expression of thought therefore tends to become more and more mechanical or prosaic. Primitive man, however, on account of the nature of his language, was constantly reduced to using words and phrases figuratively: he was forced to express his thoughts in the language of poetry. The speech of modern savages is often spoken of as abounding in similes and all kinds of figurative phrases and allegorical expressions.[14]

This conclusion, moreover, is less inevitable than it appears. In fact, as these writers discover that all words are derived by metaphor, synecdoche, and so forth, we might expect them to see contemporary language as figurative, while the original language would be nonfigurative, "proper"; whereas in principle they are asserting just the opposite. Vico contends that these transfers of meaning had already taken place, at the outset, and that today we have forgotten the metaphoric origin of most words; thus the past, and not the present, is indeed the era of metaphor. For Condillac, there is a qualitative difference between the tropes of the earliest periods and contemporary ones: the former were authentic, being born of necessity (very few words were available), whereas the latter are a sign of decadence and of imminent death, for they serve only as ornaments (here again is the opposition between tropes of meaning and tropes of beauty that we found in Quintilian); thus it is the tropic mechanism and not individual tropes that entitle the past to be known as the figurative era. Jespersen, too, argues that if there are so many dead tropes in today's language, it is because they were once alive: thus the first language was figurative, and so on. Whatever the explanation, the conclusion is the same: primitive signs are grounded in the possibility of motivation.

The second major stage in the search for original language consists in the passage to onomatopoeia and to interjection (depending on whether the researcher is relying on a mimetic or an expressive theory of language). Condillac, who defends interjection, says that "the cries of the passions contributed to enlarge the operations of the mind, by giving occasion naturally to the mode of speaking by action" and, speaking of the first men, that "the

14. *Progress in Language* (London, 1894), p. 353, or *Language* (London, 1922), p. 432.

natural cries served them for a pattern, to frame a new language."[15] Renan, a partisan of onomatopoeia, contends in turn that "the decisive motive for the choice of words must have been, in most cases, the desire to imitate the object that they wanted to express. . . . The language of the first men was thus, in a way, only the echo of nature in human consciousness" (p. 136). A. W. Schlegel sums up these theories amusingly: "So here are the first men: except for their inarticulate cries of joy, sorrow, or anger, they are busy whistling like the wind, roaring like the waves on a stormy sea, making noises with their voices like rolling stones, howling like wolves, cooing like doves, braying like donkeys."[16]

Let me point out that these theories have their supporters among contemporary linguists. A Soviet author, A. M. Gazov-Ginzberg, presents a new version of the mimetic thesis in his book entitled *Was Language Representative at Its Source?*[17] Here onomatopoeia is awarded the ennobling name of *mimeme*, and its study that of *mimology*. Gazov-Ginzberg divides mimemes into four classes, according to the origin of the sound: (1) reproduction of internal human sounds; (2) reproduction of external sounds; (3) sonic rendering of gestures and nonsonic mimic by mouth and nose; (4) babbling (baby-talk), in which the easiest combinations of sounds designate the most accessible situations and experiences. The author then analyzes the roots of proto-Hebraic language and shows the presences of onomatopoeia in 140 cases out of 180, the others being words of foreign or unknown origin.

In a book entitled *La Reconstruction typologique des langues archaïques de l'humanité*, another linguist, Jacques van Ginneken, illustrates recent forms of the theory of interjection.[18] Van Ginneken in his turn broadens the notion of interjection and replaces it by that of the *click*. The click is a sonic complex that often includes sounds unknown to the phonological system of the language; it is born of the natural movements of man. Van Ginneken writes: "The movement the mouth makes in the click-sign was and is a truly innate and universally human movement that helps in the

15. *An Essay on the Origin of Human Knowledge*, trans. T. Nugent, 1756 (facsimile reproduction: Gainesville, Fla., 1971), p. 174.
16. "De l'étymologie en général," *Oeuvres écrites en français* (Leipzig, 1846), 124–125.
17. *Byl li jazyk izobrazitelen v svoikh istokakh?* (Moscow, 1965).
18. Amsterdam, 1939.

infant's sucking action; its accidental differentiations were later adapted to serve as signs of our various states of consciousness. . . . In the absence of the mother, every normal child, in the second or third month of his existence, feels the desire to suck and begins to have imaginary meals" (p. 63).

Van Ginneken's examples are drawn from all the "archaic languages of humanity."

Finally, the third state in the search for original language leads us to gestural language, or, as it was called in the eighteenth century, the language of action. Vico, William Warburton, and Condillac in particular describe it in detail. In the first chapter of his *Grammaire*, Condillac writes: "Gestures, facial movements, and inarticulate accents, these, my Lord, are the first means men possessed to communicate their thoughts. The language that is formed with these signs is called *language of action*."[19]

This language is at once natural (that is, motivated) and acquired; it is the only language that conforms to what it expresses, for it is not subject to the constraint of linearity; now ideas themselves arise simultaneously and not successively ("the language of simultaneous ideas is the only natural language" [p. 430]).

What remains for Condillac a purely intellectual view unsupported by empirical data (although he speaks of the "establishment for the instruction of deaf-mutes" directed by Abbé de l'Epée, p. 429) becomes the subject of concrete research in the nineteenth and twentieth centuries. In particular, the discovery of gestural codes among North American Indians encourages research on an autonomous and even primary "language of action." Here we must mention one study in particular that left its mark on research in this area, F. H. Cushing's "Manual Concepts."[20] But it is once again Van Ginneken who tries to systematize all the data on gestural language in order to establish this as the absolute origin of language. According to him, the gesture is primordial, for it is part of the action that it designates; we reach the zero degree of the sign, since this sign signifies itself. "The gesture in this case is nothing but the work begun in the outdoor air, and that the manual concept brings to life again inside. Thus it is

19. In *Oeuvres philosophiques*, I (Paris, 1947), 428.
20. In *American Anthropologist*, 5 (1892), 289–317.

natural language. For here there is no convention. The sign is the natural sign, for it is the signified itself" (p. 127).

To complete the picture, we should recall the parallel research on writing. Vico had already established a rigorous parallelism between the "three languages" of humanity and the three writing systems (hieroglyphic, symbolic, and epistolary) of the Egyptians. And Warburton, bishop of Gloucester and one of Vico's contemporaries, developed this analogy at length in *The Divine Legation of Moses* (1738), a part of which was immediately translated into French under the title *Essai sur les hiéroglyphes des Egyptiens* (1744).[21] The states of language are abstract contemporary language, metaphorical language, and language of action; as for writing, these are its stages:

"The first essay towards writing was a mere picture" (p. 23); the example invoked is that of the Aztecs, which is a reference, broadly speaking, to the pictogram. Then comes the stage of hieroglyphics. The passage from the first to the second stage was achieved in three ways. "The first way was, *to make the principal circumstance in the subject stand for the whole*. Thus when they would describe . . . a tumult, or popular insurrection,—*an armed man casting arrows* . . ." (p. 25): we would call that a synecdoche. "The second, and more artful method of contraction, was by putting the instrument of the thing, whether real or metaphorical, for the thing itself. Thus an *eye*, eminently placed, was designed to represent God's omniscience" (p. 25); the instrument for the thing, in rhetorical terms, is a metonymy (possibly already metaphorical, Warburton cautions us). The Egyptians' "third, and still more artificial method of abridging picture-writing, was *by making one thing to stand for, or represent another, where any quaint resemblance or analogy in the representative could be collected from their observations of nature, or their traditional superstitions*" (pp. 25–26). Here we confront the metaphor. Within this second stage itself, two phases are distinguishable: that of hieroglyphics, and that of Chinese ideograms, highly stylized. As for the third stage, it consists of alphabets, unmotivated marks.

Let us note, finally, that Warburton does not stop at establishing the formal identity of hieroglyphics and tropes, but extends

21. On Warburton's role, see M.-V. David, *Le Débat sur les écritures et l'hiéroglyphe aux XVII et XVIII⁰ siècles* . . . (Paris, 1965). Warburton is quoted from the 1837 London edition, vol. ii, bk. iv, sec. iv.

this same type of relation to other symbolic activities, particularly dreams (we sense the influence of Clement of Alexandria once again). Analyzing Artemidorus's *Oneirocritica*, he observes that the way to interpret dream images is none other than the one we see at work in the hieroglyphic and in the trope. "The *Egyptian priests*, the first interpreters of dreams, took their rules for this species of DIVINATION, from their *symbolic* riddling, . . . for by this time it was generally believed that their gods had given them *hieroglyphic writing*. So that nothing was more natural than to imagine that these gods, who in their opinion gave *dreams* likewise, had employed the same mode of expression in both revelations" (p. 67). "The *oneirocritics* borrowed their art of diciphering from symbolic hieroglyphics" (p. 68). Does the interpretation of dreams originate then in hieroglyphics?[22]

Let us consider the complete set of data. The dominant feature, the one that determines the others, directly or indirectly, could be formulated in the following manner: original language is conceived in terms of increasing proximity between the sign and what it designates, or, as I said above, in terms of the referent's presence in the sign. The language of action is the most original of all, because it signifies itself and because in so doing it achieves the maximum degree of presence: it *is* the thing designated more than it is the designator of that thing (we are reminded of Goethe's and Schelling's formulations). The fantasm of primitive language is at the same time a fantasm of the fading away of language, since things take the place of signs and the gap introduced by the sign between man and the world is finally reduced.

We must recall that this conception of language is at the opposite pole from what is believed today to be its true nature. In a synchronic perspective, as the founders of modern semiotics have

22. I do not mean to suggest by this that Warburton prefigures Freud. The classification of tropes (relations between two meanings) in classical antiquity is based on that of psychic associations (relations between two mental entities). That seems to go without saying. Thus it is difficult to understand insistent assertions that Freud's great discovery consists in having baptized metonymy "displacement" and metaphor "condensation," and Lacan's in having "recognized [in the Freudian terminology] two essential figures designated by linguistics: metonymy and metaphor." Is this truly a step forward? Especially considering that the condensation/displacement opposition *is not* equivalent to the opposition between these rhetorical figures. See, among others, J.-F. Lyotard, *Discours, figure* (Paris, 1971), pp. 239–270, and J. Bellemin-Noël, "Psychanalyser le rêve de Swann?", *Poétique*, No. 8 (1971), p. 468. We shall dwell at length on this issue in the next chapter.

often repeated, the object denoted has only a "slight effect" on the sign (C. S. Peirce), it is an "exterior being" (Saussure). Diachronically, it is impossible to conceive of the origin of language without postulating the *absence* of objects at the outset; As Leroi-Gourhan writes, "that amounts to making language the instrument of liberation with respect to the object-world (*le vécu*)."[23] On the other hand—and this is the point that justifies all the premodern reflection on language—the symbolizer may be part of the symbolized, or vice versa.

One consequence—or variant—of this first feature attributed to original language is the belief that the latter must be composed exclusively of concrete nouns. Since the object must be present in the sign, abstraction will always be considered a later development, being already an absence in itself. This opinion (the canonical formulation of which appears in Locke's *Essay*[24]) serves as the corner stone of a large portion of contemporary etymological research. Now Benveniste's counteranalysis (in *Problems*, pp. 256ff.) shows quite clearly how the "concretist" prejudice may oblige linguists to close their eyes to the facts. Benveniste is dealing here with the etymological family *trust, true, truce*, terms all linked to the idea of fidelity and related phonetically and morphologically to the terms used for "tree" in Greek, Sanskrit, English, and so forth—"sometimes 'oak' in particular or 'wood' in general" (p. 257). The traditional explanation, given by Hermann Osthoff,

establishes the Indo-European word represented by Gr. *drûs* 'oak' as the point of departure of the whole morphological and semantic development, and claims that the moral values implied in *Treue* and *truste* proceed from it. The Gothic adjective *triggws*, O.H.G. *gitriuwi* 'getreu, faithful,' would, then, properly signify 'firm like an oak.' In the Germanic mentality, the "oak" would have been the symbol of firmness and confidence, and the image of "oak" would have inspired the whole set of the representations of "fidelity." [P. 257]

23. *Le Geste et la parole*, II (Paris, 1965), 21. In this sense, writing marks one further step in "humanization": it implies the possible absence not only of the referent but also of the interlocutors.

24. "I doubt not but, if we could trace them [words] to their sources, we should find, in all languages, the names which stand for things that fall not under our senses to have had their first rise from sensible ideas" (Book III, ch. 1, 5). Lévi-Strauss has demonstrated convincingly (in the opening pages of *The Savage Mind*) the impossibility of defending this viewpoint.

Benveniste has no difficulty demonstrating the inconsistency of this universally accepted explanation, which would so well illustrate the precedence of the concrete over the abstract. First of all, the root *drū* signifies "oak" only in Greek, whereas a look at the other Indo-European languages proves beyond doubt that its meaning is that of "wood," "tree" in general. Even in Greek the other meaning is relatively recent; this is perfectly comprehensible, given that the oak tree does not grow in the territory of any of the Indo-European languages. Resuming his analysis, Benveniste shows that the Indo-European meaning could not have been anything but " 'to be firm, solid, sound' ":

> Hence it is this common signification that the designation of "tree" shares in the same degree. Contrary to Osthoff's reasoning, we consider that *derwo-*, *drwo-*, *dreu-* in the sense of 'tree' is only a particular use of the general sense of "firm, solid." It is not the "primitive" name of the oak which created the notion of solidity; on the contrary, it is by the expression of solidity that trees in general and the oak in particular were designated. [P. 258]

And Benveniste goes on to cite a series of similar cases.

A third general feature of "primitive" language arises from the initial status of all words as proper nouns. Here we are only pushing the preceding characteristic to the extreme: if words are to be seen as more and more concrete, we end up by establishing a name for each thing. Adam Smith notices this: "The assignation of particular names to denote particular objects, that is, the institution of nouns substantive, would, probably, be one of the first steps towards the formation of language";[25] the other words are subsequently derived through antonomasia (according to the model "He is a Caesar"). The original words are the proper names of objects; language is a nomenclature. We find analogous affirmations in the writings of Rousseau.

On this point, Saussure has a very explicit passage. He writes:

> The ground of language does not consist of nouns. It is an accident when the linguistic sign happens to correspond to an object that is well defined for the senses, like "horse," "fire," "sun," rather than to an idea such as "he set forth." However important this case may be, there is no apparent reason to take it as the type for language; indeed, the opposite is true. . . .

25. *A Dissertation on the Origin of Languages* (Tübingen, 1970), p. 31.

We find here, implicitly, a tendency that we cannot fail to recognize, nor to challenge, concerning what would be the ultimate constituent of language, namely, a nomenclature of given objects. *First* the object, then the sign; hence (a claim we shall always deny), an exterior basis for the sign, and the shaping of language by the following relation:

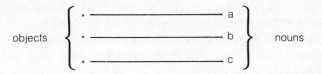

whereas the actual shape is a a-b-c, without connection to any knowledge of a real, object-based relation such as *——a. If an object could be, at any point whatsoever, the term on which the sign is fixed, linguistics would immediately stop being what it is, from top to bottom.[26]

A fourth characteristic of original language: since the word is close to the thing, it exists by itself (it signifies "naturally") and, unlike words today, it does not need to belong to a rigid system. Renan therefore concludes that "language was never more individual than at the origin of man" (*De l'origine du language,* p. 176). The user of language enjoys a certain liberty in the choice of a particular sign, since signs are all motivated in nature and thus immediately comprehensible. Do we not seem to be reading, once again, a description of the metaphoric use of our *own* language?

I shall not dwell on certain other characteristics that are likewise derived from the preceding ones: the affective, or irrational, or syncretic nature of original language.[27] Sign and symbol remain confused in these speculations; however, their principal features are outlined there—among other assertions, to be sure, that are hard to accept. But does this not suffice to give the lie to W. D. Whitney, and many others after him, who affirmed with reference to research on the origins of language, that most of what has

26. "Notes inédites," *Cahiers Ferdinand de Saussure,* XII (1954), pp. 68–69; *Cours de linguistique générale,* critical edition (Wiesbaden, 1967), fasc. 2, nos. 1089–1091, p. 148.

27. Syncretic in the sense that the subjective and the objective are not distinguished. Renan writes, for example: "It seems as though primitive man did not live with himself but rather lived spread over the world, from which he scarcely distinguished himself" (p. 211), and he quotes Maine de Biran approvingly as saying that primitive man exists wholly outside himself (*Oeuvres,* [Paris, 1841] III, pp. 42–43).

been said and written on the subject is no more than castles in the air?

SAVAGE LANGUAGE

Let us turn now to a second variant of the same attitude; in this case a writer describes the symbol while claiming to focus on what others call sign. We are no longer dealing with another time but with another place: time is replaced by space, and history by ethnography.

Lévy-Bruhl is a typical representative of this attitude. Typical, and not isolated: this fact justifies our attention to his work in spite of a certain discredit in which it is held today. We need not go back over the already established criticisms of his principal ideas. On the other hand, there is a need to uncover and formulate the theory of the symbolic that he traces, in part unwittingly.

Once again, we have to begin with the *presence* of the symbolized in the symbolizer: "It is not a perceived relationship, still less a convention that gives rise to [symbols]. The symbol is felt as being, in a way, the being or the object that it represents, and "representing" here takes on the literal meaning of actually rendering present. . . . The jawbone of a dead child is the child's 'representative,' in the strong sense, for its mother; it enacts the child's actual presence."[28]

The relation is not one of identity, as others have thought (in that case there would no longer be symbolization), but of belonging; the symbol *is* the being in the sense that it is part of it. From appurtenance to symbol, as primitive people understand it, the transition may be imperceptible. For the symbol, like the appurtenance, participates in the being or object that it "represents," and in this way assures its actual presence (*L'Expérience mystique*, pp. 200–201).

This conception of the symbol applies not only to gestures and objects (like the jawbone of the child), but also to words, to the extent that words denote (and denotation is close to symbolization); proper names would then be, as we might expect, the privileged example.

The name, for them, is something entirely different from a convenient means of designating someone and of recognizing him

28. *L'Expérience mystique et les symboles chez les primitifs.*

among others, a sort of label attached to each individual, which may be chosen arbitrarily and changed if need be, and which remains exterior to the individual without any connection to his intimate personality. On the contrary, the real name . . . is an appurtenance, in the full meaning of that word, consubstantial, like other appurtenances, with the one who bears it. [Ibid., p. 236]

We have already seen that this "uncivilized" attitude was shared by Lévy-Bruhl himself, who refused to change labels in spite of his need to do so.

Might one not also recall, in this connection, that belonging is the basis for a rhetorical trope, synecdoche? One senses that the variety of names (appurtenance, participation, *pars pro toto*, synecdoche) has contributed, as it was thought to have done only for the primitives, to hiding the identity of the thing. "Observers have for a long time noted the bold applications that primitive peoples make of the formula *pars pro toto*, without seeing any difficulties there. . . . If primitives make such ample use of this formula, it is because this is how they express the intimate participation that they feel between the parts of a living thing and its entirety, between its appurtenances and itself" (ibid., pp. 176–178). Lévy-Bruhl also writes in his *Notebooks*: "Then one understands that a part may appear 'to represent the whole,' that is to say to act as a sign or symbol . . .: by a sort of convention (p. 85).

But if symbols are related to tropes, can we still claim that they are the exclusive perquisite of savages? Lévy-Bruhl is astonished that, for savages, colors are not designated by abstract names as they are for us, but by the names of objects bearing that color (a generalizing conceptual synecdoche); he forgets that we speak in just the same way of *orange* (taking the fruit for the color) or *rose*. We could find other tropes without difficulty among his examples. This does not prevent one of his disciples from writing that "our language initiates us into logical thought and is incapable of translating any other form of thought."[29]

Moreover, Lévy-Bruhl himself notes the formal resemblance between primitive symbolism and rhetorical tropes, but he rejects it: "Let us get rid of the idea that this may be only a metaphor, a 'figure' enacted" (*L'Expérience mystique*, p. 270). If we try to find the reasons for this rejection, we discover that for Lévy-Bruhl metaphor, being "play," is opposed to what is "serious." But to

29. E. Cailliet, *Symbolisme et âmes primitives* (Paris, 1935), p. 145.

see the poetic trope as a superfluous ornament is after all just one (false) idea among others. It is not the figure that Lévy-Bruhl is rejecting here, but one of its descriptions.

There is a second reason for the failure to recognize tropes in primitive symbols: it is that we are in the habit of reducing all tropes to metaphor alone, and even to a single variety of metaphor, the one that depends upon material resemblance, and we are no longer able to identify the others. This leads a perplexed Lévy-Bruhl to write, on one occasion: "The symbols of primitive peoples . . . do not necessarily consist in reproductions, or images, of these beings or objects" (ibid., p. 180); and again: "In order to *be* in this way the dead that they represent, it is by no means necessary that the symbols reproduce their features" (p. 204). Upon what relation, then, does the symbol depend? Lévy-Bruhl cites the example of the house, for the person who lives in it, or the following description from the classic work of Baldwin Spencer and Francis James Gillen: "The natives when asked the meaning of certain drawings such as these will constantly answer that they are only play-work and mean nothing; but what are exactly, so far as their form is concerned, similar drawings, only drawn on some ceremonial object or in a particular spot, have a very definite meaning."[30] And, in his *Notebooks*: "The footprints are in no way a 'part' of the man or animal of which they are an appurtenance, although they *may be* him since to act on them is to act on him" (p. 155).

Lévy-Bruhl explains these facts by the presence of a new type of abstraction that he calls mystical. However, it suffices to analyze his examples in order to see that he is dealing here with what rhetoric calls *metonymy*. The portrait is not a cause for concern so long as it is not painted by the ethnologist: the metonymic relation between agent and action counts for more than the metaphoric (or synecdochic) relation between the image and the being represented. A given design has meaning only when it is engraved on a particular object; it acquires meaning by way of the metonymic relation of place. The same is true for the house symbolizing its inhabitants, or the footprint symbolizing its maker. The apparent absence of tropes is only the presence of tropes other than metaphor.

30. *The Native Tribes of Central Australia* (London, 1899), p. 617, quoted in Lévy-Bruhl, *Les Fonctions mentales dans les sociétés primitives* (Paris, 1910); I have used the 1951 edition.

The properties of symbolic systems derive logically from the definition of the symbol.

First, the level of isolated symbols. Initially, everything that touches the name (or the symbol) touches the being, since the one is part of the other, or, as Lévy-Bruhl writes, "to act upon the symbol of a being or an object is to act upon the being or object itself" (*L'Expérience mystique*, p. 225). Here is an example. According to J. Mooney, the Indian looks upon his name not as a simple label but as a distinct part of his individual self, just like his eyes or his teeth. He believes that he would suffer just as surely from a malevolent use of his name as from an injury inflicted upon a part of his body (*Fonctions*, p. 46). Are we all Indians, then?

As a second consequence, the identity of names signifies the identity, at least in part, of the beings named. We have seen that Lévy-Bruhl was able to formulate this principle but did not understand that it applied to his own discourse as well. The following example is from Cailliet's book: "Another play on words was circulating based on the name of the 'Mission Society.' This title was linked to the Malagasy words *asosay ity* (which sound very much like the English word "society") meaning 'Introduce them into our home.' These envoys from abroad, it was said, had been given the mission of incorporating into their homeland the land of the Hova." And Cailliet concludes: "The sound of words matters more than their meaning. Where we look for synonyms, uncivilized peoples seek homonymy: they look at words just as they have looked at things (pp. 120–121).

A third consequence of the fact that the symbolizing entity is part of what it symbolizes: to represent or to say a thing is already to bring it into existence. Thus predictions are realized not because soothsayers know how to read the future, but because their words give life to what they designate. Lévy-Bruhl recounts cases in which something is named in the indicative so that it will come about (*L'Expérience mystique*, pp. 286–288). Cailliet tells of the fright provoked by a warning in the face of trouble: the word itself already brings the misfortune into being to a certain extent.

A fourth consequence: uncivilized people confuse temporal succession with causality. According to Gray, if one of them, walking down a road, sees a snake fall on him out of a tree, and learns the next day or the next week that his son is dead in Queensland, he will relate these two facts (*Fonctions*, p. 72). Lévy-

Bruhl sums up these theories in the following way: "Primitive peoples confuse the antecedent with the cause. This would be the very common error in reasoning that is known as the *post hoc, ergo propter hoc* sophism" (ibid., p. 73). He himself is more inclined to see in this "a mystical relation . . . between antecedent and consequent" (p. 74). But this feature is one more consequence of the constituent properties of the symbol. Since the symbolizing entity is part of what it symbolizes, and since homonymy entails synonymy, the proximity of symbolizing entities implies that the entities symbolized are also in proximity; it is not "by chance" that two symbols are found side by side. In this connection, let us recall Roland Barthes's definition of the law of narrative, literary or not: "The mainspring of narrative activity is the very confusion between consecutivity and consequence, what comes *after* being read in the narrative as *caused by*; narrative in this case would be a systematic application of the logical error denounced by the Scholastics in the formula *post hoc, ergo propter hoc.*"[31] And Freud—each is speaking of the object he knows best—found this same uncivilized logic at work in dreams: "In a psycho-analysis, one learns to interpret propinquity in time as representing connection in subject-matter. . . . [Dreams] reproduce *logical connection* by *simultaneity in time*. . . . Causation is represented by temporal sequence."[32]

Shall we have to limit narratives and dreams to savages or to mystical participation?

As far as the symbolic *system* is concerned, Lévy-Bruhl's conception still can be grasped only by inversion. Indeed, according to him the characteristic feature of the use of symbols is the absence of system, a position he justifies in these terms: "What [symbols] 'represent' seems to be defined only very vaguely in the primitive mind" (*L'Expérience mystique*, p. 195). But we may wonder whether this vagueness, this purported absence of system is not instead the indication of a different system, one that Lévy-Bruhl is incapable of recognizing but that we might attempt to bring to light on the basis of his examples.

31. "Introduction à l'analyse structurale des récits," in R. Barthes et al., *Poétique du récit* (Paris, 1976), p. 22.
32. *The Interpretation of Dreams,* in *The Standard Edition of the Complete Psychological Works of Sigmund Freud,* ed. James Strachey, 24 vols. (London, 1953–74), iv, 247, 314, 316.

A single symbolizing entity evokes several symbolized entities, not through lack of system, but because each entity symbolized can be converted in turn into a symbolizer. Lévy-Bruhl gives the following example: the leaf fallen from a tree symbolizes the footprint left on it (through metonymy); this footprint refers us to the man who has walked on the leaf (again through metonymy); the man symbolizes the tribe he belongs to (through synecdoche) (ibid., pp. 230ff.).

A particularly eloquent example of conversion appears in Cailliet's book, *Symbolisme et âmes primitives*. It can be summarized in one sentence: "Persons born under a red moon will become kings." This assertion is explained by the fact that the color red is associated with blood and thus with power. The process of symbolization involved might be presented in the chart:

Blood symbolizes power (through metonymy) but it is symbolized by red (through synecdoche). Red symbolizes blood and is symbolized by the moon, more precisely by a certain phase of the moon (another synecdoche). Now this phase itself (having acquired the meaning of power) comes to be symbolized by the people who were born in it, through a temporal metonymy. Each symbolizing term is in its turn symbolized; the conversion unfolds in a chain that may go on indefinitely; and each new symbolizing term acquires the symbolized terms of the previous symbolic processes: thus red takes on, through the intermediary of blood, the "meaning" of power (just as a certain phase of the moon, or the persons born in this period, take on the same meaning) even though there is no direct symbolic relation between them. Then this process stops and the relation changes (I have designated the new one by a double arrow, as opposed to the single arrows used before): the king also symbolizes power; two distinct symbolic chains can meet here thanks to the identity of one of the symbolized terms ("power"). Thus we are confronted with a new relation, proper to symbolic systems, that we might call *equalization*.

Another operation characteristic of symbolism is overdetermination. If it goes unrecognized, it, too, may be taken as an indication of a lack of system. Cailliet gives the following example: "A young native, having lost a first son, called the second *Roalahy*. At my request he explained: 'I gave him that name, Roalahy (= two + man), because he is himself and he replaces the first one, and also because his name sounds something like Roland, and Roland was a famous white man, I understand'" (p. 119).

So Joyce did not invent this device: every user of symbolic systems does as much.

To be continued. . . .

8

Freud's Rhetoric and Symbolics

In his work on jokes and dreams, Freud describes a particular mechanism that he most often calls "(dream-)work," and that he takes to be peculiar to, and thus characteristic of, the unconscious.[1] The mechanisms that Freud points out, such as condensation, indirect representation, displacement, and punning, must be attributed not to dreams in particular, according to him, but to all the activities of the unconscious—and to these alone. "There is no necessity to assume that any peculiar symbolizing activity of the mind is operating in the dream-work, but that dreams make use of any symbolizations which are already present in unconscious thinking . . ." (ID, 5, 349).[2] When he goes on to compare dreams

1. In the French version of this book, the discussion introduced here is supported by a detailed analysis of Freud's descriptive work in *Jokes and Their Relation to the Unconscious* (pp. 285–315) and it is supplemented by an appendix entitled "Freud on Enunciation" (pp. 361–369).

2. All quotations from Freud are from *The Standard Edition of the Complete Psychological Works of Sigmund Freud*, ed. James Strachey, 24 vols. (London, 1953–74; abbreviated *SE*). The particular texts quoted are identified as follows: for *The Interpretation of Dreams* (abbreviated *ID*), volume and page numbers are given; for *Introductory Lectures on Psychoanalysis* (*SE*, vol. 15; abbreviated *IP*), and for *New Introductory Lectures on Psychoanalysis* (*SE*, vol. 22; abbreviated *NP*), the lecture number is given in roman numerals, followed by a page number in arabic numerals.

and hysteria, Freud maintains the same position, even more force-fully: dream-work and hysterical symptoms have a common origin. *"A normal train of thought is only submitted to abnormal psychical treatment of the sort we have been describing if an unconscious wish, derived from infancy and in a state of repression, has been transferred to it"* (*ID*, 5, 598; Freud's italics).

Now a detailed analysis, undertaken elsewhere, of *Jokes and Their Relation to the Unconscious* (*SE* 8; this text is more convenient to analyze, for my purposes, but the results would be no different for *The Interpretation of Dreams*) proves the contrary: the symbolic mechanism that Freud has described lacks specificity; the operations that he identifies are simply those of any linguistic symbolism, as they have been inventoried, most notably, by the rhetorical tradition. Benveniste pointed this out in a study that appeared in 1956: as he described dreams and jokes, Freud unwittingly rediscovered the "old catalogue of tropes."[3]

Not that all of Freud's distinctions and definitions were already available in some rhetorical treatise; but the nature of the phenomena he describes is precisely the same. On certain points, his descriptions fall short of those the rhetoricians produced: for example, on verbal jokes and the characterizations of figures such as paronomasia, antanaclasis, and syllepsis. In other cases he ends up with results similar to those of the rhetoricians: for example, the way he confuses phenomena that are present simultaneously on the one hand, present and absent on the other, mirrors the rhetoricians' inability to define clearly the difference between figure and trope. Finally, he sometimes identifies and describes verbal phenomena that had escaped the rhetoricians' attention, for example, displacement—notwithstanding the uncertainties that have been noted in his use of this term. If we add that in this period (the beginning of the twentieth century) the rhetorical tradition had fallen into oblivion, it is clear that Freud deserves all the more credit: *Jokes and Their Relation to the Unconscious* is the most important text on semantics of its time.

Certain passages of *The Interpretation of Dreams* reveal that Freud was almost aware of the fact that he was describing the forms of all symbolic processes, not those of an unconscious symbolism. So it is on the famous first page of the chapter "Dream-

3. The expression is from Emile Benveniste, "Remarks on the Function of Language in Freudian Theory," in *Problems in General Linguistics* (Coral Gables, Fla., 1971), p. 75.

Work," where Freud globally defines this work as transposition, *Übertragung*, a very precise translation of the term *metaphora* in Aristotle's *Poetics*: "The [manifest] dream-content seems like a transcript of the [latent] dream-thoughts into another mode of expression. . . . The dream-content . . . is expressed as it were in a pictographic script, the characters of which have to be transposed individually into the language of the dream-thoughts" (*ID*, 4, 277).

The subsequent description of pictographic script and of the rebus device particularly calls to mind the work of Clement of Alexandria (see above, pp. 32ff.). Freud contrasts image and rebus: Clement made this same opposition between the first and the second degree of symbolic hieroglyphics, and we have seen that that difference paralleled the one between proper meaning and transposed meaning or trope. The dream, then, speaks in tropes.

Returning to the connection between dream mechanisms and metaphor as defined by Aristotle, we find that it crops up once in Freud's text itself. After noting that certain logical relations are absent in dreams, Freud writes: "One and only one of these logical relations is very highly favoured by the mechanism of dream-formation; namely, the relation of similarity, consonance or approximation—the relation of 'just as'. This relation, unlike any other, is capable of being represented in dreams in a variety of ways" (*ID*, 4, 319–320). A footnote adds the following: "Cf. Aristotle's remark on the qualifications of a dream-interpreter quoted above on p. 97, n. 2." And in said note 2, we read: "Aristotle remarked in this connection that the best interpreter of dreams was the man who could best grasp similarities." But we recall that, for Aristotle, this property characterizes dreams and tropes alike, since "a good metaphor implies an intuitive perception of the similarity in dissimilars" (*Poetics*, 1459a). Moreover, Freud, like Aristotle, uses "similarity" to mean any symbolic equivalence; *metaphora* includes synecdoches and metaphors for Aristotle; and for Freud, transposition includes resemblance, but also "harmony" and "contact."

For the parallel but inverse process of symbolization, Freud uses the general term *interpretation*. "The work which transforms the latent dream into the manifest one is called the *dream-work*. The work which proceeds in the contrary direction, which endeavors to arrive at the latent dream from the manifest one, is our *work of interpretation*" (*IP*, xi, p. 170; Freud's italics). "The dream-work . . . restricts itself to giving things a new form" (*ID*, 5, 507). But does this not define any symbolization?

Contrary to what he himself must have believed, Freud's original contribution to the theory of symbolism in general does not lie in the description of dream-work or of the technique of joking; he is original here only in details. By and large, he is content to rediscover the rhetorical distinctions and to apply them systematically to a new field. On the other hand, in the area of *interpretation* Freud is truly an innovator. Indeed, he identifies two interpretative techniques, *symbolic* and *associative*; or, in his own words, "a combined technique, which on the one hand rests on the dreamer's associations and on the other hand fills the gaps from the interpreter's knowledge of symbols" (*ID*, 5, 353). Now the characterization and description of the associative technique (more important than the other in Freud's eyes) had never been undertaken before.

The symbolic technique, annexed to the other, consists in using a repertory established once and for all, such as a "key to dreams," in order to translate dream-images, one at a time, into latent thoughts. This technique is to be applied only to one part of the dream, the part that is made up of symbols (in the narrow sense), as its name indicates. The defining feature of the symbol, for Freud, is that its meaning does not vary: symbols are universal. "Many of the symbols are habitually or almost habitually employed to express the same thing" (*ID*, 5, 352). "A constant relation of this kind between a dream-element and its translation is described by us as a 'symbolic' one, and the dream-element itself as a 'symbol' of the unconscious dream-thought" (*IP*, x, p. 150). However, this constancy of meaning does not preclude plurality: "As contrasted with the other dream-elements, a fixed meaning may be attributed to them, which, however, need not be unambiguous" (*NP*, xxix, p. 13).

The difference between Freud's symbolics and popular keys to dreams (in this connection Freud also uses the term "decoding": *ID*, 4, 97) does not lie in their logical form but in the source that is tapped in the search for latent meaning. "In the case of symbolic dream-interpretation the key to the symbolization is arbitrarily chosen by the interpreter; whereas in our cases of verbal disguise the keys are generally known and laid down by firmly established linguistic usage" (*ID*, 5, 341–342). The fixed expressions of a language reveal to us these universal equivalences, as do myths, popular tales, and other common forms: "This symbolism is not peculiar to dreams, but is characteristic of unconscious ideation, in particular among the people, and it is to be found in folklore, and in popular myths, legends, linguistic idioms, proverbial wisdom and current jokes" (ID, 5, 351). Another enumeration has this symbolism deriving "from folklore (that is, from knowledge about popular manners and customs, sayings and songs) and from poetic and colloquial linguistic usage" (IP, x, p. 159).

Once again, then, Freud concedes that dream symbolism is not limited to dreams; but he believes that it is peculiar to "unconscious ideation" alone. Whatever one may think about the existence of universal and constant symbols, one cannot help but observe that Freud unhesitatingly declares that the symbolism in a whole series of endeavors, from manners to poetry, is "unconscious." This is the price he has to pay in order to maintain his assertion that a specific unconscious symbolism exists. Let us also note in passing that Freud's use of the word "symbol" is opposed to that of the romantics (for whom fixed meaning corresponds rather to allegory); Freud is antiromantic, moreover, when he affirms that latent thoughts are in no way different from any other thoughts, in spite of their symbolic mode of transmission: for the romantics, on the contrary, the symbols's content differs from that of the sign, and that is why the symbol is untranslatable.

If the defining feature of symbols, and thus of the technique of symbolic interpretation, is their constant and universal meaning, the associative technique is defined for its part, as we might suppose, by its individual character, the individual in question being obviously not the interpreter but the producer. "The technique which I describe in the pages that follow differs in one essential respect from the ancient method: it imposes the task of interpretation upon the dreamer himself. It is not concerned with what occurs to the *interpreter* in connection with a particular element of the dream, but with what occurs to the *dreamer*" (ID, 4, 98, n. 1; Freud's italics). This technique consists in asking the dreamer, as soon as he has finished the account of his dream, to state everything that the elements of this dream arouse in him; the associations thus established are considered to be the interpretation of the dream. "We ask the dreamer . . . to divert his attention from the dream as a whole on to the separate portions of its content and to report to us in succession everything that occurs to him in relation to each of these portions—what associations present themselves to him if he focuses on each of them separately" (*NP*, XXIX, pp. 10–11). This interpretation of the dream contains, first of all, one portion of its latent thought (the other portion is revealed to us through knowledge of symbols), and, second, a series of "explanations, transitions, and connections" (*NP*, XXIX, p. 12) that link latent thoughts and manifest content. These associations on the part of the dreamer, recorded at a particular moment in his life, are, as we might expect, devoid of any universality. One symbolizing element may evoke innumerable symbolized elements; conversely, one symbolized element may be designated by an infinite number of symbolizers. "Not only are the elements of a dream determined by the dream-thoughts many times over, but the individual dream-thoughts are represented in the dream by several elements" (*ID*, 4, 284).

I shall not pass judgment on the rightness of Freud's method (that is best left to specialists in oneirology). I shall limit myself to pointing out his originality, which lies[4] in his valorization of the associations that arise during the moment that follows the narration of the dream—thus, in the way he assimilates one type of relation—based on contiguity of signifiers—to another, the symbolic relation. His detailed presentation of this technique also allows us better to understand the process of condensation. Since to interpret is to associate, it goes without saying that the symbolic utterance is always "condensed": condensation is an inevitable effect of interpretation.

To say that unconscious symbolism, if it exists, is not defined by its operations is to make an observation with numerous consequences. I shall consider just one of them here. An interpretative strategy may codify either its destination point (the meaning to be discovered) or the trajectory that links the text with which one begins to the text reached at the end: it may be either "finalist" or "operational." Freud presents the psychoanalytical interpretation, in accordance with his scientific requirements, as a strategy that does not prejudge the final meaning, but discovers it. Now, we know today that the interpretative operations described by Freud are, apart from terminology, those of any sym-

4. I am leaving aside here the role played by transference. It is discussed in the French version of this work, pp. 366–369.

bolism. No particular operational constraint weighs upon the psychoanalytical interpretation; it is thus not the nature of these operations that accounts for the results obtained. If psychoanalysis is really a specific strategy (as I believe), it can only be such, on the contrary, through an a priori codification of the results to be obtained. Psychoanalytical interpretation can only be defined as an interpretation that discovers in the objects analyzed a content in harmony with psychoanalytical doctrine.

The evidence for this is provided, moreover, not only by an analysis of Freud's practice but also, occasionally, by his own theoretical formulations. We have seen that Freud was conscious of the fact that the relation between symbolizer (manifest content) and symbolized (latent thoughts) was in no way different from that pertaining between the two meanings of a trope or the two terms of a comparison. Not of just any comparison, however. Freud writes:

> The essence of this symbolic relation is that it is a comparison, though not a comparison of *any* sort. Special limitations seem to be attached to the comparison, but it is hard to say what these are. Not everything with which we can compare an object or a process appears in dreams as a symbol for it. And on the other hand a dream does not symbolize every possible element of the latent dream-thoughts but only certain definite ones. So there are restrictions here in both directions. [*IP*, x, p. 152; Freud's italics]

In fact, Freud did not stop at these suspicions alone, especially insofar as the choice of latent ideas was concerned. In *The Interpretation of Dreams*, he sets a limit to the multiplication of meanings, a place where the references from one meaning to another come to a halt: there exist ultimate symbolized elements, which are no longer convertible in turn into symbolizers.

> Dreams frequently seem to have more than one meaning. Not only, as our examples have shown, may they include several wish-fulfillments one alongside the other; but a succession of meanings or wish-fulfillments may be superimposed on one another, the bottom one being the fulfillment of a wish dating from earliest childhood. And here again the question arises whether it might not be more correct to assert that this occurs "invariably" rather than "frequently." [*ID*, 4, 219]

The desires of early infancy close the symbolic circuit here.

The same limitation of possible meanings, which makes psychoanalytic interpretation a finalist interpretation, is maintained elsewhere. "The range of things which are given symbolic representation in dreams is not wide: the human body as a whole, parents, children, brothers and sisters, birth, death, nakedness. . . . The very great majority of symbols in dreams are sexual symbols" (*IP*, x, p. 153). This passage defines the interpretative strategy of psychoanalysis, one of the most powerful of our day. Its "finalist" character is patent, and parallels with that other great finalist strategy, that of Patristic exegesis, can hardly be avoided. The substance of the terms aside, does the sentence just quoted not recall one that figured in Origen's remote treatise *On First Principles*? Here is how the Christian practitioners of hermeneutics are characterized in that text:

> Therefore it is chiefly the doctrine about God, that is, about the Father, Son and Holy Spirit, which is indicated by those men who were filled with the divine Spirit. Then, too, the mysteries relating to the Son of God, how the Word became flesh, and for what reason he went to the length of "taking upon him the form of a servant," have also been made known by those who were filled, as we have said, with the divine Spirit. [IV, II, 7; in Butterworth trans., p. 283]

In both texts, it is foreknowledge of the meaning to be discovered that guides the interpretation (which does not mean that psychoanalysis is a religion).[5]

Our examination of the texts Freud devoted to rhetoric and symbolics might be summarized in one sentence. Freud's contribution to these areas is considerable, but it does not always lie where he thought it did, nor where his disciples have seen it. It is no less pertinent for all that.

---

5. Marthe Robert has strongly emphasized the fact that, in a manner opposed to that of religious interpretations, the Freudian trajectory always moves from the spiritual to the carnal (*Sur le papier* [Paris, 1967], p. 239).

9

Saussure's Semiotics

===

Glossolalia moved from the province of religion into that of medicine around the middle of the nineteenth century. In the early 1800s, the German Justinius Kerner could still take the incomprehensible phonic sequences of the "seer of Prevorst"[1] to be revelations from on high. But the positivist spirit was waiting in the wings, and by the end of the century we hear of "glossolalia" or "speaking in tongues" every time someone utters a series of sounds that are incomprehensible to anyone else but that the speaker considers part of an unknown language. The Irvingian sect in England, the collective mystical ecstasies in Sweden, and a visionary German pastor, Paul (not to mention his illustrious namesake, Saint Paul), are treated by psychologists and doctors as if they are no different, qualitatively, from the extravagant American Le Baron (a pseudonym) who thinks he can converse with the Egyptian pharaohs; all these people suddenly imagine that they understand and speak a foreign language when in fact they do not know a word of it except when they are in these ecstatic states.[2]

---

1. *Die Seherin von Prevorst* 2d ed. (Stuttgart and Tübingen, 1832).
2. For overviews, see Jean Bobon, *Introduction historique à l'étude des néologismes et des glossolalies en psychopathologie* (Paris and Liège, 1932); and W. J. Samarin, *Tongues of Men and Angels* (New York, 1972).

Linguists lose no time in pointing out that these so-called languages have nothing to do with the idioms to which they lay claim, but that, on the contrary, they are "deformed" products of languages known by the same person in a normal state. Thus Wilhelm Grimm had shown that the "divine" language of one of the most famous glossolalists, Saint Hildegard, was nothing but a mixture of German and Latin.

Of the many cases recorded, one merits special attention, because of the reactions it aroused. This is the case of a young girl, known under the pseudonym Mlle Hélène Smith, who lived in Geneva at the end of the nineteenth century and the beginning of the twentieth. She attracted the attention of local psychologists because of her somnambulism and her mediumistic trances, states in which psychologists of the day took special interest. She was a remarkable subject for observation, being cooperative and frank; moreover, she never sought to profit financially from her capacity as a medium. In the course of her trances, she began to "speak in tongues"; this phenomenon intrigued one of her observers to such an extent that he soon afterward published a thick volume containing a detailed description of her case. The writer in question was Theodore Flournoy, professor of psychology at the University of Geneva; his book was called *From India to the Planet Mars*.[3]

Indeed, Mlle Smith lived two "novels," as Flournoy called them: in one she visited the planet Mars and communicated with stellar beings; in the other she experienced an Oriental adventure that took place partly in India. Flournoy consequently identified and transcribed two "languages," Martian and Hindu (or Sanskritoid). As his knowledge of Hindi-based languages was very limited, he called upon several colleagues at the University of Geneva, and most importantly upon the "eminent Orientalist, M. Ferdinand de Saussure."[4] These events took place between 1895 and 1898.

The analysis of the "Hindoo" language seems to have fascinated Saussure to a degree that is difficult to fathom. He took

3. Trans. D. B. Vermilye (New York and London, 1900): quotations are from this text except where otherwise indicated. As the published translation is incomplete, certain passages have been translated directly from *Des Indes à la planète Mars* (Paris and Geneva, 1900; abbreviated *DI*).

4. The expression is from E. Lombard, *De la glossalie chez les premiers chrétiens et des phénomènes similaires* (Lausanne, 1910), p. 62.

the greatest care in commenting upon Mlle Smith's linguistic productions; he attended seances and suggested possible interpretations of her case. As a result, fully half the chapter in which Flournoy deals with the Hindu language is composed of excerpts from Saussure's letters.

To begin with, there is the puzzling fact that Mlle Smith has never learned a single word of Sanskrit (her probity cannot be questioned; this is not a hoax); yet her Hindu discourse strongly resembles Sanskrit. Several solutions come to mind: perhaps she lived in India in a former life, or perhaps her soul travels there while her body remains in Geneva, speaking Hindu, under the professors' watchful eyes. Or else—a more acceptable solution for scientific psychology—she grasps other people's knowledge, through telepathic communication; yet there is apparently no one in her surroundings who knows Sanskrit. Saussure attended his first seance two years after her initial glossolalic productions. Or else, finally, there is the possibility that Mlle Smith has heard a student of Sanskrit in Geneva reciting his conjugations aloud in the next room; or else, perhaps while taking a walk, she has happened upon a treatise on Sanskrit and this fact has been effaced from her memory. This would be the most satisfying solution, but Flournoy never succeeds in verifying it.

Here is Saussure's general characterization of Mlle Smith's Sanskritoid language:

"As to the question of ascertaining whether all this really represents Sanscrit, it is evidently necessary to answer, *No.* One can only say:

"First: That it is a medley of syllables, in the midst of which there are, incontestably, some series of eight to ten syllables, constituting a fragment of a sentence which has a meaning . . .

"Secondly: that the other syllables, of unintelligible aspect, never have an anti-Sanscrit character—i.e., do not present groups materially contrary or in opposition to the general figure of the Sanscrit words." [Pp. 328–329]

At the same time, Saussure points out a series of incompatibilities or contradictions. Here are two examples:

"The most surprising thing," remarks M. de Saussure, "is that Mme Simandini [the Indian reincarnation of Mlle Smith] spoke Sanscrit, and not Pracrit [Indian women speak Prakrit and not Sanskrit] . . . But the idiom of Simandini, even though it be a

Sanscrit very hard to recognize, is not in any case the Pracrit"
[Pp. 320–321]

And, commenting upon another example of her discourse:

"*Sumina*," says M. de Saussure, "recalls nothing. *Attamana*, at
most *âtmânam* (accusative of *âtmâ*), *l'âme*, 'the soul'; but I hasten
to say that in the context in which *attamana* figures one could
not make use of the Sanscrit word which resembles it, and
which at bottom only signifies (*âme*) 'soul' in philosophical language, and in the sense of *l'âme universelle*, or other learned
meanings." [P. 324]

Flournoy tells the story of the last episode of Saussure's inter-
vention as follows: "The preceding pages had already gone to
press when M. de Saussure had an ingenious and appealing idea.
. . . He decided to compose a text for their benefit [i.e., for
readers who did not know Sanskrit] that would be to the language of Livy or Cicero as nearly as possible what Simandini's
Sanskrit is to that of the Brahmans" (*DI*, p. 315). The para-Latin
text and its commentaries follow. Saussure concludes:

"Two important conclusions impose themselves:
"1. The text does not confuse 'two languages.' However
little these words may resemble Latin, at least we see no third
language, such as Greek, Russian, or English, intervening. . . .
2. It also has particular value in that *it presents nothing contrary to
Latin*, even in the places where it corresponds to nothing because the words are without meaning. Let us abandon Latin
here and return to Mlle Smith's Sanskrit: this Sanskrit *never*
contains *the consonant f*. This is an important detail, though a
negative one. In fact *f* is foreign to Sanskrit; now in free invention, the chances would be twenty to one that the speaker
would have created Sanskrit words including the letter *f*, that
consonant appearing as legitimate as any other to the unini-
tiated. [*DI*, p. 316]

The troubling absence of *f* remains incomprehensible, and
Flournoy ends up perplexed: how can we explain that Mlle Smith
has guessed such a specific feature of the Sanskrit language without recourse to occult powers (since deception is ruled out from
the start)? Would it have sufficed to glance through a treatise on
Sanskrit to notice this?

But the story of Mlle Smith and the missing *f* does not stop
there. As soon as Flournoy's book appeared, it fell into the hands

of another linguist, a professor of Sanskrit like Saussure; full of enthusiasm for the curious linguistic matter it presents, Victor Henry rapidly wrote a little book that was published the following year as *Le Langage martien*.[5] Now this work does focus on the interpretation of Martian and not of Hindu (the Martian language is given a much fuller treatment); furthermore, Henry bows to the authority of his eminent colleague Saussure, who has commented at length on the Sanskritoid texts. There is only one limited point on which he allows himself to make a suggestion: it concerns precisely the absence of *f*. But his suggestion throws a surprising light on all that precedes. Victor Henry writes: "If one general thought completely occupies Mlle Smith's subconscious at the time she is assembling the sounds of Sanskritoid or Martian, it is surely that 'French' must be entirely avoided: her entire attention must be focused on that point. Now the word 'French' (*français*) begins with an *f*, for this reason, *f* must appear to her as the "French" letter *par excellence*, and thus she avoids it as much as she can" (p. 23).

Thus the absence of the letter *f* would be explained not by a supernatural knowledge of Sanskrit, but by Mlle Smith's attitude with regard to her native tongue: the significance of *f* is determined by the mechanism of acrophony that has been well known since the earliest studies of the history of writing. To make this discovery, one has only to recognize that the logic of symbolism is *not* necessarily the same as that of language; or even, more simply, that alongside language there exist other modes of symbolism that we must first learn to perceive. The letter *f* symbolizes "French" owing to a relation that is not characteristic of language conceived as a system of signs.

Now Saussure does not admit diversity among symbolic systems. If we reexamine his comments at this point, we notice that he is more prepared, confronted as he is with an apparently insoluble problem, to acknowledge the supernatural (transmigrations of Mlle Smith's soul) than to modify his method of investigation—which touches here upon the principles of symbolic functioning. Rather than relate these Sanskrit utterances to French (for it is obvious that Mlle Smith does not know Sanskrit), he confines himself to a logic of referential plausibility: why does this language resemble Sanskrit when women ought to speak Prakrit

5. Paris, 1901.

(as if Mlle Smith, alias Simandini, had really attended the ceremonies that she describes, ceremonies that took place tens of
centuries earlier and thousands of miles away)? Why does she
use philosophical words in an everyday context? Unable to look
squarely at the symbolic relation itself, Saussure attends only to
the referential context—an all-the-more paradoxical approach in
that, unless we accept transmigration of the soul, this context
is purely imaginary. Repression where the symbol is concerned
proves stronger than the prevailing scientific taboo ruling out
recourse to the supernatural. Flournoy tends in the same direction when he invites Saussure to a seance in order to assure a
more faithful transcription of the Sanskritoid language: "M. de
Saussure, very much better qualified than we are to distinguish
the Hindoo sounds" (p. 326). But in order to produce "Hindoo
sounds," Mlle Smith has to have visited India, which she has not
done in this lifetime. Thus both men have implicitly accepted the
supernatural version of these events, professors though they are,
and at Geneva no less: all for want of admitting the existence of a
logic of symbolism other than that of language (confused with
that of reason). An (analytic) eavesdropper would have usefully
replaced the practiced ear of the Sanskrit expert.

The phenomenon is all the more striking in that, in Flournoy's
book, unceasing attention is paid to the *subconscious* (and he cites
approvingly the studies in *On the Psychical Mechanism of Hysterical
Phenomena* by Breuer and Freud). Saussure, in a way, is not far
from the solution. He makes a significant lapsus in presenting his
Latinoid: he writes that "the text does not confuse *two* languages"
and immediately adds that "at least we see no *third* language,
such as Greek, Russian, or English intervene" (emphasis added).
Two becomes three through the addition of the mother tongue,
French, which, significantly, does not appear among the languages cited as possible examples. And at another point he
writes:

> "Let us suppose that Simandini wants to say the following sen-
> tence: *I bless you in the name of Ganapati.* Placed in the Sivroukian
> state, the only thing that does not come to her mind is to utter,
> or rather to *pronounce* that sentence in the French words which
> remain the theme or the substratum of what she is going to say;
> and the rule her mind obeys is that these familiar words must
> each be replaced by an exotic-sounding substitute. It scarcely
> matters how: it is essential only, and above all, that these
> sounds not resemble French in he own view." [*DI*, pp. 304–305]

Saussure thus finds himself very close to the solution, but it escapes him. Like so many who come after him, he has an inkling of the right path, but he is unable to transcend the limits of his own premises, and so he stops short on the threshold of discovery.

Let us return now to Mlle Smith's other language, Martian.

Her Martian utterances are more numerous than the Hindu ones. Moreover, some time after she has produced them, she provides a literal translation of each one: the complete transcription of both versions is available in Flournoy's book. Flournoy himself launches the work of interpretation as he opts rapidly for a basic hypothesis: "The 'Martian' is, in my opinion, only an infantile travesty of French" (p. 241). In support of this opinion, Flournoy relies initially upon phonic and graphic properties: "Martian phonetics, in a word, are only an incomplete reproduction of French phonetics" (p. 246). And where writing is concerned: "Here again we are in the presence of a feeble imitation of our system of handwriting" (p. 247). In the second place, and here the evidence speaks for itself, Flournoy relies on the morphological system, in particular on the fact that French homonyms are homonyms in Martian as well: "At all times the Martian translates the French word, allowing itself to be guided by auditive analogies without regard to the real meaning, in such a way that we are surprised to discover in the idiom of the planet Mars the same peculiarities of homonyms as in French" (p. 250).

Thus the French preposition *à* and the verb *a* are rendered by the same Martian word *é*; the French words *si, le, de, te,* and so on receive similar treatment. What resists analysis, however, is the Martian lexicon itself: it appears to Flournoy to be perfectly arbitrary.

Deciphering this lexicon, or more precisely its mode of production, is the task Victor Henry takes on in his book on Martian language. Here we must recall that, five years earlier, the same Henry had published a work of general linguistics entitled *Antinomies linguistiques*,[6] a book rich in new and bold ideas whose third chapter has some bearing on the questions that concern us. This chapter considers whether language is conscious or unconscious by nature: Henry resolves this "antinomy" in the following way: "Language is the product of the unconscious activity of a conscious subject" (p. 65); and, further on: "If language is a conscious

6. Paris, 1896.

phenomenon, its mechanisms are unconscious" (p. 78). Among other examples of unconscious mechanisms we find cases of lapsus, contamination of several words or phrases, popular etymology, transfer of meaning through the use of tropes, and so on.

This idea serves as the basis for Henry's study of Martian language, since the author supposes that Mlle Hélène Smith unconsciously used these same mechanisms of language in general in creating the Martian language: "The language created by a glossolalist will reproduce, and allow us to grasp, with the clarity that results from direct observation, the unconscious and subconscious mechanisms of normal language" (p. v). Certain pathways are not available to conscious thought in the waking state. We must not conclude from this that an ordinary subject cannot follow them, for such a subject also possesses a subconscious and an unconscious self. The other place where the subconscious manifests itself spontaneously (outside of linguistic creation) is the dream; and Henry repeatedly justifies his own approach by referring to the logic of dreams: "The logic of dreams is not at all that of the man who is awake and fully conscious" (p. 23). "The logic of dreams is bolder and vaguer than that of a waking subject" (p. 48). Thus we witness the dawning of that other logic whose existence Saussure was unwilling to recognize.

The mechanisms that Henry sets forth are familiar to any specialist in etymology (or, more generally, in rhetoric, since the mechanisms of etymological derivation are, as we have seen, only a projection of the tropic matrix onto history). On the level of the signifier, we encounter addition, suppression, and permutation (metathesis). On the level of the signified, which we shall consider at greater length, we rediscover the basic tropes.[7] Here, to begin with, are some synecdoches: *miza*, derived from Fr. *maison*, "house," signifies "movable pavilion" (a particularizing material synecdoche) in Martian; *chéké*, from Fr. *cheque*, "check," signifies "paper" (a generalizing conceptual synecdoche); *épizi*, from Fr. *épine*, "thorn," means *rose*, "rose(color)" (this is a double synecdoche: the thorn for the rose, through a particularizing material synecdoche, and the rose for the color, through a particularizing conceptual synecdoche). Here are several examples of metonymy: *zati*, from Fr. *myosotis*, "forget-me-not" (the French common name in the exact equivalent), means *souvenir*, "memory" (the sign for

7. In this context I am using the terminology proposed by Jacques Dubois et al., *Rhétorique générale* (Paris, 1970).

the thing); *chiré*, from Fr. *chéri*, "dear," "cherished," means *fils*, "son" (the quality for the thing); *ziné*, from Fr. *Chine*, "China," means *porcelaine* (the place of origin for the thing). And an antiphrasis: *abadâ*, from Fr. *abondant*, "abundant," means *peu*, "little."

Other mechanisms are more interesting, owing to the complexity of the operations they put into play. To begin with, there are contaminations (portmanteau words): the Martian word *midée*, a contraction of *misère*, "misery," "poverty," and *hideux*, "hideous," signifies "ugly"; *forimé*, from *forme*, "form," and *firme*, "firm," means "marks (of writing)." There are also cross-language word plays (Henry leans heavily on Mlle Smith's knowledge of German and Magyar, limited though it is). Thus the Martian word *nazère* derives, in his opinion, from the word *Nase*, which means *nez*, "nose," in German and also *trompe*, "(elephant's) trunk; in Martian it signifies the first person plural, singular, of the verb *tromper*, "to deceive": (*je*) *trompe*, "I deceive." The homonymy of *trompe* in French makes it possible to designate one of its meanings by the German equivalent of the other (this mechanism is also widespread in the history of writing systems, under the name of "rebus"). Another example: the Martian word *tiziné* would come from the Magyar *tiz*, which means *dix (doigts)*, "ten (fingers)"; now ten fingers make *deux mains*, "two hands":' and *tiziné*, in Martian, means *demain*, "tomorrow"!

This last example brings us closer to Freud's interpretations of his patients' dreams; the next two, multilingual transformations, attest to a degree of mental acrobatics that makes verification difficult. The proper name *Esenale*, in the Martian novel, corresponds unmistakably to a person who lived on earth, a certain Alexis; but how can we account for the shift from Alexis to Esenale? The sequence *-al-* remains intact, moving from the beginning of the first name to the end of the second; *exis* recalls the Magyar *csacsi*, which means *âne*, "donkey," a word rendered in German by *Esel*; the *l* becomes *n* through dissimilation, and *Alexis* becomes *Esenale*. A final example: the Martian word *éréduté* means *solitaire*, "solitary." The transformation comes about as follows. First *éréduté* is decomposed into *éréd-* (which gives *Erde* by metathesis—German for *terre*, "earth"), *-ut-* (the name of the musical note *sol*, G, and *-é*, which is changed into the neighboring vowel *i*, *sol-i-terre* produces *solitaire*.[8] Henry succeeds in demon-

---

8. But *ut* means *do* and not *sol*. . . . Has Henry forgotten, or is Mlle Smith confused?

strating in this way the process by which nearly all the terms constituting the Martian lexicon were created.

Just as Freud claimed to have learned everything from his hysterical patients, we hardly know which to admire the more: Victor Henry's ingenuity, or that of Mlle Hélène Smith's "subconscious self." It is clear, however, that even if we can make some connections (which are striking because of the chronological coincidence), Henry's pages remain merely *haunted* by a Freudian spirit that never truly inhabits them. The new linguistics misses its first opportunity to embark upon the road of the symbolic (and thus its opportunity to open itself to psychoanalysis at its inception). The opportunity will not arise again for decades. *Le Langage martien* has no effect whatever on the evolution of science.

At least the conclusion that Victor Henry draws is clear: "invented" and "meaningless" words are in fact derived from other words. The language of the glossolalist is a *motivated* language. Henry writes: "Even a person making an unstinting effort to create a language *that resembles nothing else* could not escape the fatal necessity of betraying this project, of hinting at the play of the secret organs that work together in the unconscious self toward the entirely mechanical elaboration of human language" (p. 7). And also: "Man could not invent a language if he wanted to: he can only speak, he only speaks, through his memories, be they immediate, mediate, or atavistic" (p. 140).

We should add at once that a complete absence of interpretation is not impossible; we even encounter this variant during another period in Mlle Hélène Smith's life. Noticing that the structures of French have been identified in her Martian utterances, she passes to another "language," discovered by herself, that Flournoy calls "ultra-Martian." This new language quite decidedly does not lend itself to interpretation, but this is precisely its meaning: to be unintelligible. Paraphrasing Jakobson, we might say that the glossolalist's neologisms are linguistic or antilinguistic, but never a-linguistic.

Another feature of glossolalic productions has attracted the attention of almost all observers: the abundance of alliterations and of rhythmic figures. As has so often been the case both before and since, this other mechanism of symbolic thought is considered an atavistic feature—or, in the best of cases, a poetic feature. Flournoy notes the "frequent use of alliteration, assonance and rhyme" (*DI*, p. 240) and relates this phenomenon to poetry.

Henry does the same thing ("as in all primitive languages," he writes) and speaks of "this subconscious ever ready to versify" (p. 34). Lombard writes that "the versifying tendency is very pronounced in glossolalists, as it is in general with prophets and seers. This is yet another regressive feature, if it is true that in all the literatures of the world poetry appeared before prose" (p. 140). We may conclude that a symbolic system such as the glossolalist's discourse, compared to language, reinforces "syntax," understood in the broad sense (that is, the relationship of constituent elements among themselves) at the expense, often, of "semantics" (the relationship of the elements with what they designate).

Saussure's first contact with the symbolic thus ends in failure. If I have insisted on presenting it here in detail, it is because it has gone unnoticed, to my knowledge, until now; but also because it prefigures in a remarkable way Saussure's relations with symbolic phenomena to the very end of his career. It is not a question of reproaching him for this, even retrospectively; the sketchy state in which *all* of Saussure's research remained, from this period onward, shows clearly enough to what extent he himself was dissatisfied with the results obtained. But his impasses have exemplary value: they anticipate those of a large sector of modern linguistics.

Although it is difficult to date Saussure's manuscripts, the first group we must consider would appear to be the studies on paragrams, undertaken between 1906 and 1909.[9] To be sure, what particularly attracts our attention in these texts is the absence of any problematics related to the symbolic dimensions of language—an absence that is all the more astonishing given that we are dealing with analyses of poetic phenomena. Saussure situates himself in the perspective of an extreme "formalism," if we may use that term for the exclusive attention paid to "syntactic" phenomena. What interests him is the configuration formed by the elements of the signifier ("couplings," "diphones," "mannequins," or what he calls "phonic paraphrase," all variants of paronomasia), never the relations of evocation or of symbolic suggestion. If the word that is the object of "phonic paraphrase" is absent from the line of verse, Saussure may become preoccupied with certain relations of evocation; but then he immediately reduces their semantic depth

9. Published in part by Jean Starobinski under the title *Les Mots sous les mots* (Paris, 1971); Eng. trans. by O. Emmet, *Words upon Words: The Anagrams of Ferdinand de Saussure* (New Haven, 1979).

to zero: the sounds "allude" not to a meaning (still less, as the romantics would have had it, to an infinite number of meanings), but only to a *name*—the word is reduced to its signifier. The "themes" that Saussure seeks and discovers in Vedic, Greek, and Latin poetry are, first and foremost, proper nouns.

In a second group of rough drafts, dating apparently from 1909–1910[10] and devoted to the study of the *Nibelungen* and other legends, Saussure deals to a greater extent with symbols. But most of the time he speaks of symbols only to affirm that there are none in these legends; that what the modern reader takes to be symbols are only unjustified projections of his own reading habits. More precisely, these ancient texts have become "symbolic" by virtue of deformations: lacunae, omissions, errors in transmission lead the modern reader toward a symbolic interpretation.

> An author of an epic or even of a historical text tells the story of a battle between two armies, and among others the combat of the leaders. Soon we hear of no one but the leaders. Then the duel between leader A and leader B becomes (inevitably) symbolic since this single combat represents the entire outcome of the battle. . . . The reduction of the battle to a duel is a natural phenomenon in semiologic transmission, produced through a lapse of time between narrations, and consequently the symbol exists only in the imagination of the critic who comes along after the fact and judges badly. [P. 30]

And again:

> One might think that a *symbol* was present, whereas there is simply an error in transmission touching on words that originally had a perfectly direct meaning. —Symbolic creations exist, but they are the product of natural errors in transmission. [P. 31]

> We may recognize a symbol that is explained as not having been a symbol at first. . . . Symbolic interpretation exists only in the hands of the critic. . . . For the person who is listening to a story being told, as for the rhapsodic narrator who is repeating the story as he heard it from his predecessor, it is the gospel truth that Hagen threw the treasure into the Rhine—and *consequently* there is no symbol in the end, as there was none at the beginning *either*. [Ibid.]

10. Excerpts from these drafts have been published by D'Arco Silvio Avalle as "La Sémiologie de la narrativité chez Saussure," in *Essais de la théorie du texte* (Paris, 1973).

If symbols exist only for someone who "judges badly," or do not even exist at all, it is because Saussure, in order to identify them, needs a category that he could have found in Augustine: that of the intentional sign (but Augustine also recognized the existence of nonintentional signs alongside of intentional ones). For Saussure, according to the psychological framework within which he is operating, intentionality is a constituent feature of the symbol; now this feature is absent from the legends in question, even though these legends may be "symbolic" for today's reader. "An *intention to symbolize* existed at no time during that period. . . . Symbolic creations are always involuntary" (p. 30). "Like all types of signs, symbols are never anything but the result of an evolution that created an involuntary relation among things: they are neither invented nor immediately self-evident" (p. 31).

Not being intentional, symbols have a hard time existing.

It is true that we find in these same notebooks another text which reserves a more important place for symbols and which proclaims the necessity of a *semiology*. But the word "symbol" is in fact used here in the place of *sign*:

—The legend is composed of a series of symbols in a sense that must be specified.
—These symbols are unwittingly subjected to the same vicissitudes and to the same laws as all other series of symbols, for example the symbols that are the words of language.
—They are all part of *semiology*. [P. 28]

This "meaning to be specified" can be discovered in the courses in general linguistics that Saussure taught between 1907 and 1911, for which unfortunately we do not have even rough drafts but only notes, often contradictory ones, taken by his students.[11] Here the general term systematically becomes *sign*; *symbol* has the meaning "motivated sign"; except for the terms themselves, we have an opposition familiar to Port-Royal, Dubos, Lessing, and so on. For example:

1131.2. The signs of language are totally arbitrary whereas in certain polite expressions they lose this arbitrary character and

11. These notes, edited by R. Engler, have been published in the *Cours de linguistique générale*, critical edition (Wiesbaden, 1967; fasc. 1 and 2 contain the sections that concern us). References to this edition consist of a first number indicating the sentence and a second indicating the notebook used (this corresponds to the column number in Engler's edition).

move closer to being symbols. . . . 1137.2. It is characteristic of the symbol that it is never completely arbitrary; the symbol is not empty. There is the rudiment of a link between the idea and the sign, in the symbol: 1138.2. The scale, symbol of justice.

Saussure's "sign" is what Ast, and sometimes Goethe, called allegory; they contrasted it, as he does, with *symbol.*

We know, however, that arbitrariness is not, for Saussure, merely one of the sign's various features, but its fundamental characteristic: the arbitrary sign is the sign par excellence. This postulate has important implications for the place of symbols within the semiology of the future: their place is of necessity extremely limited. The *Course* edited by Charles Bally and Albert Sechehaye is in this respect particularly blunt: it affirms that all signs have to be understood on the model of the linguistic sign, and that all of semiology must be modeled on linguistics. "Signs that are wholly arbitrary realize better than the others the ideal of the semiological process; that is why language, the most complex and universal of all systems of expression, is also the most characteristic; in this sense linguistics can become the master pattern for all branches of semiology although language is only one particular semiological system.[12]

What the manuscripts say is more moderate. The proposition "that is why language . . . is also the most characteristic" finds no support there; only one student (Albert Riedlinger) notes the last proposition, and in particular the expression "master pattern for all branches of semiology"; the most common formulation is the following: "276.4. Language is not the only sign system, but it is the most important one." Moreover, Riedlinger notes a restriction that Bally and Sechehaye omit: "290.2. But from the outset it must be said that language will occupy the principal subdivision of this science [semiology]; it will be the master pattern. But this will be *by chance* [emphasis added]: theoretically, it will only be *one* particular branch [of semiology]."

The editors have thus hardened Saussure's thought; but they have not betrayed it. Now, such an affirmation clearly means that there is no place for symbols within semiology; this latter domain accepts signs other than linguistic ones only to the extent that they are in no way different from linguistic ones! Broader in its

12. *Course in General Linguistics,* trans. W. Baskin (New York, 1959), p. 68.

extension, semiology coincides exactly with linguistics in its comprehensiveness. Thus Saussure can say: "1128.2. When semiology is organized, it will have to see whether systems other than arbitrary ones will also fall within its domain. 1129.2. In all cases it will be particularly concerned with arbitrary systems." The question remains open, as indeed the editors of the *Course* observed; we can read the following exchange in the margin of the manuscript that they were establishing: "288.6. *A.S.* Does semiology study signs and symbols? *Ch.B.* De Saussure responds somewhere that this remains to be seen!"

Not only do nonlinguistic symbols not really warrant a place in semiology, but even the symbolic aspects of the linguistic sign are neglected: as symbols in language, Saussure envisages onomatopoeia and interjection ("exclamation"), but never tropes or allusions (it is true that the latter exist only in what he calls "speech" [*parole*], not in "language" [*langage*]. Someone like Lessing has much more to teach us in this respect. The only suggestion that might have led to a true typology of signs remains undeveloped: we read in the notes: "276.2. In language, signs evoke ideas *directly*. . . ." "276.5. It might be said that almost all institutions are based on signs, but these signs do not evoke things directly." Not only will this opposition between the direct and the indirect not be taken up again or made explicit, but we note that it appears only in the juxtaposition of two versions of the same part of Saussure's discourse (none of his students noted both sentences).

Saussure's work appears remarkably homogeneous today in its refusal to accept symbolic phenomena. In his correspondence with Flournoy, Saussure simply leaves these phenomena aside; this accounts for the failure of his attempts to explain the language of Mlle Smith. In his research on anagrams, he pays attention only to the phenomena of repetition, not to those of evocation; when he is obliged to attend to the latter, he limits himself to the identification of a word, most often a proper noun, that opens up no symbolic trajectory. In his studies of the *Nibelungen*, he recognizes symbols only in order to attribute them to mistaken readings: since they are not intentional, symbols do not exist. Finally, in his courses on general linguistics, he contemplates the existence of semiology, and thus of signs other than linguistic ones; but this affirmation is at once limited by the fact that semiology is devoted to a single type of signs: those which are arbitrary, like the linguistic signs. There is no room for the symbolic in Saussure.

Curiously, the effects of the romantic crisis are almost imperceptible in the human sciences around 1900. In their condemnation, explicit or implicit, of the symbol, in their very conception of what the symbol is, Saussure, Lévy-Bruhl and even Freud—in varying degrees, to be sure, and for aspects of their thought that have unequal importance—are neoclassics rather than romantics, contemporaries of Condillac much more than grandchildren of Moritz, Goethe, or F. Schlegel. Saussure is romantic when he grants special importance to systems, or in his refusal to explain meaning through some relation to an external referent; he ceases to be romantic when he turns a deaf ear to symbolics.

10

Jakobson's Poetics

Whenever one attempts to survey the work of a theoretician of poetics, an initial question arises: what is literature?

It so happens that this question—and its answer—permeate the writings of Roman Jakobson, to such an extent that one of his studies bears the title *Qu'est-ce que la poésie?* (What is poetry?). His answer, despite minor terminological changes, remains astonishingly consistent. In 1919, Jakobson wrote: "For me, the unique and essential moment of poetry is the expressive intent of the verbal mass. . . . Poetry is nothing other than *an utterance aiming to express*" (*QP*, pp. 20, 14).[1] In 1933: "The content of the notion of

1. The following abbreviations are used in references to Jakobson's work: *QP: Questions de poétique* (Paris, 1973); *LP*, "Linguistics and Poetics," in *Essays on the Language of Literature*, ed. Seymour Chatman and S. R. Levin (Boston, 1967), pp. 296–322 (also in Thomas Sebeok, *Style in Language* [New York, 1960], pp. 350–377); *MN*: "Marginal Notes on the Prose of the Poet Pasternak (1935)," in *Pasternak*, ed. Donald Davie and Angela Livingstone (Nashville and London, 1970), pp. 135–151; *RA*: "On Realism in Art," in *Readings in Russian Poetics*, ed. Ladislav Matejka and K. Pomorska (Ann Arbor, Mich., 1971), pp. 38–46; *PS*: "A Postscript to the Discussion on Grammar of Poetry," *Diacritics*, 10, no. 1 (Spring 1980), pp. 22–25; *TA*: "Two Aspects of Language and Two Types of Aphasic Disturbances," in *Fundamentals of Language*, by R. Jakobson and M. Halle (The Hague and Paris, 1956), pp. 69–96 (also in *Selected Writings* II [The Hague, 1971], pp. 239–259).

poetry is unstable and it varies over time, but the poetic function, *poeticity,* as the Formalists have singled it out, is a unique element, *sui generis.* . . . But how does poeticity manifest itself? In that the word is felt as word and not as a simple substitute for the object named, nor as an explosion of emotion" (*QP,* pp. 123, 124). And in 1960: "The set (*Einstellung*) toward the MESSAGE as such, the focus on the message for its own sake, is the POETIC function of language" (*LP,* p. 302).

The poetic use of language is distinguished from other uses through the fact that, in poetry, language is perceived in itself and not as a transparent and transitive mediator of "something else." The term thus defined is, in 1919, *poetry;* it later becomes *poetics* (the poetic function), that is, the abstract category that is grasped through the perceptible phenomenon. But the definition itself has not changed. Poetic language is autotelic language.

Where does this definition come from? One of Jakobson's recent texts confirms the reply that a reader of the preceding chapters might offer to this question. Reflecting on the influences that have marked him, Jakobson writes:

> But already much earlier [than 1915, when he read Husserl], about 1912 [that is, when he was sixteen years old], as a secondary-school student who had resolutely chosen language and poetry as the object of his future research, I came across the writings of Novalis, and I was delighted to discover in his work, as at the same time in Mallarmé, the inseparable conjunction of the great poet with the profound theoretician of language. . . . The so-called Russian Formalist school was in its germination period before the First World War. The controversial notion of *self-regulation (Selbstgesetzmässigkeit) of form,* to use the poet's language, underwent an evolution in this movement, from the earliest mechanistic stances to an authentically dialectical conception. This latter had already found a fully synthetic incitation, in Novalis's famous "Monologue"—which had from the beginning astonished and bewitched me.[2]

Novalis and Mallarmé in fact are two names that appear in Jakobson's writings from the very beginning. Moreover, the latter source has its own origin in the former, although the affiliation is indirect: Mallarmé lived after Baudelaire, who admired Poe, who absorbed Coleridge—whose theoretical writings were a condensed version of the writings of the German romantics, and

2. *Form und Sinn* (Munich, 1974), pp. 176–177.

thus of Novalis. Mallarmé presented to his French (and Russian) readers a synthesis of romantic ideas on poetry—ideas that had found no echo in what was called romanticism in France. And in fact in the Jakobsonian definition of poetry we have no trouble recognizing the romantic idea of intransitivity expressed by Novalis and his friends, in the "Monologue" and other fragments. It was indeed Novalis and not Jakobson who defined poetry as an "expression for expression's sake." And no great distance separates Novalis's *Selbstsprache*, autolanguage, and Khlebnikov's *samovitaja rech'*, autonomous discourse; Khlebnikov is still another intermediary between Novalis (or Mallarmé) and Jakobson.

Jakobson and the Russian formalists are not the only recent champions of the romantic definition. After having been forgotten for a hundred years or so, this definition has become the watchword of all avant-garde poetic schools (even those that take a stand against what they call romanticism) since the turn of the century. I shall call upon only one witness here, Jean-Paul Sartre. After declaring that "nobody has ever asked himself . . . what is writing," Sartre reformulates the romantic topos as follows:

> Poets are men who refuse to *utilize* language. . . . The poet has withdrawn from language-instrument in a single movement. Once and for all he has chosen the poetic attitude which considers words as things and not as signs. For the ambiguity of the sign implies that one can penetrate it at will like a pane of glass and pursue the thing signified, or turn his gaze toward its *reality* and consider it as an object.[3]

People have often been tempted to confuse the formalist conception of poetry with the doctrine of art for art's sake. That the two have a common origin (here called "German romanticism") is obvious. For Jakobson, the link is explicit; as for the first formulations of the "art for art's sake" idea, they are only French echoes of German ideas: Benjamin Constant's, after a conversation with Schiller in 1804; Victor Cousin's, after a visit to Solger in 1817. But the differences are equally important: the formalist conception of poetry has to do with the function of language in literature (or of sound in music, and so on); the "art for art's sake" doctrine deals with the function of literature, or art, in social life. Thus Jakobson is right to object to the unwarranted accusations: "Nei-

---

3. *What Is Literature?*, trans. Bernard Frechtman (New York, 1965), foreword, p. xviii, pp. 6–7.

ther Tynianov, nor Mukařovský, nor Shklovskii, nor myself—none of us preaches that art suffices unto itself; we show on the contrary that art is a part of the social edifice, one component in correlation with others" (QP, p. 123).

The social function of poetry that is of particular interest to Jakobson (in Qu'est-ce que la poésie?, for example) is precisely the one summed up by the Mallarméan precept: "give a purer meaning to the words of the tribe."[4] Jakobson writes:

> Poetry protects us against the rust that threatens our formula of love and hatred, of revolt and reconciliation, of faith and denial. The number of citizens of the Czechoslovakian Republic who have read the works of Nezval, for example, is not very great. To the extent that they have read and accepted them, they will—without intending to do so—joke with a friend, insult an adversary, express their emotion, declare and live their love, talk politics, in a slightly different way.[5] [QP, p. 125]

At the same time, Jakobson's thinking on this question does not remain fixed, and its evolution is instructive. In 1919, the total rejection of representation, of any relation between words and what they designate, is, if not the norm of all poetry, at least its ideal. "Poetry is indifferent to the object of the utterance." "What Husserl calls *dinglicher Bezug* is absent" (QP, pp. 14, 21). In 1921, Jakobson devotes an entire study to "realism in art"; he denounces the polysemy of the term, but he does not take a stand on the existence or nonexistence of a relation of representation. Ten years later, dissociating poetics from poetry, he sees the latter as a "complex structure" of which poetic autotelism is only one component. In the study devoted to Pasternak, he considers that the "tendency toward the suppression of objects" is characteristic only of certain poetic schools, such as Russian futurism ("we have identified [a tendency] in the work of Pasternak and his contem-

---

4. "The Tomb of Edgar Poe," in *Mallarmé*, ed. Anthony Hartley (Harmondsworth, England, 1965), p. 90.

5. T. S. Eliot develops the same argument ten years later: "We may say that the duty of the poet, as poet, is only indirectly to his people: his direct duty is to his *language*, first to preserve, and second to extend and improve. . . . So far, I have only suggested the final point to which I think the influence of poetry may be said to extend; and that can be put best by the assertion that, in the long run, it makes a difference to the speech, to the sensibility, to the lives of all the members of a society, to all the members of the community, to the whole people, whether they read and enjoy poetry or not" ("The Social Function of Poetry," in *On Poetry and Poets* [New York, 1957], p. 9 and pp. 11–12).

poraries to make the sign radically independent of its object":
MN, p. 150). Finally, in 1960, he writes: "The supremacy of poetic
function over referential function does not obliterate the reference
but renders it ambiguous" (LP, p. 303). Thus in the span of some
forty years Jakobson has managed to traverse the entire course of
romantic aesthetics.

In order to go beyond the doctrine of pure autotelism, Jakobson (in harmony with the other formalists on this point) indicates
two major directions. The first is the study of *motivation*: "From
time to time, the consistent motivation and justification of poetic
constructions have also been called realism" (RA, p. 45); thus we
are to study not the "reality" that literature designates, but the
means whereby the text gives us the impression of doing this—
the plausibility of literature rather than its truth.

In the second place, the analysis of nonsignificative elements
(sounds, prosody, grammatical forms) is to be extended to the
semantic realm, to "thematic structure"; once more, it is not "reality" as such that becomes the object of analysis, but its mode
of presentation in the text. The unsurpassed model of this type
of work remains the "Marginal Notes on the Prose of the Poet
Pasternak," in which, through a genuine *tour de force*, Jakobson
encompasses in a single "figure" not only the rhetorical play and
semantic or narrative configurations ("we have tried to deduce
the themes of Pasternak's and Mayakovsky's work from the basic
structural features of their poetics": MN, p. 149), but also the
poetic (as opposed to the anecdotal) biography of the writer:
"in this way we have deduced from the semantic makeup of
Mayakovsky's poetry both its actual libretto and the core of the
poet's biography" (MN, p. 140).

But the difference between Novalis (or Sartre) and Jakobson is
not just that the first two define poetry as pure autotelism, whereas the third makes it possible to see the interaction of two components, imitation and play. There is more: Novalis's poetic or
prophetic discourse and the pamphleteer's discourse adopted by
Sartre are qualitatively distinct from Jakobson's *scientific* discourse.
There is perhaps considerable resemblance between the formulas
of the first two and the third, out of context; but their dissimilarity
appears to be (and is) just as important, as soon as we consider
the use that is made of them. Their meaning is nearly the same,
but not their function. What interests Jakobson is not proffering
revelations or denouncing his adversaries, but laying the ground-

work on the basis of which description, *knowledge* of particular literary phenomena will be possible.

In his very first text on literature, Jakobson wrote: "The object of literary science is not literature but literariness. . . . If literary studies want to become scientific, they have to recognize the *device* as their sole 'actor'" (*QP*, p. 15). And, fifty years later, in the "Post-scriptum" to his *Questions de poétique*: "Literariness, in other words, the transformation of a verbal act into a poetic work, and the system of devices that bring about such a transformation, is the theme that the linguist develops in his analysis of poems" (*PS*, p. 23).

The object of science is not, has never been, a real object, taken in itself; thus in the case of literary studies, literary works themselves are not the object (just as "bodies" are not the object in physics, chemistry, or geometry). This object must be constructed: it is made up of abstract categories that a given point of view permits us to identify within the real object, and of the laws governing the interaction of these categories. Scientific discourse has to account for perceived phenomena, but it does not have *as its goal* the description of the phenomena in themselves. The study of literature, which Jakobson later calls *poetics*, will have as its object not works but literary "mechanisms."

This fundamental choice situates Jakobson's discourse within the perspective of science. Here we must set aside two common and complementary misunderstandings. The first is the one that "technicians" commit: they believe that science begins with mathematical symbols, quantitative verifications, and austerity of style. They fail to understand that, in the best of cases these are instruments of science, and that scientific discourse does not need them in order to constitute itself; this discourse consists in the adoption of a certain attitude with regard to the facts. The second is that of the "aesthetes": they cry sacrilege as soon as anyone speaks of abstraction, threatening thereby to obliterate the precious singularity of the work of art. They forget that the individual is ineffable: we enter into abstraction from the very moment that we consent to speak. We do not have the choice of using or not using abstract categories, but only of doing so knowingly or not.

A problem that warrants our attention is nonetheless posed by the simultaneous evocation of science—in the framework of which poetics is located—on the one hand, and of semantics ("at present the linguist is preoccupied with semantic problems at all levels of language, and when he seeks to describe what makes up a poem, then its meaning—in brief, the semantic aspect of the poem— appears precisely as an integral part of the whole," Jakobson writes in 1973 [PS, p. 22]) on the other hand. Unlike the other sectors of linguistics, semantics does not have a universally accepted doctrine; the very possibility of its existence as a discipline continues to be debated today. Literary critics, whose testimony is important in the present context, would find themselves aligned with the skeptics in this debate. To hear them talk, as soon as we are dealing with meaning, there is no longer an impassable border between description and interpretation (thus, here, between science and criticism); any specification of meaning is subjective. This would account for the extraordinary abundance of different interpretations of a single text, the interpretations varying over time or even simply from one individual to another. Do the poetic readings of a linguist allow us to overcome these objections? Do they bring us to import scientific certainty even into the problems of meaning?

To situate Jakobson's nuanced position better in relation to this problem, let us look more closely at some examples of his own literary analysis.

One section of his study of Dante's sonnet "Si vedi li occhi miei" is devoted to the semantic level. What type of phenomena does he consider? He picks out four terms, *pietà, giustizia, paura, virtù*, and remarks that "*anguish* and *fright* are the respective responses of the poet and of everyone, responses inseparable from the suffering inflicted upon *justice-virtue*" (QP, p. 308); he also notes that "direct references and displaced references follow one another in regular alternation," and that "a close link is established between *pietà* and *virtù*" (ibid.). In the analysis of one of Du Bellay's sonnets, Jakobson affirms that "the reality of *i'adore* comes to replace the potential mark [Fr. *cachet*] of the verb *pouras*" (QP, p. 351), or that "the two circumstantial expressions designate respectively maximum distance—*au plus hault ciel*—and the most intimate proximity in space—*en ce monde*" (QP, p. 352). Speaking of Baudelaire's *Spleen*, he notes that "the subject, *Anguish*, a personified abstract noun, in contrast with the *hearses* of the first clause, belongs to the spiritual sphere. Now the action of this abstract subject, like the direct object it governs, is, in contrast, entirely concrete" (QP, p. 432), and so forth.

What unifies these diverse examples of semantic analysis? In an initial stage, we might distinguish two series: to the first belong all the phenomena of *syntagmatic* semantics, all the cases in which Jakobson identifies the positional, relative value of a given linguistic segment with respect to some other (relations of parallelism, contrast, gradation, subordination, and the like). A second group is constituted by the phenomena that are established not in *praesentia* now but *in absentia*, in the framework of a *paradigm* of which only one term figures in the poem analyzed: thus we shall observe that one noun is abstract, another concrete; that a given stanza participates in substance, another in accident; that the real in one place is opposed to the virtual in another, and so on. In fact, the two series of phenomena, syntagmatic and paradigmatic, are unified by virtue of being, both of them, *relational* phenomena. Without calling *anguish* by any other name, we shall specify that it is related to *dread* and is articulated with *virtue*. We shall not state what *sky* "means" for Du Bellay, but we shall point out that it belongs to the class of distant objects—and thereby contrasts with the terms belonging to the opposite class of nearby objects. We shall not speak of *the* meaning, but always and only of *the meanings*.

Thus in the debate that both connects and opposes semanticists and critics, Jakobson's attitude amounts to attributing to each group its own special field, one with which that group alone is qualified to deal. To the critic who affirms the subjectivity of meaning, Jakobson implicitly opposes the fact that the relation of meanings is identifiable in and through language: words speak among themselves. To the semanticist eager to take command of the area of meaning in its totality, Jakobson opposes a different argument, just as implicitly: only formal relations (including those among meanings) can be *described* in coherent, unchallengeable language; individual semantic contents do not lend themselves to metalanguage, but only to paraphrase—which remains the business of the critic. Closer to Saussure than he seems at first glance, Jakobson reserves for linguistics only relational semantics, made up of differences and identities of terms within syntagmas and paradigms; he leaves to interpretation (to the critic) the task of specifying the meaning of a work—for a given period, setting, or sensibility.

But let us return to the set of "mechanisms" that Jakobson has made the object of poetics. What are they? Their identification follows from the definition Jakobson has given of poetry: a language that tends to become opaque. Thus all devices deployed by poets lead us to perceive language in itself, and not as a simple substitute for things or ideas: figures, plays on time and space, special vocabulary, sentence construction, epithets, derivation and poetic etymology, euphony, synonymy and homonymy, rhyme, word decomposition. . . .

One tendency of poetic language in particular engages Jakobson's attention: the tendency toward repetition. For "the form of a word is not perceived unless this form is repeated within the linguistic system," he writes in 1919 (QP, p. 21). And in 1960, asking "according to what linguistic criterion the poetic function is recognized empirically," he formulates the following answer: "The poetic function projects the principle of equivalence from the axis of selection into the axis of combination" (LP, p. 303). This accounts for the particular attention he pays, throughout his work, to the various forms of repetition and, more specifically still, to parallelism (which includes resemblance as well as difference). He likes to quote the following sentence from Gerard Manley Hopkins: "The artificial part of poetry, perhaps we shall be right to say all artifice, reduces itself to the principle of parallelism,"[6] and he himself writes: "On every level of language, the essence of poetic artifice consists in recurrent returns."[7]

Internal coherence is the best way to achieve intransitivity: here Jakobson sets up a relation that was familiar to the German romantics. The very details of this affirmation, an essential one for Jakobson (that poetic rhythm attests to the fact that discourse finds its finality in itself, and that, owing to such mechanisms, language ceases to be arbitrary) were established by A. W. Schlegel in the following passage:

The more prosaic a discourse is, the more it loses its musical stresses, and only articulates itself drily. The tendency of poetry is exactly the opposite, and therefore in order to announce that it is a discourse having its end in itself, that it serves no external interests and that it thus will intervene in a temporal succession determined elsewhere, it has to form its own temporal succession. It is only in this way that the listener will be drawn away from reality and situated in an imaginary temporal sequence, that he will perceive a regular subdivision of the sequences, a

6. "Poetic Diction," in The Journals and Papers of Gerard Manley Hopkins, ed. H. House and G. Storey (London, 1959), p. 84.

7. "Grammatical Parallelism and Its Russian Facet," Language, 42 (1966), 399.

measure in the discourse itself; whence arises the marvelous phenomenon according to which, in its freest appearance, when it is used as pure play, language willingly rids itself of its arbitrary character, whose rule is solidly established elsewhere, and submits to a law apparently foreign to its content. This law is measure, cadence, rhythm. [*Die Kunstlehre*, pp. 103–104][8]

In practice, Jakobson explores three textual levels from the standpoint of the principle of parallelism: sounds or letters, prosody, and grammatical categories; but his choice is dictated by practical rather than theoretical concerns. Since 1960 he has concentrated on illustrating this principle with the help of concrete analysis of poems, deliberately choosing them from different languages and from widely separated periods. This universal sampling includes texts of Dante and Shakespeare, Pushkin and Baudelaire, Mácha and Norwid, Pessoa and Brecht. These analyses have a dual purpose: theoretical, in that they tend to illustrate Jakobson's hypothesis about the functioning of poetry (although the initial theorem almost disappears under the abundance of evidence), and historical, in that they make possible a better understanding of certain key texts of the European literary tradition. To state the meaning of an individual work, as we have seen, is not among the tasks of poetics, any more than is the explanation of the work's aesthetic effect; but the exact description of the poetic mechanisms involved makes it possible to *invalidate* unsound interpretations. To be convinced of this, we have only to read the conclusion of Jakobson's study of a Shakespearean sonnet:[9] a good dozen among the previous readings of this sonnet are shown to be inconsistent, once they are confronted with the rigorous description of the verbal structures characteristic of the text.

Valéry used to say that "literature is, and can be nothing but, a sort of extension and application of certain properties of lan-

8. In the painstaking analysis he has made of Jakobson's poetics (*Mimologiques* [Paris, 1976], pp. 302–312), Gérard Genette has brought to light an ambiguity that I have not taken into account here. A number of passages bear witness to a position that Jakobson confuses with the one he believes he is defending, whereas the two are far from identical: Jakobson would be as much a partisan of vertical motivation as of horizontal repetition; while remaining within the wake of romanticism, he would belong with A. W. Schlegel rather than with Novalis. The facts Genette has established cannot be denied; nevertheless, I am left with the impression that he exaggerates their importance.

9. R. Jakobson and L. G. Jones, *Shakespeare's Verbal Art in "Th'expence of Spirit"* (The Hague and Paris, 1970), 34 pp.

guage"; and Paulhan avers "that every literary work is essentially a machine—a monument, if one prefers—of language, this is evident from the very first." Some twenty or thirty years earlier, Jakobson had already dedicated his life to the *passion for language*—and thus, necessarily, to literature. Those who accuse him of "formalism," or who hasten to assure us that formalism is outmoded, are not aware that their accusations depend upon a preliminary dichotomy opposing "form" to "substance" or to "ideas." Jakobson's choice—never to stop perceiving language, not to let language fade into transparency and into "naturalness," whatever the pretext—has a much more serious ideological and philosophical signification than this or that "idea" that may have currency today. However, the refusal to recognize the autonomy of language, the refusal to seek to know its specific laws, is part of a secular stance that underlies a major part of our culture—and it would take far more than one Jakobson to combat it.

If Jakobson is at once a linguist *and* a theoretician of poetics, it is not by accident: he interrogates literature as the work of language. And it is not just at the level of the sentence that the observation of linguistic forms is relevant to knowledge of literature, but also at the level of discourse. The types of discourse, traditionally called genres, are formed, according to Jakobson, around the expansion of certain verbal categories. The two most extensive literary genres, lyric poetry and epic poetry (or, at another level but in parallel fashion, poetry and prose), have attracted his attention most often. A German romantic, Jean Paul, had already established a similar affiliation: between past and epic, present and lyric, future and drama. Jakobson wrote in 1934: "If we reduce the question to a simple grammatical formula, we can say that the point of departure and the main theme are, for the lyric, invariably the first person of the present tense; for the epic, the third person of the past tense" (*MN*, p. 138). And later, he specified:

> Epic poetry, focused on the third person, strongly involves the referential function of language; the lyric, oriented toward the first person, is intimately linked with the emotive function; poetry of the second person is imbued with the conative function, and is either supplicatory or exhortative, depending on whether the first person is subordinated to the second one or the second to the first. [*LP*, p. 303]

But it is the way he connects these same two types of discourse with two rhetorical figures, metaphor and metonymy, that constitutes Jakobson's most celebrated attempt to observe the projection of verbal categories onto transphrastic units. In 1923, another formalist, Boris Eikhenbaum, made a similar identification of the two great poetic schools of the day, the symbolist and the acmeist, in his book on Anna Akhmatova, one of the major representatives of acmeism:

> The symbolists place the emphasis precisely on metaphor ("setting it apart among all the representative devices of language": André Biély), as a way of bringing together widely separated semantic series. Akhmatova rejects the principle of extension, which depends upon the associative power of the word. Words are not grounded upon other words, but touch each other like the pieces of a mosaic. . . . In place of metaphors we find, in all their variety, the lateral nuances of words, based on periphrases and metonymies.[10]

In his study on Pasternak, Jakobson generalizes this observation, applying it to the two basic genres, and he concludes, twenty years later: "For poetry, metaphor, for prose, metonymy is the line of least resistance" (TA, p. 96).

There is no sharp dividing line between those of Jakobson's writings that have to do with linguistics and those that deal with problems of poetics, and there cannot be. His work as a grammarian may interest the literary specialist just as much as the work he devotes to prosody—since the verbal categories are in fact projected onto the organization of discourse. Others have tried to pursue this line of research, starting from the theory of double types (citation, proper name, antonymy, shifters) or with the functions of language; still others, no doubt, will one day be able to find in Jakobson's "linguistic" writings a source of inspiration for an investigation of discursive forms, poetic and otherwise.

All discursive categories come from language; but in order to identify them it is necessary first to recognize the multiplicity of systems that function within language. Jakobson has ceaselessly tried to combat reductionists of all stripes, all those who seek to reduce language to any single one of the systems that manifest themselves through it. Just as people had to recognize finally that Europe was not the center of the earth, nor the earth the center of the universe, so, in the same movement of differentiation

10. The quote is taken from B. Eikhenbaum, *O poèzii* (Leningrad, 1969), pp. 87–88 and 133.

between the self and others, the same struggle with infantile egocentrism, we have to stop identifying language with the part of it we know the best; we have to recognize the "doubles" of language.

Conversely, the same figures, the same mechanisms are found outside of language: in film, in painting. For language in itself cannot be the immediate object of a science, any more than literary works can. "Many poetic features belong not only to the science of language but to the whole theory of signs, that is, to general semiotics" (LP, p. 297). Thus the various types of semiotic process are to constitute the object of each discipline, and not the various substances. Metaphor and metonymy are defined by the (differently) motivated relation between two meanings of a word; but every image includes a motivated relation between itself and what it represents. It would thus be appropriate to study all the motivated relations of signification simultaneously, and, in another context, all the unmotivated ones. So the very movement that earlier led literary studies to poetics will one day lead from poetics to semiotics and to symbolics.

If I had to choose one detail from Jakobson's biography to use as a symbol, it would be the following. At age eighteen, an adolescent is inflamed by the verse of three contemporary poets, only a little older than he: Khlebnikov, Mayakovsky, Pasternak; he promises himself never to forget this experience. Even if this event never actually took place, it is necessary to our understanding of the guiding lines of Jakobson's career.

There is, first of all, something like a wager: to be a linguist and at the same time to experience an audacious poetry with intensity. The easy way out would have been to practice linguistics but to read only "average" texts; or, conversely, to be passionately devoted to poetry but to leave aside the science of language. Jakobson was unwilling to give up anything, and he "won": his theory of language is exceptional in that it does not recognize the opposition between the norm and the exception. If a linguistic theory is correct, it must be able to account not only, let us say, for neutral utilitarian prose, but also for the wildest verbal creations of a Khlebnikov, for example. It is in this respect that Jakobson appears to me to be a particularly exemplary figure.

This same experience has been decisive for his poetic theory. Not only has he devoted three major studies to the above-mentioned poets, but his entire conception of poetry rests on a generalization of his early experience. Would he have had the same luck with Pushkin? Not without being born a hundred years earlier: contemporary language is part of the structure of the text, poetry is to be consumed while it is hot. His experience would never have been as intense with poets of another era, and thus could not have determined in the same way his vision of poetry in general. He was able to read Pushkin through the intermediary of Mayakovsky; the inverse would have given the mediocre result that is familiar to us all, from our years of university study. The moral, for the young theoretician of poetics: you must live the poetry of your time.

There is more. To commit one's life to the investigation of phenomena, as every scientist wishes to do, attests both to a powerful ambition and to a great humility: humility, in this case, because the project is merely to describe and explain what others have done; ambition, because these others are called Pasternak, Mayakovsky, Khlebnikov. It is to renounce both the facility of nonreferential discourse and the boredom of superfluous description. In this, too, Jakobson wins: he offers quite as much knowledge, today, as he does food for thought—or for dreams.

Openings

===

In 1767, on the eve of the romantic crisis, there appeared the last great work of classical linguistics: Beauzée's *Grammaire générale*. In 1835, when the new system was already well in place, perhaps the most important text for all of modern linguistics appeared: Wilhelm von Humboldt's *Linguistic Variability and Intellectual Development*.[1] The distance between classics and romantics can be measured by the distance between the two projects that these titles announce. In the place of generality we find variability; the affirmation of identity gives way to that of difference.

To recognize the irreducible difference of phenomena, to give up the search for a unique and absolute essence of which phenomena would be more or less perfect manifestations is indeed a romantic invention. This change is consciously adopted by Humboldt, and it follows from a reversal that we were able to observe in the course of the romantic crisis: the shift of attention from imitation to production. In an imitative or representative perspective (concerning art or language), unity predominates:

1. For texts mentioned or quoted in this section, see the Bibliographical Notes for Chapter 6.

works are determined by their referent, which is the world, and which is one. But if we judge that the decisive moment lies in production, and thus in the relation between producer and product, which leads to expression, then diversity comes to the fore: it grows out of the variety among the subjects that are expressing themselves.

Language is first of all expression of the individual. "The first factor is naturally the personality of the speaker himself, who is in constant and direct contact with nature, and who cannot possibly fail to express in language his own ego in contrast to it," Humboldt writes (vii, 104; *LV*, p. 74). But the most significant threshold of variance in the domain of language is that of the languages themselves; the most important expression is that of a people. "The spirit of the nation is reflected in its language," Humboldt wrote as early as 1821 (iv, 55; Herder had been saying the same thing since the end of the eighteenth century), and he never gave up repeating it afterward: Languages "always have a national form" (iii, 38; *LV*, p. 20). "From every language, . . . conclusions can be drawn with respect to the national character" (vii, 172; *LV*, p. 132). It is even the privileged expression of the spirit of a people, so that the people is formed in turn by its language: "Every language receives a definite individuality from the nation and reacts in a uniform manner upon it" (vii, 170; *LV*, p. 130).

If language is expression first and foremost, then languages are inherently diverse: "The innumerable details which the use of the language necessitates must be drawn together to form a unit, regardless of how speech is to be practised. And this unit cannot be other than an individual one, inasmuch as the language sinks its roots into all the fibres of the human intellect" (vii, 245; *LV*, p. 187). And as expression is inherently national, so too is diversity: the difference between languages is more important than the difference between individuals, or between dialects: "The structure of languages in the human race varies because and to the extent that it is the intellectual idiosyncrasy of nations themselves" (vii, 43; *LV*, p. 25). "A unique cosmic viewpoint reposes in every tongue" (vii, 60; *LV*, p. 39).

To the synchronic variability of languages is joined a diachronic variability, that of periods (synchrony is clearly not opposed to diachrony, but both together are opposed to the panchrony, or even achrony, that is implied by general grammars). In time as in

space, language differences are irreducible, and by the same token
are more important than similarities: history, not in the sense of
chronology nor of exemplification of some eternal essence, but in
the sense of an irreversible and irreducible unfolding, is another
romantic invention (once more in the wake of Vico and Herder).
History (the study of variations in time) is not opposed to ethnol-
ogy (the study of variations in space); both arise from the romantic spirit that enthrones difference in the place of identity.

A. W. Schlegel provides a good illustration of this new role of
history in literary studies. In the classical view, there is only one
ideal in literature; it is generally located in the past, and in the
place of "history" we find a series of more or less successful
attempts to attain this same unique ideal. What characterizes the
romantics is precisely their renunciation of the unique ideal: romantic art is not a degraded classical art, but a different art. Here
again, it is the relation of production, and thus of expression, that
justifies the change. "I, for my part, am disposed to believe that
poetry, as the fervid expression of our whole being, must assume
new and peculiar forms in different ages" writes A. W. Schlegel
(*Vorlesungen*, I, 47; *Lectures*, p. 50). There is no longer one ideal
but several, and no one period is privileged with respect to others
(to paraphrase his brother Friedrich: periods are like the citizens
of a republic). "There is no monopoly of poetry for particular ages
and nations; and consequently that despotism in taste, which
would seek to invest with universal authority the rules which at
first, perhaps, were but arbitrarily advanced, is but a vain and
empty pretension" (I, 18, *Lectures*, p. 18). The time of despotic
monarchies has passed, the spirit of the bourgeois revolution
breathes on the arts as on the sciences, and along with it comes
history, that is, the recognition of irreducible differences.

It is this new viewpoint that allows us to value both the ancients and the moderns: each may be "models *in their kind*" (I, 19;
Lectures, p. 20; emphasis added). The classical attitude consisted
in believing in the immutable essence of poetry, which was identified with its manifestation among the Greeks, and in con-
demning modern poetry in consequence. "Maintaining that nothing could be hoped for the human mind but from an imitation of
antiquity, in the works of the moderns, they only valued what
resembled, or seemed to bear a resemblance to, those of the ancients. Everything else they rejected as barbarous and unnatural"
(ibid.). According to the romantic viewpoint that Schlegel illus-

trates, on the other hand, each period has its own ideal, and the efforts of its artists are directed toward the realization of this ideal. "They were compelled by their independence and originality of mind, to strike out a path of their own, and to impress upon their productions the stamp of their own genius" (ibid.); they brought to light "the peculiar spirit of *modern* art, as contrasted with the *antique* or *classical*" (I, 21; *Lectures*, p. 21). The notion of originality and the valorization of this notion make their appearance under the pressure of the romantic postulates.

Nevertheless, Humboldt and A. W. Schlegel are not romantic extremists. They seek to reconcile unity and diversity. Schlegel writes that "the groundwork of human nature is no doubt everywhere the same; but in all our investigations, we may observe that, throughout the whole range of nature, there is no elementary power so simple, but that it is capable of dividing and diverging into opposite directions" (ibid.); and according to Humboldt, "in language the individualization within general conformity is so marvelous that we may state with equal correctness that the entire human race possesses but a single language and each human possesses a particular one" (VII, 51; *LV*, p. 31). Each writer also attempts to explain this submission to conflicting principles by recourse to appropriate metaphors. Schlegel turns to the metaphor of body and spirit: "It is evident that the spirit of poetry, which, though imperishable, migrates, as it were, though different bodies, must, so often as it is newly born in the human race, mould to itself, out of the nutrimental substance of an altered age, a body of a different conformation" (*Vorlesungen*, II, 110; *Lectures*, p. 340). Humboldt draws upon the metaphor of means and ends: "The form of all languages must be fundamentally identical and must always achieve a common objective. The variety among languages can lie only in the media and the limits permitted the attainment of the objective" (VII, 251; *LV*, p. 193). That said, even though these writers do attempt to maintain an equilibrium, the context in which they state their messages causes us to hear one half much more loudly than the other. Identity has given up its place to difference.

To observe, during the very process of writing the "history" of the passage between classics and romantics, that the idea of diversity and history is a romantic and anticlassical idea, is of course to make a statement full of consequences. Two conflicting solutions seem to be available to someone who is trying to recon struct the conceptual systems of the past, as I have been in the foregoing pages—but how could anyone formulate such a project without already embarking upon one path or the other? Both solutions are caught up in similar distortions. Either we are to believe in the eternal and immutable essence of things and concepts, in which case system dominates history: changes in time are only variations provided for by the initial combinatorial system; they do not modify the unique framework. Or else we postulate that changes are irreversible, differences irreducible: history dominates system, and we give up the unique conceptual framework. We may write a treatise or a history. Now even if the choice is in some sense free in other cases, it ceases to be so when the object of study is precisely the place where the idea of treatise and the idea of history confront each other. One is already romantic if one writes the history of the passage from the classics to the romantics; one is still classical if one perceives the two as simple variants of a unique essence. Whatever solution is chosen, the writer adopts the viewpoint proper to one of these periods in order to judge—and distort—the other.

Confronted with this paradoxical constraint, then, one might dream of defining a third position, neither classical nor romantic, on the basis of which both sides could be evaluated.

There is no question, here at the end of a work, of establishing such a program; it is too late for that. The question, rather, is one of turning back upon oneself the observing look that has been directed toward others, of asking oneself what this (re)search means, not in terms of the explicit content of the discussions that make it up, but in terms of its very existence, and of the forms it has found itself taking. Is it classic or romantic? Have I written a systematic book or a historical book? Or something else again?

Let me note what encourages me to believe that a third position is possible, that such a position is even in the process of being established, and that—ultimate presumption!—it is manifest throughout the present research (there can be no question of personal merit here, since meaning establishes itself through the text, not in it, somewhat as in Novalis's "Monologue"—but in a very much lengthier and heavier way!) Consider the very possibility of describing romantic ideology today: of describing it, and no longer simply repeating it as if it were the truth. In certain areas and under certain conditions, romantic doctrine still retains a revolutionary force: it can lead those who practice it to judge that, far from being merely one doctrine among others, it constitutes the advent of a truth. There is no reason to regret this. But so long as one shares in a doctrine, one is unable to grasp it as a whole, thus to grasp it as doctrine; conversely, to be able to do so is already to be part of it no longer. I was "romantic" when I began to write these pages; having reached the end, I could no longer remain so: I see myself changed.

The present is obviously neither the simple repetition nor the total negation of the past. If one were to believe the romantics' descriptions of themselves and of the classics, one might imagine a sort of mirror image, a perfect symmetry, only with the minus sign regularly replaced by the plus sign. This image is false. The romantics did not invert the propositions of the classics; they did not replace them with propositions that were rigorously contradictory. We are dealing with a global reorganization, not with a term-for-term symmetry. Individual classic propositions are not necessarily negated; rather, they are granted a different role to play (we became aware of this in connection with the example of imitation). The relations, the hierarchies are (in particular) the things that change; isolated elements can always be found among earlier writers.

The same holds true for us today, with respect to the romantics (and to the classics too, for that matter). What characterizes our attitude is not necessarily different from the past, once we break it down element by element. But the organization of the whole is different, the privileged values have changed; the servants, to use Dubos's imagery, have often become mistresses.

Classical rhetoric (the rhetoric that extends from Quintilian to Fontanier) saw only one norm in language; the rest was deviation, either in the signifier or in the signified—a deviation that was desirable and nevertheless always threatened with condemnation. The romantic aesthetic, taken at the extreme, affirms that each work is its own norm, that each message constructs its own code. I believe today in a plurality of norms and of discourses: not one only, nor an infinite number, but several. Each society, each culture possesses a set of discourses whose typology can be established. There is no reason to condemn one of these in the name of another (we might just as well consider ice to be deviant water, I. A. Richards used to say), but that does not mean, either, that each discourse is individual and resembles no other. Between discourse in general and examples of discourse there are *types* of discourse.

Classical rhetoric and aesthetics (to the extent that the latter existed) attributed a purely transitive role to art and to language. Art is functional, and this functionality is reduced finally to a single objective: the imitation of nature. Language is equally transitive, and its function is just as unique: it serves to represent, or to communicate. We are familiar with the romantic reaction: it rejects all function, and affirms the intransitivity of art (Moritz) as well as that of language (Novalis). We no longer believe today in art for art's sake, and yet neither do we accept the idea that art is simply utilitarian. This is because between classical unicity and romantic infinity (zero) the path of *plurality* can be affirmed. Language has mutiple functions; so does art; their distribution, their hierarchy, do not remain constant in different cultures during different periods.

For Lévy-Bruhl, Freud, and Saussure, neoclassics all (in very different ways), the symbol is a deviant sign, or an inadequate one. For Augustine too, the symbol is only a different way to say what a sign says. The romantic position, although it is the inverse, shares in a comparable asymmetry: the sign, for Wackenroder, becomes an imperfect symbol. Nevertheless, in Augustine as in Goethe, we saw the development of a typological vision: an effort to recognize the difference between sign and symbol and to describe this difference in structural terms (as an opposition between direct and indirect). Others—Creuzer, Solger—were to demonstrate in turn the possibility of refusing to valorize one term of the opposition at the expense of the other (the difference between symbol and allegory was the one under discussion at the time), of refusing to present one as the degradation of the other. We are prepared today to affirm *heterology*: the modes of signifying are multiple, and each is irreducible to any other; their difference lends itself to no value judgments whatsoever; each one, as A. W. Schlegel would say, may be exemplary in its kind.

These are only a few examples by means of which I am trying to pinpoint the contemporary position with respect to that of the classics and that of the romantics. Rather than a middle road, or a conciliatory mix of the two, I see the contemporary attitude as opposed, on the whole, to both (even though the oppositions may take varying forms). Neither classic nor romantic, but typological, plurifunctional, heterological: this is how I see the perspective that allows us today to read the past—or, more concretely, the one that has led me to write these pages. History or treatise? The historical opposition of classics and romantics has concerned us as much as the sytematic opposition between sign and symbol; and yet we do not have a simple alloy. I have not said much about this, I know; but to do so, one would have to try one's own hand at a "theory of the symbol," a task that could not be appropriately undertaken here. Such a theory can be produced only by the construction of a *symbolics of language.*

Bibliographical Notes

CHAPTER 1

All quotations from Aristotle are from the W. D. Ross edition, 12 vols. (Oxford, 1908–52). The works of Sextus, Diogenes, Quintilian, and Plutarch are quoted from the Loeb Classical Library editions. For Artemidorus, quoted material is from *The Interpretation of Dreams: Oneirocritica*, trans. R. J. White (Park Ridge, N. J., 1975). Clement is quoted from *The Writings of Clement of Alexandria*, in W. Wilson, *The Ante-Nicene Christian Library* (Edinburgh, 1869), vol. xii. The excerpts from Augustine's sermons and letters are translated from the French (Bibliothèque augustinienne); all other quoted material from Augustine comes from the following sources: *Against Lying*, trans. H. B. Jaffee, in *Treatises on Various Subjects*, The Fathers of the Church, vol. 16 (New York, 1954), pp. 111–179; *Concerning the Teacher*, trans. G. B. Leckie (New York and London, 1938); *Confessions*, trans. E. B. Pusey (Chicago, 1952); *De Dialectica*, trans. B. D. Jackson (Dordrecht and Boston, 1975); *Divine Providence and the Problem of Evil*, trans. R. P. Russell, in *Writings of St. Augustine*, The Fathers of the Church, vol. 1 (New York, 1948), pp. 227–332; *The First Catechetical Instructions*, trans. J. P. Christopher (Westminster, Md., 1946); *Lying*, trans. Sr. M. S. Muldowney, in *Treatises on Various Subjects* (see above), pp. 45–110; *On Christian Doctrine*, trans. D. W. Robertson, Jr. (New York, 1958); *On the Trinity*, in *Basic Writings*, trans. W. J. Oates (New York, 1948).

Additional references complementary to those given here can be found in the histories of the various disciplines that I consulted, for example: R. H. Robins, *A Short History of Linguistics* (London, 1969); William and Martha Kneale, *Development of Logic* (Oxford, 1962); R. Blanché, *La Logique et son histoire* (Paris, 1970); C. S. Baldwin, *Ancient Rhetoric and Poetic* (Gloucester, 1924); George Kennedy, *The Art of Persuasion in Greece* (Princeton, 1963), and *The Art of Rhetoric in the Roman World* (Princeton, 1972); J. Cousin, *Etudes sur Quintilien* (Paris, 1935); Jean Pépin, *Mythe et Allégorie* (Paris, 1958).

The most complete study of Augustinian semiotics is that of B. D. Jackson, "The Theory of Signs in Saint Augustine's *De Doctrina christiana*," *Revue des études augustiniennes*, 15 (1969), 9–49, reprinted in R. A. Markus, ed., *Augustine* (Garden City, N.Y., 1972), pp. 92–147; this is a good source for references to earlier studies, to which we can add Jean Pépin, *Saint Augustin et la Dialectique* (Villanova, 1976). On the other hand, we can leave aside R. Simone, "Sémiologie augustinienne," *Semiotica*, 6 (1972), 1–31. I have not been able to consult C. P. Mayer, *Die Zeichen in der geistigen Entwicklung und in der Theologie des jungen Augustinus* (Wurzburg, 1969).

CHAPTER 2

The modern texts to which I refer are Albert Yon, "Introduction" à Cicéron, *L'Orateur* (Paris, Les Belles Lettres, 1964), pp. xxxv–cxvi ("La rhétorique"); J. Pépin, "Saint Augustin et la fonction protreptique de l'allégorie," *Recherches augustiniennes* (Paris, 1958), pp. 243–286. Tacitus is quoted from the H. W. Benario translation: *Agricola; Germany; Dialogue on Orators* (Indianapolis, 1967). Cicero and Quintilian are quoted from the Loeb Classical Library editions. For Augustine, quotations from *On Christian Doctrine* are from the translation by D. W. Robertson, Jr. (New York, 1958); the quotation from *Against Lying* is from the H. B. Jaffee trans., in *Treatises on Various Subjects*, The Fathers of the Church, vol. 16 (New York, 1954), p. 154. Other texts quoted are Macrobius, *Commentary on the Dream of Scipio*, trans. W. H. Stahl, Records of Civilization, Sources and Studies, no. xlviii (New York, 1952); Johann Jakob Breitinger, *Kritische Abhandlung von der Natur, den Absichten und dem Gebrauche der Gleichnisse, 1740* (Facsimile edition, Stuttgart, 1967); Pierre Fontanier, *Les Figures du discourse* (Paris, 1968); Immanuel Kant, *The Critique of Judgement*, in *The Critique of Pure Reason; The Critique of Practical Reason and Other Ethical Treatises; The Critique of Judgement*, trans. James Creed Meredith (Chicago, 1955); and John Locke, *An Essay Concerning Human Understanding*, 2 vols., ed. A. C. Fraser (New York, 1959). Virgil of Toulouse, known as Virgilius Maro the Grammarian, is translated from the text given in D. Tardi, *Les Epitomae de Virgile de Toulouse* (Paris, 1928).

CHAPTER 3

The following editions are quoted: C. C. Du Marsais, *Des tropes*, 1818, reprinted in Geneva in 1967 (abbreviated *DT*); for Du Marsais's other texts, *Oeuvres*, 7 vols., ed. Duchosal and Millon, 1797. N. Beauzée, *Grammaire générale*, 1767; for his articles, *Encyclopédie méthodique, Grammaire et littérature*, 3 vols., 1782, 1784, 1786 (abbreviated *EM* with volume number). Condillac, *Oeuvres philosophiques*, 3 vols., ed. Georges Le Roy (Paris, 1947; *De l'art d'écrire*, abbreviated *AE*, appears in vol. ɪ). P. Fontanier, *Commentaire raisonné sur les tropes de Du Marsais*, 1818, reprinted in Geneva in 1967 (abbreviated *CR*); and *Figures du discours* (Paris, 1968; this single volume, abbreviated *FD*, brings together the two parts of the treatise). Quintilian, *Institutio Oratoria*, Loeb Classical Library edition. 1968 edition of *Figures du discours*, pp. 5–17; J. Cohen, "Théorie de la figure," *Communications* 16 (1970), 3–25; Genette, *Figures III* (Paris, 1972), pp. 21–40; M. Charles, "Le Discours des figures," *Poétique*, 4 (1973), 340–364; Paul Ricoeur, *La Métaphore vive*, Paris, 1975, pp. 63–86. G. Sahlin's solid study, *C. C. Du Marsais . . .* (Paris, 1928), deals very little with Du Marsais's rhetorical work.

CHAPTER 4

I quote Diderot's writings from the following editions: *Lettre sur les sourds et muets*, in *Diderot Studies*, 7 (Geneva, 1965); *Oeuvres esthétiques* (Paris, 1968; abbreviated *OE*): *Oeuvres romanesques* (Paris, 1962; abbreviated *OR*); *Oeuvres complètes*, ed. Assezat-Tourneux, 20 vols. (Paris, 1875–1877; abbreviated *OC*, with volume number). Three English translations served as sources for certain quotations (identified by editor or translator in the text): *Diderot's Selected Writings*, ed. L. G. Crocker, trans. Derek Coltman (New York and London, 1966); *Diderot's Thoughts on Art and Style*, trans. B. L. Tollemache (New York 1893, repr. 1971); *Rameau's Nephew* and *D'Alembert's Dream*, trans. L. W. Tancock (Harmondsworth, England, 1966).

CHAPTER 6

For Friedrich Ast, I quote the following works: *System der Kunstlehre* (Leipzig, 1805); *Grundriss der Philologie* (Landshut, 1808); *Grundlinien der Grammatik, Hermeneutik und Kritik* (Landshut, 1808).

Clement is quoted from *The Writings of Clement of Alexandria*, in W. Wilson, *The Ante-Nicene Christian Library* (Edinburgh, 1869), vol. xɪɪ.

For Friedrich Creuzer: *Symbolik und Mythologie der alten Völker* (1810), 1819, vol. ɪ, is quoted.

Goethe's works are quoted from the Jubiläumsausgabe (abbreviated JA) or else from the Weimarer Ausgabe (abbreviated WA). The reference to the edition is followed by volume and page numbers. Quotations from the *Theory of Colours* are from the translation by C. L. Eastlake (London, 1840).

Quotations from Wilhelm von Humboldt come from the Prussian Academy edition (Berlin, 1903–36, 17 vols.), or else, where appropriate, from *Linguistic Variability and Intellectual Development*, translation of *Über die Verschiedenheit des menschlichen Sprachbaues und ihren Einfluss auf die geistige Entwicklung des Menschengeschlects* by G. C. Buck and F. A. Raven (Coral Gables, Fla., 1971; abbreviated *LV*). In references to the German edition the volume number is given first in roman numerals, followed by the page number.

Kant's *Critique of Judgement* is quoted from the J. C. Meredith translation: *The Critique of Pure Reason; The Critique of Practical Reason and Other Ethical Treatises; The Critique of Judgement* (Chicago, 1955).

For Heinrich Meyer, I quote in one context his *Kleine Schriften zur Kunst* (Heilbronn, 1886), and in another his notes on Winckelmann's *Werke* (Dresden, 1808–1825, 11 vols.), vol. II, 1808.

The works of Karl Philipp Moritz are quoted from *Schriften zur Aesthetik und Poetik*, Kritische Ausgabe (Tübingen, 1962; abbreviated *S*), or else from *Götterlehre, oder mythologische Dichtungen der Alten* (Lahr, 1948).

For Novalis, except as noted, the reader is referred to the French edition: *Oeuvres complètes*, ed. A. Guerne, 2 vols. (Paris, 1975). References to vol. II give the section number in roman numerals followed by the fragment number in arabic numerals; for vol. I, the volume number is followed by the page number. I have not always followed Guerne's translation, which is sometimes incorrect and very often imprecise. A better (but less complete) French version is offered by M. de Gandillac, under the title *L'Encyclopédie* (Paris, 1960). Two English translations were the source of certain quotations: *The Novices of Saïs*, trans. Ralph Manheim (New York, 1949), and *Henry von Ofterdingen*, trans. P. Hilty (New York, 1964).

Origen's *On First Principles* is quoted from the G. W. Butterworth translation (New York, 1966).

For Schelling, I quote the original edition: *Sämmtliche Werke*, Stuttgart and Augsburg; the roman numeral indicates the volume number (of the first series, unless otherwise noted) and the arabic numeral indicates the page. Where indicated, quoted material comes from *The Philosophy of Art: An Oration on the Relation between the Plastic Arts and Nature*, trans. A. Johnson (London, 1845), and *System of Transcendental Idealism*, trans. P. Heath (Charlottesville, Va., 1978).

For A. W. Schlegel, I refer to the following editions: *Vorlesungen über schöne Literatur und Kunst*, vol. I, *Die Kunstlehre* (Stuttgart, 1963; identified as *Die Kunstlehre*), and *Vorlesungen über dramatische Kunst und Literatur* (Stuttgart, vol. I, 1966, vol. II, 1967; identified as *Vorlesungen*). Quotations from this second work are taken from the J. Black translation, *A Course of Lectures on Dramatic Art and Literature*, 2d ed., rev. (London, 1904; identified as *Lectures*).

For Friedrich Schlegel's writings I have adopted the following abbreviations: the fragments published during his lifetime are designated by a letter indicating the name of the collection (*L* = *Lyceum*, *A* = *Athenaeum*) and by a number indicating the fragment; the text referred to is in vol. II of the Kritische Ausgabe, 18 vols. (Munich, 1958–79). For the Lyceum fragments, the translation used is that of Peter Firchow, *Friedrich Schlegel's Lucinde and Fragments* (Minneapolis, 1971). As for his posthumous fragments, *LN* followed by a fragment number designates *Literary Notebooks*,

1797–1801 (London, 1957); "Philosophie der Philologie" refers to J. Körner, "Friedrich Schlegels 'Philosophie der Philologie.'" *Logos,* 17 (1928), 1–72 (the page number is given); finally, vol. xviii of the Kritische Ausgabe is designated by its number, followed by the section number (roman numeral) and the fragment number (arabic numeral). *Gespräch über die Poesie* is in vol. ii of the Kritische Ausgabe; quotations from this work are from *Dialogue on Poetry and Literary Aphorisms,* trans. E. Behler and R. Struc (University Park, Pa., and London, 1968).

In the case of Friedrich Schleiermacher, I quote *Hermeneutik* (Heidelberg, 1959).

For K. W. F. Solger, I quote *Erwin* (Munich, 1971; reprint of the 1907 edition) and *Vorlesungen über Aesthetik,* 1829.

For W. H. Wackenroder, quotations are from the M. H. Schubert translation: *Confessions and Fantasies* (University Park, Pa., and London, 1971).

Index